# A Roman Empire of
# Our Very Own???

# A Roman Empire of
# Our Very Own???

Harry D. Hurless

Library of Congress Control Number:     2009905311
ISBN:          Hardcover          978-1-4415-4161-1
               Softcover          978-1-4415-4160-4

**To order additional copies of this book, contact:**
Xlibris Corporation
1-888-795-4274
www.Xlibris.com
Orders@Xlibris.com
63593

# PREFACE

★★★★★★★★★★★★★★★★★★★★★★★★★★★★★★★★★★★★★★★★★★★★★★★★★★★★★★★★★★★★★★★★

There is nothing wrong with America that
the faith, love of freedom, intelligence
and energy of her citizens cannot cure.


Dwight D. Eisenhower

★★★★★★★★★★★★★★★★★★★★★★★★★★★★★★★★★★★★★★★★★★★★★★★★★★★★★★★★★★★★★★★★

This may be the most important book that you will ever read; in terms of the benefits for your personal welfare and for the salvation of our nation. **We are living in ominous times.** Our federal government, many state governments and numerous other very significant publicly and privately managed segments of our society are on life-support. Their survival is in doubt! The nation's financial system, at the highest levels, is in utter chaos; with the "domino effect" seriously impacting, in a negative way, the financial systems of nations around the world. Some of our largest banks and other financial institutions which had previously been thought to be "rock solid" have failed. Chrysler and the General Motors Corporations are in Chapter 11 bankruptcy, future projections are grim.

Failure of the huge Fannie Mae and Freddie Mac, federally-backed and managed real-estate financing organizations was a primary contributing factor in the evolution of these problems. Ineptitude of the involved members of both political parties in the Legislative Branch, especially in the House of Representatives, the lackluster performance of the Senate and the Executive Branch in their oversight responsibility and the illiterate and uninvolved response of the mainstream, mass media and it's punditry all share responsibility for this tragic, possibly terminal, situation.

However, it is especially important at this time to recognize the primary responsibility of the citizen voter, you and I, for creating and tolerating the gross incompetence that has existed in our public arena for at least the last three decades.

Abraham Lincoln correctly characterized our government as being "Of the People, By the People, and For the People". Successful operation of such a "people-oriented" government carries with it a required level of intellectual capability and absolute responsibilities of the citizen-voter.

1. The voter needs to have a good working knowledge as to how the system of government is supposed to work. We have a problem! Effective civics courses were eliminated from our kindergarten—12th grade curricula decades ago.

2. The voter needs to vigilantly observe the effectiveness of the total system operation; and especially of the persons in those positions that he/she votes into office. Impossible, if one lacks the knowledge specified in #1 above.

3. Every eligible voter must critically analyze the efficacy of his/her political agents in representing his/her best interests and those of the nation. Duty then requires that he/she regularly vote in elections. Lacking the information noted in #1 above, many voters will be unable to judge what course of action best fits the needs of the nation. The system is broke! Many, (most?) citizens including many of those who vote are not qualified to do so intellectually. Selection of the best qualified candidate suffers.

As is evidenced by the publication of this book, which was actually written in the early 1990's, astute observation of conditions at that time demonstrated a critical need for drastic changes of direction in our political arena. It was the authors hope that publication of the book at that time would inform the people and stimulate corrective action. Inability to find a publisher stymied those hopes. In the intervening time, our broken system has continued to deteriorate to the point, that today the critical problems we face confirm the accuracy of the author's foresight; his worst fears are materializing!

At the time this book was written it appeared that our debilitating problems were primarily the result of the predominant control of our government by the Democratic Party over the years. The advent of an eight year Republican administration has since demonstrated that to not be true. Democratic policies are misdirected and will destroy the nation if left unchallenged. However, experience demonstrates that the Republican Party today has no constructive vision for the future, and they do not have the managerial ability to implement it if they did.

It is important to understand that the ongoing, inane national debate pitting Democrats versus Republicans, conservatives versus liberals, right-to-life versus abortion rights, feminine versus male, ethnicity versus ethnicity, etc. etc. will never solve any of our problems. This is a generational problem. Our public education system has been debased to the point where graduates of our high schools are not educated to the point where they can successfully perform the citizenship duties required of them by our system. The "Baby Boom" generation which is now approaching retirement age has done an abysmal job of perpetuating the adequate; if not perfect, societal environment they inherited. I can think of no situation in our society that is not orders of magnitude in worse condition than it was when they took over!

As the nation has struggled with its ongoing problems there has been some speculation as to whether or not conditions will get as bad for our citizens as they were during the Great Depression. The author lived through the Great Depression in stark poverty. He shares his concerns today in an effort to try to assure that this and future generations will not have to experience such hardships.

It is extremely important that each reader of this book understand that the fears expressed in the title, "A Roman Empire of Our Very Own???" go far beyond the nation's experience with the Great Depression. The problems that resulted in the Great Depression were largely internal and therefore, correctable by national reform. The problems that we face today are being exacerbated by foolish, inexperienced, Boomer management actions. Tentacles of the problems span the globe. When the "Boot Finally Falls", if it falls, resolution will be in the hands of foreign entities to which we have become indebted and to those who have invested in our real estate, commerce, and manufacturing assets.

Recovery of our economy will not solve the problem; the proposed insane spending must be drastically curtailed!

The Roman Empire disappeared as a society! That could be our fate!

The author posits the following thoughts for your careful consideration:

> - There is a possibility, however so slight, that our nation can recover from problems exacerbated by actions taken as of today; with one exception. Follow through with all of the spending included in the President's new budget, recently approved by Congress, is beyond the pail! Discovery of major new adverse conditions might also invalidate that possibility. The author believes that a desirable, positive outcome can only happen if citizens become more involved in the process

and force our leadership to move in a more sane direction. Where possible proposed bailouts and handouts should be cancelled, no bailouts to any state or anyone else, no new huge, costly programs—exercise some common sense!

-The nation has been encumbered by a staggering amount of new debt during the last few months of the Bush administration and these first months of the Obama administration. No one knows if, or the degree to which these expenditures might contribute, at all, to the solution of our problems. The new debt imposes a very heavy present and future burden on our citizen-taxpayers. But, the new administration is undaunted; it is actively pursuing plans for gross additional expenditures which have been quantified by the statement that the plan will lead to a national debt of $10,000,000,000,000 in 10 years. The insanity of this proposal is characterized by the fact that some foreign leaders have smiled or broke into a laugh when it has been discussed in their presence. The author sees no hope for survival of this nation if that is allowed to happen.

## SO! WHAT TO DO?

All citizens who are intellectually able to understand the extreme gravity of the situation must dedicate themselves to unite; Democrats and Republicans, men and women, all races and ethnicities, with others and do what they can to change the course of our government. The great silent majority, those who understand that we have serious problems but who feel a sense of futility about changing it must rally around this effort. After all! This is our country, our freedom, our lives, our very existence which is threatened. We must unite as individuals; as <u>Americans</u> not as members of special interest groups if we are to succeed.

Our salvation, maybe only hope, lies in the fact that Obama cannot do this by himself. He must convince the legislative branch to approve his proposals. The recent situation in which a large majority of senators voted down the money for his proposal to close the Guantánamo Bay prison provides a glimmer of hope. We don't know whether they did this of their own volition or in response to a fusillade of citizen-contacts. But, it showed us that it can happen. It demonstrated the presence of some patriotism, intellect, and conscious that has been hidden there for a long time.

The willingness in both the House and the Senate, within both parties to blindly follow misdirected party-line proposals of their leadership boggles my mind. After all! They and their loved ones will share in the great loss with all of the rest of us. Unbelievable! That they are unable to understand; or that they just don't care!

The recent "tea parties" and polling data tell us that a huge segment of the population understands the gravity of these problems and probably are willing to do what they can to correct the situation. That "something" should include a continuing barrage of contacts, on a daily basis if necessary, with their senators and representatives, demanding true representation of the people's interest.

If those in elective positions of authority and trust continue to defy the people's wishes, they must go. Vote them out! A purge of incumbents would be healthy for the country.

In closing, it seems productive; to consider what the country and its citizens might face, if in fact, the outcome of our present situation emulates that of the Roman Empire. As things are developing, China holds the largest amount of our national debt. Proceeding with the Obama plan would result in a national debt of $10 trillion in 10 years. Some have speculated that China might refuse to accept more US debt at some point in time. An interesting scenario can be drawn in which that would not be true.

China has been around for thousands of years. Its population numbers over 1.3 billion people. Its government leaders have demonstrated the ability and willingness to do what is necessary for the country to survive. The term "Cool Hand Luke" comes to mind as you consider their modus operandi. They are not diverted by the multitude of trivial, insidious, and intellectually vacuous issues driving decisions in this country.

Assume that China continues to accept U. S. debt and that at the end of 10 years they hold $7 or $8 trillion of that debt. What happens when payment comes due? The US, of course, has no plan for repayment of any of its debt! We do not even pretend to feel it necessary to balance our annual budget! And, the debt grows. What might the Chinese demand as payment? That is an awful lot of money! A penniless society cannot finance an effective military complex. A bloodless coup could well result. The Chinese will be looking for and demand title to those of our assets that will help them provide for their own citizenry. With little or no bargaining power our nation and its citizens would be at their mercy. We can guess that their "no nonsense" policies will result in little or no sympathy or empathy for the devastated condition that results for the American people. A tragic end that none of us want to comprehend; the specter of which should energize all of us, including our leaders to do what is necessary to avert such a cataclysmic end!

This book will provide you with a great deal of information and will help you develop your own strategic plan to help in this all-important effort. To succeed, we will need the participation of massive numbers of our citizens. Discussing the information presented here with your fellow citizens, helping to promote the wide distribution of the book by giving it as a gift or recommending it to others, along with your own active and overt support for this total effort will be critical. This may well be our last opportunity to save this nation and the system of government that has done so much for all of us in the past!

Harry D. Hurless
June 5, 2009

# GLOSSARY OF TERMS

Much of the discussion in this book is about normal activities and events casually observed or experienced by citizens of this country as they proceed down the pathway of life. Most of us subscribe to Abraham Lincoln's theory that ours is a nation governed by the concept, "Of the People, By the People, and For the People".

Acceptance of that description implies that all of our people are interested in, involved in, and dedicated to forming, managing, and controlling the destiny of the country. That, in turn, implies that everyone carefully follows and is able to understand all that transpires in the life of the nation. And, that they will react in their role as citizens, to maintain a course that will achieve that destiny.

With those thoughts in mind, this book has been carefully written for easy reading and comprehension. But, there are a few terms used that may unnecessarily intimidate or otherwise affect the easy flow of ideas or understanding in the reader's mind. Information in this glossary is intended to minimize any such problems.

## ROMAN EMPIRE

Any simple suggestion that your understanding this treatise requires a background of study of the Roman Empire will, in and of itself, intimidate most readers in the target audience for the book. It is, therefore, important that we put that fear to rest as soon as possible.

Properly understood, the relationship between our discussion and the implications of the title are summary in nature, but they are important.

No one knows, for sure, how or when Rome was founded. According to one tradition it was founded in 753 B.C. The Roman Empire was the major "super power" of its time. At its height, it occupied most of what is now known as Europe, the Middle East, and the northern coastal area of Africa. Its several millions of people spoke many languages and they worshiped different gods. Roman traits included a deep sense of duty, seriousness of purpose, and a sense of personal worth; all of which were cherished ideals during the first 150 years of our own country!

Although its boundaries changed many times, the empire continued to exist for about 1300 years. My sense is that during most of that 1300-year existence, Roman citizens would never have accepted as a valid scenario, the suggestion that their empire would fail and disappear as a viable entity. We can guess that clues may have been available to them at times that, "all was not well in their corner of the world". But, most of their people lived with the same sense of denial that we see in our country today.

The similarities of the Roman situation and our own seem important enough to warrant our attention. The Roman Empire dominated in its time, as we do today. The Empire and its people had their "day in the sun"; and then, after several hundred years, it was over for them. As citizens of this country, our journey of discovery has to begin with the realization that the same fate is surely in store for us and our nation. The big question we face is not "if the end of our domination will come"! But "when will it come". Only then can we recognize that the duration of our "time at the top" and the nature and scope of our fall from supremacy are dependent upon the intelligence and dedication with which we conduct ourselves and the affairs of the nation while we occupy this eminent position of world leadership.

My concern about the low level of intelligence and dedication being brought to the job of governing our nation led to my decision to begin writing this book in 1989. As the finishing touches are being added to it in the early 1990's, very little, of consequence, has changed for the better.

The lack of concern that we; as a people demonstrate, and the idiocy that we tolerate in the positions of supreme power and importance in our government institutions will surely be viewed at some future day of reckoning as the greatest dereliction of duty of all time. It is hoped that this book will increase awareness to the situation we face and instill passion in its readers to do what they can to implement corrective action. (For more information surf the World Wide Web using search words—Roman Ruins.)

## EMOTIONAL PLAGUE - ERA OF EMOTIONAL IDIOCY

These two related conditions in our society are introduced here for the first time that I am aware of. They represent an important new concept in diagnosing and analyzing the problems we are facing. So important, in fact, that before the country can even begin to solve its problems; it must establish a pecking order for considerations that must be a part of the total resolution process. Factors such as the lessons of past experiences; knowledge of the interacting relationships between humans, and between humans and their universe; intelligence as to the laws of science and the universe that cannot be waived as an expediency to making the resolution easier; and finally empathy, and compassion, which with the introduction of the mothering instincts inherent in the female point of view into the process has tended to make them all-important; far beyond any realistic level that can be supported by intelligent analysis.

The EMOTIONAL PLAGUE, like the regular plague, strikes one person at a time. Let me introduce you to this subject in this way. Some time ago the National Broadcasting Network (NBC) carried a program entitled, Robert F. Kennedy; the Man and the Memories. In one touching scene of that program, an influential person, with connections to high places in government, was shown with a group of people, many of them children, who were living in circumstances that left much to be desired. (Conditions, co-incidentally that I have experienced in my own life.) This person made a statement to the effect that she had to try to get Robert Kennedy to come down and see for himself the conditions that existed here. Efforts to accomplish that were successful. He eventually had many opportunities to view such situations. That is how people in positions of power are exposed to, "and catch" the emotional plague.

Ordinary people like you and I are exposed in the same way. In addition we encounter forced exposure when the hard media includes articles on the subject of deprivation in this country and abroad into its publications; or when the electronic media regularly includes items on the subject in the evening news scene. It is obvious that such exposure fulfills a part of the media's commitment to assure that our people are aware of the existence of such situations; and to sustain the "Era Of Emotional Idiocy" as a viable controlling factor in our society.

The disease is highly infectious. The rate at which exposed people are infected is very high! As a result it has permeated our "halls of public and political power" in epidemic proportions for decades.

The affect of the plague and the epidemic it creates in the halls of political power is quite unusual. We all know that attributes of emotion, empathy and compassion are powerful personal motivating forces. However, at a personal level, most of us are able to keep the situation under control. We are moved by exposure to such conditions and most of us will give to the extent we are able. But our giving ceases at that point where the continued viability of our own living unit begins to be jeopardized.

The reaction of our agents and leaders in the power structure is much different; strikingly more destructive! The tug of the emotional plague at their souls does not seem to be as great as it relates to <u>their</u> giving of <u>their</u> own personal resources for such causes. I can not recall of ever hearing of such people's devotion and substantial personal giving to these causes. Not-withstanding that fact, the tug and pull of this plague is there in their souls and it is powerful. And they react with generous gifts, <u>of my resources and yours</u>; no strings attached! Our individual ability to pay is totally ignored. They demand you give your share—<u>off the top</u>. If your contribution to their preferred charities does not leave you and your family with enough to buy food, clothing and the other necessities of life; that is too bad! You have a problem—but it does not serve as an excuse for you not to support their wacky programs!

Personal experience has reinforced this concept in my mind. Our residence is located in a moderately up-scale neighborhood which includes the homes of several local elected officials. Over the years, I have never seen one of them or a member of their family call house to house to collect for these charitable "causes". On the other hand, my wife and I have volunteered many times to do those jobs for all sorts of drives—the March of Dimes, the Cancer Fund, the Heart Fund, etc.. These elected officials, who are our neighbors, publicly support, in a vocal way, all of these and other charitable drives. But, in all of the times I have done the job, they have never donated to our request for help! It makes all of the difference in the world; <u>whose money they are giving away</u>!

When the penetration of the emotional plague reaches epidemic proportions; the "ERA OF EMOTIONAL IDIOCY" presents itself. The possibility of reasoned, intellectual decisions based on experience, knowledge, and criteria that are all important considerations no longer apply. The chaos that exists today in our public arena is the net result.

## FEEDBACK

This book goes to some length to define this term. And, it provides examples of how the concept fits into "closed loop" control systems and into the use of the "scientific method of problem solving". None-the-less, I have been made aware that for those to whom the term is new, the concept is still difficult to understand.

Simply stated, feedback in a control system, involves asking the question, "How are we doing? And a link is provided for feeding the answer to that question back into the guidance system. If the answer is, "We're right on", there is no signal to the feed-back link and no correction is necessary. If the answer is, "We are going too fast", a signal to that affect is sent back and actions are taken to decrease the speed. The process of asking this question and providing a correction signal may occur several times per second; or it may go on continuously. Each application is different. These systems may or may not include a human link.

When used in the problem solving methodology, the question is the same. "How are we doing?" Are we achieving the expected results? If the answer is yes, no correction is applied. If the answer is, "No we are not", the deviation is analyzed and a corrective action is taken.

The point of this discussion in the book is that for decades our leaders have insisted on origination, continuation, and expansion of hundreds of government programs, at monumental, financial sacrifice to all of us. It has never occurred to them to even ask that first, all-important question "Is this program working?" If it had been asked, the answer would almost always have been, "No it is not". And the funds wasted on them year after year, decade after decade, could have been applied to something more productive!

## MERIT

What an impossible twist of fate, that anyone should feel the necessity to include this simple word in a glossary such as this. The concept of "merit-based personnel systems" is discussed in chapter 16 of this book. As related there, the concept of a "merit system" was introduced into our government operations in the early 1880's. National leaders at the time, recognized that with the continuing growth of our government, its operation and management was becoming more complex and difficult. They realized their responsibility for maximizing the effectiveness of its operation. It was apparent to them that the "spoils system" of staffing that had been in use was totally ineffective. They took the position that "the people's business" justified hiring the best qualified people available. The Civil Service Act of 1883 was passed and served the nation well for many decades. It established a "merit system" of personnel management in the Federal government that eliminated "the spoils system", with its identifying features of nepotism and political patronage by those in power!

Having worked within the confines of the Federal Civil Service "merit system" for years, its strengths are perfectly clear to me. The fact that communication of the true meaning of the contents of this book requires inclusion of the author's intended definition of the word, "merit" is just one more harbinger of serious decay within our society. Revisionist's prostitution of the word <u>merit, in some circles of society</u>, is a recent discovery for me. Is nothing safe from their reckless, moronic exploits?

I first encountered this situation in a story out of Chicago. In the past, promotions in that city's police department have been criticized as being biased and politically motivated. During his term as mayor of that city, outside experts advised mayor Richard M. Daley to spend $5,000,000 to have a consultant redesign and administer the recruitment testing to remedy that problem. In a subsequent application of the new system, the list of test results for lieutenant positions came back with just 13 minority names among the top 175 scorers.

"In an effort to <u>be fair</u>", the mayor and police chief promoted 13 officers who had not achieved qualifying scores on the exam; to meet diversity quotas! Most of the 13 were members of minority groups. Of course, their selection eliminated the promotion opportunity for 13 other candidates who; having proven themselves to be "best qualified" by the department's testing system, should have been next in line.

This story, as related to this point, is not all that unusual. This kind of miscarriage of justice has become common-place in our society in recent decades; especially in the public service. What stunned me, and the reason I felt it was necessary to include an item on "merit" in the glossary; was the fact that the 13 positions filled outside their normal selection system; were referred to in some media coverage, as "<u>merit</u>" positions! What a sham!

The word "merit" is defined as follows in the Fifth Edition of the Webster's Collegiate Dictionary:

Merit

> 1. Due reward or punishment; usually reward deserved; a mark or token of excellence, of approbation. 2. Quality, state, or fact of deserving well or ill; desert; as, each according to his merit. 3. Worth; excellence. 4. That which is counted to one as a cause or reason of deserving well; a praiseworthy quality, act, etc.
> — v.t. To earn by service or performance; deserve.

This word has no viable application in the hiring action for the 13 lieutenants for the Chicago force discussed above. <u>Merit</u>, as defined above had nothing to do with their selection! Those people were hired on the basis of the color of their skin, their sex, their race, etc.; To meet quotas and diversity goals.

It is important to understand that the word merit, as used in this book, conforms to the above definition of the word! The best qualified are sought out and hired. A concept that is totally incompatible with the hokey meaning applied to it by the activists in the above encounter.

It is interesting to note that rank and file members of the Chicago police force, as well as minority leaders of the community were angered by the bogus action taken by the mayor and the police chief.

## REFERENCE SOURCE FOR THIS BOOK (World Book Encyclopedia ©1965)

I have been asked why I used The World Book Encyclopedia, Copyright 1965, as a primary reference for parts of this book. That is a fair question that I suspect many others will also wonder about.

One answer is that I bought a set of those books for our two children to use while they were growing up. Since it has been around our house all these years, I have had many occasions to refer to it for my own research. In the process, I have learned to trust it as a source of accurate, unbiased information. "I've had it available, so I have used it."

But more importantly, I have used it precisely because of its 1965 copyright date. At that point in time the activists, the revisionists and the pseudo intelligentsia had not yet set about the irresponsible, inane, idiotic pursuit of remaking our society, our history, and our literature into their version of what they think it should be! In my mind, this information resource from the early to mid 1960's can be trusted to be intellectually sound; free of bias, and free of the self-serving actions of such groups.

# CHAPTER 1

Many years ago a young patriot of our nation spoke the following words:

"No man thinks more highly than I do of the patriotism, as well as abilities, of the very worthy gentlemen who have just addressed the House. But different men often see the same subject in different lights; and, therefore, I hope that it will not be thought disrespectful to those gentlemen, if, entertaining as I do, opinions of a character very opposite to theirs, I shall speak forth my sentiments freely and without reserve. This is no time for ceremony. The question before the House is one of awful moment to this country. For my own part I consider it as nothing less than a question of freedom or slavery; and in proportion to the magnitude of the subject ought to be the freedom of the debate. It is only in this way that we can hope to arrive at truth, and fulfill the great responsibility which we hold to God and our Country. Should I keep back my opinions at such a time, through fear of giving offence, I should consider myself as guilty of treason towards my country and of an act of disloyalty towards the majesty of the heaven, which I revere above all earthly kings."

"Mr. President, it is natural for men to indulge in the illusions of hope. We are apt to shut our eyes against a painful truth and listen to the song of that siren, till she transforms us into beasts. Is this the part of wise men, engaged in a great and arduous struggle for liberty? Are we disposed to be of the number of those who, having eyes, see not, and having ears, hear not, the things which so nearly concern their temporal salvation? For my part, whatever anguish of spirit it may cost, I am willing to know the whole truth; to know the worst and to provide for it."

The words he spoke at that time, on March 23, 1775 have become a part of our treasury of foundation documents for our government and our Nation.

As a result of the love, ardor, and conviction with which he expressed his thoughts and ideas to the other members of the Virginia Convention of Delegates, his words have indelibly etched themselves into the minds and hearts of succeeding generations of Americans.

He continued:

> "What is it that gentlemen wish? What would they have? Is life so dear, or peace so sweet, as to be purchased at the price of chains and slavery? Forbid it, Almighty God! I know not what course others may take; but as for me, give me liberty, or give me death." (End of quote)

The man who spoke those words was, of course, Patrick Henry. The vision, courage and dedication to his country, that he displayed on that occasion, earned him a place in the history of the United States.

Quoting Patrick Henry here, helps us to deal with several questions and reservations that each of us must confront, in our own way, as we proceed to consider, form opinions on and react to the pressing issues of national importance that confront us, today.

We are not implying here, that each and every one of us, can and will be able to affect the future of our country to the same degree that he did. However, it is a fact that the quality of government and the quality of life we receive in this country is the result of the actions of all of our citizens who actively participate in those opportunities that present themselves. Each individual must give such participation a high priority in the competition for his/her time and effort.

Even though you and I may not be masters of the history of this country, we can gain some insight into the conditions that, even then, confronted dedicated, active citizens and politicians of those times; and relate them to our present situation.

He recognized the patriotism and abilities of his peers and fellow members of the Virginia Convention of Delegates to whom he was speaking. He carefully acknowledged that in expressing his point of view, he was not being disrespectful to those who shared and had expressed opposing points of view. Effective resolution of "questions . . . of awful moment to this country," would only result from honest, all-out, debate of the facts, issues and possible consequences of various points-of-view and actions that might be taken. To quote, "It is only in this way that we can hope to arrive at truth, and fulfill the great responsibility which we hold to God and our Country."

He acknowledged his personal belief that to express his opinions and to press for resolution of the problems facing the Nation in ways that were compatible with his beliefs was his solemn duty; as a member of the Convention of Delegates and as a citizen of his country. If he were to do less he, "should consider himself as guilty of treason towards his country, and of an act of disloyalty towards the majesty of the heaven, which he revered above all earthly kings."

He recognized the natural tendency of man to, "indulge in the illusion of hope." And to, "shut our eyes against a painful truth", to seek and take the easy way out whether or not it is the best action in terms of benefit to our Nation. (Think about that carefully. Does that concept have application in our situation today?)

He asks several very thought-provoking questions; questions that we might ponder in light of conditions in our country today. He goes on to provide his own thoughts with respect to them.

> "Is this the part of wise men, engaged in a great and arduous struggle for liberty? Are we disposed to be of the number of those who, having eyes, see not, and having ears, hear not, the things which so nearly concern their temporal salvation? For my part, whatever anguish of spirit it may cost, I am willing to know the whole truth; to know the worst and to provide for it."

He sums up his perception of the situation with which they are confronted and what he sees as the only way out.

> "There is no longer any room for hope. If we wish to be free—to preserve inviolate those inestimable privileges for which we have been so long contending—if we mean not basely to abandon the noble struggle in which we have been so long engaged, and which we have pledged ourselves never to abandon until the glorious object of our contest shall be obtained—we

must fight!—I repeat it, sir, we must fight; an appeal to arms and to the God of Hosts is all that is left us!"

The point of view expressed by Mr. Henry ultimately prevailed; the state of war was not long in coming. On April 19, 1775 minutemen and british redcoats clashed at Lexington and Concord. The strife continued for several years with the outcome remaining in doubt through much of that time.

The decisive battle occurred at Yorktown in October of 1781 when General Washington's troops defeated a large force of British redcoats under General Cornwallis. The final peace treaty was signed on September 3, 1783. The last British troops pulled out of New York in November of that same year.

## A NEW NATION WAS BORN

The new nation owed its existence to the loyal support given to the effort by the colonists; to effective leadership and to the intense dedication and selfless sacrifice of those patriots who made up the militia at the time. All driven by the perceived need to throw off the bonds of subservience to Great Britain and to establish a new democratic, citizen-oriented form of government that would fit their needs.

# CHAPTER 2

*******************************************************
* No man is good enough to govern another
* without that others consent.
*
* Abraham Lincoln
*******************************************************

The colonies that prevailed over the British in the Revolutionary War were voluntarily associated with each other and pursued their common goal of freedom living under the provisions of an Articles of Confederation (AOC), which had been drafted and presented to Congress in June 1776 and approved by the Congress on November 15, 1777, after lengthy debate. It was not until almost four years later in 1781 that it was endorsed by all of the states.

In the struggle with the British the loose, non-binding Articles of Confederation proved to be adequate. It provided an acceptable framework of rules and relationships during that period. The specter of what defeat, at the hands of the British, would mean to the individual colonists and to the aspiring new nation, served to strengthen the sense of cooperation, cohesiveness and singleness of purpose among the colonists. They were determined to gain new control of their own destiny.

Following their victory against the British, the colonists and the states changed the focus of their attention to the pursuit of their own interests. In this mode of operation, it soon became apparent, that the government structure provided by the AOC was inadequate to serve their needs and those of the Nation on a continuing, peace-time basis.

The AOC provided for a central Congress which consisted of one representative from each of the thirteen states. Delaware, a small state, had the same representation as did Virginia and some others that were many times larger. The powers given to the Congress were very limited. It could regulate the post offices, metal money, standards for weights and measures and it could make treaties. It could obtain money or men for the army from the states only if those states were willing to contribute. The Congress had no way of enforcing its laws.

Government which conformed with the Articles did not provide for a President and a Supreme Court. The realization came early that the government's limited status, authority and power would impede the new nation's ability to manage internal affairs as well as all-important trade, commerce and other relationships with the nations of the world.

And so! in modern parlance, we would say that the colonists found themselves, "between a rock and a hard spot". Having just cast aside the bonds of oppression they had experienced under the heavy hand of the British rulers, they were determined not to reestablish conditions that would, once again subject them to such conditions. On the other hand, they recognized an impelling need to establish a central government that could provide for the common defense, could govern interstate and international commerce, and could levy taxes to pay for the *necessary* expenses of such activities. It would need to have authority to adjudicate problems between the states. Provisions for enforcing the laws were needed. Finally, they recognized that as times and conditions changed, it would be necessary for future generations to alter or amend the provisions of the document; they devised a practical procedure for doing this.

In early May 1787 the states sent delegates to Philadelphia to try to amend the "Articles of Confederation" to satisfy the nation's on-going needs. The difficulty of the task to be under-taken there was recognized. The delegates that gathered in Philadelphia were leaders of the country at that time. Many had distinguished themselves in ways that uniquely qualified them to contribute to the success of the effort. Statesmanship, the art of debate, of give and take, the ability to keep the needs and interests of the individual colonists and their states in the forefront of their consideration—but to be willing and able to subordinate that, *to the documented, authentic needs of the nation* was a common virtue. They were dedicated to the concept of the individual citizens maintaining preeminent control of their own destiny and of their government. History tells us that the debate was on occasion rancorous and stormy to the point that there was often fear that the effort would fail. But that did not happen.

And so it was that on September 17, 1787, the Convention, by unanimous consent; the States represented there subscribed to an amended Articles of Confederation. It was renamed, "The Constitution of the United States". The document was signed by the delegates to the Convention and sent out to the states for ratification. It took nine months to gain the approval of the required nine states.

Some measure of the success of this effort may be gleaned by the fact that neither the colonists nor the states was entirely satisfied with the provisions of the new Constitution. Individuals, working people, felt that they had not been adequately represented; that the wealthy, owners of property, etc. would gain all of the benefits. There was a widespread fear that the new government would be tyrannical and infringe upon the rights of the individual and/or usurp the power of the states. (A situation that speaks well of their vision and perception of what might happen. Although this was not a problem in their lifetimes, it has evolved into a major problem during the last half century.)

The Constitution developed in Philadelphia in 1787 has served as a major foundation block of our government in the intervening years. There have been 26 Amendments to it. The first ten amendments were all adopted at the same time in 1791. They carry the subtitle of "The Bill of Rights".

The Constitution provided for a basic configuration of the government that included:

1. A Congress to make the laws; to consist of two houses. Members of the lower house (The House of Representatives to be elected to two-year terms. Representatives of the upper house (The Senate) to be elected to six-year terms with one third of the membership to be up for re-election every two years. All bills seeking to raise revenues are to originate in the Congress. (Article I; revised by Amendments 16 and 17)

2. A President, who is charged with the basic responsibility of enforcing the provisions of the Constitution and the laws of the land. Who will serve as the Commander-in-Chief of the Armed Services. Who shall make treaties which must be approved by "two-thirds of the Senators present". The President, with the advice and consent of the Senate shall, "appoint Ambassadors, other public ministers and consuls, judges of the Supreme Court and all other officers of the United States, whose appointments are not herein established by law". The President is up for re-election every four years. (Article II; Amendment 22)

3. A Supreme Court and such inferior courts as the Congress may from time to time ordain and establish. The judicial power shall extend, "to all cases, in law and equity, arising under this Constitution, the

laws of the United States, and Treaties made or which shall be made under their authority; . . . etc.". The judges, "shall hold their offices during good behavior". That is, they are appointed for life, barring some misdeed that might justify their impeachment. (Article III)

The national government was given some important new powers:

1.  To levy and collect taxes,
2.  To raise and support armies,
3.  To regulate trade,
4.  To make all necessary and proper laws required to exercise the powers granted to it.

Laws passed by the Congress under the Constitution apply to all states and persons in the Nation. States may not make laws contrary to them.

The states retained full authority to control local matters such as marriage laws, property laws, education, public utilities, etc. The states were also left with the authority to decide who might vote.

An important provision stipulated that future amendments may be proposed, "whenever two-thirds of both Houses shall deem it necessary. Amendments may also be proposed, "on the application of the Legislatures of two-thirds of the several states". They become part of the Constitution when then ratified by, "the Legislatures of three-fourths of the several states, or by conventions in three-fourths thereof".

The first ten Amendments to the Constitution—The Bill of Rights—were adopted as a group about four years later in 1791. The rights of the general citizenry of the country are enumerated clearly in several of these Amendments. For example, Amendments 1, 4, 7, 9 and 10.

The following premise is included here to serve as a basis for your continuing exploration of the thesis of this book:

All of our future references to the "Constitution" will be to the total document; the original document and all of its amendments. The Constitution is the defining document of our nation. In its original form, it provided the basic foundation for the government that Abraham Lincoln labeled, "government of the people, by the people, and for the people". Reference here to its original form is for the purpose of contrasting that early document and the government that the people enjoyed under its sincere, ethical application in our society; to conditions that prevail in the country today! In that original form of the Constitution, the Judicial

Branch of our government is charged with the responsibility of protecting the rights of the *people* (all of the people) and of assuring that relationships and transactions within society—including all government actions—comply with the provisions of the Constitution. Unfortunately however, in the intervening years since its creation, we the people have **blindly** delegated the responsibility for this work to the justice system. The checks and balances built into the Constitutional system have been totally ineffective; especially during the past five or six decades. The Executive and the Legislative Branches of the federal government sat idly by, twiddled their thumbs, and did nothing to challenge their actions! And the people, who are also charged with oversight responsibility of all government actions, did nothing! As a result, the justice system has overtly evolved into a form of legislative system in its own right, issuing interpretations and decisions which reflect the personal and corporate biases of the "actors" there. Actions based, not on interpretations of the Constitution; but instead, upon what will conform to their personal biases and work to achieve their personal vision as to what the country should become.

Although it goes beyond the thesis of our work here, a good case can be made that our system of government will never operate to its fullest potential as long as there are millions of citizens who have never so much as even read the Constitution! Or who read it and lazily conclude that it is too complicated for them to understand? That is a "copout"! You owe it to yourself and to the country to read it carefully and thoughtfully and to develop your own personal opinion of its meaning and intent.

Continued reliance by the millions on the erroneous concept that only lawyers, judges and others in the legal system can understand it, and that they *must* interpret it for us—the lay people of the country—can only lead to further erosion of the system.

It should not be too difficult for us to understand that! We all know people who choose to study law and become attorneys and to work in the justice system. What motivates these people? Are they driven by a selfless, inner passion to serve society? To sacrificially dedicate their lives to achieve the best interests of the nation and its citizens in an honest, objective interpretation of laws of the land! A few of them may be.

This would be akin to comparing them with another small group of people in our society who turn their backs on career choices that would present them with possible opportunities for gaining fame and fortune; and who, instead dedicate themselves to sacrificial service to humanity and to the Lord's work.

If, in fact, that was the prevailing mind-set of the majority of those who work in and administer our justice system, then *maybe* we could rationally delegate all of our responsibilities for maintenance of law and order to them. Maybe even then, that would not be wise!

As a matter of fact, most who choose the legal profession as a career do so for the same reasons that any of us choose a line of work. It corresponds to our interests and abilities. We envision opportunities for acceptance in it; possibly even fame and fortune. In the pursuit of those ends, "looking out for number one", becomes a high priority; with legal professionals, as with most others! Continuation of the present, "total delegation" concept, means that to participate in or influence the system you must pay the "insiders" their rates and play by their rules.

An important, question poses itself. Where are the lines drawn between: *what is good for the practicing individual, for the ordinary citizens, and for the country?* To go one step further, what priority will preserving *your* rights, *my* rights, and those of *all individual citizens* receive in the considerations and actions of those practitioners of the justice system as it is presently constituted and operating? Keep in mind that there are only so many rights and benefits to go around. When governments give individuals, minority (as contrasted to majority) groups, special interest groups, etc., special benefits; they do so at the expense of the rest of us. If you are not a beneficiary of such actions, you are one of the losers!

Success of our form of government demands your participation; it demands that you read the Constitution; it demands that you develop a philosophy as to how it should work, and theories as to how it should apply to contemporary situations. Our government, including—especially—the system of justice, must work for us! or it will not work at all!

To summarize: it is important to stress the fact, that in addition to being **the nation's** Constitution; this document is **your** Constitution and **mine**. This system of government cannot work **for the people** unless it is government, **of the people**, and **by the people**! **The people** must be involved.

*That means **you** and **me**!*

# CHAPTER 3

During the past several years we have celebrated the 200th birthday of our Constitution and our nation. The oratory on such occasions naturally goes into the history of events during the intervening time. The nation has survived a number of serious challenges to our sovereignty and freedom, from outside our borders. In these instances the citizens and the states reacted with much the same singleness of purpose and dedication as was exhibited by the colonists in the earlier encounters.

It survived terrible internal conflict, in which many families suffered the agony of brother fighting against brother, in the armies of the north and the south. The Civil war raged, from April 1861 to May 1865. Freedom for the slaves, most of whom were owned and used in the south was given as the primary issue. At the time of that war the total population of the United States was about 21,000,000 of which about 3,500,000 were slaves. The significance of the estimated 360,000 casualties suffered in the conflict can be best appreciated when that figure is equated to the fact that there existed only about 5,100,000 men between the ages of 15 and 40 in the country at the time.

As the new nation grew in size, in population, in industry and commerce, in influence in the family of the world's nations, and following its emergence as a member of the victorious side in World War II, it reacted with much empathy to nations, on both sides of that conflict. It provided massive amounts of assistance, especially to those who had experienced physical destruction of their property, industry, infrastructure, etc.

It also was empathetic to and provided much assistance to disadvantaged nations and their people around the world. It became immersed in some serious conflicts, in which our way of life, as a people and as a nation, were not in immediate jeopardy. These activities could be more accurately defined as policing actions. Designed to prevent the spread of communism, the prevailing form of government in many countries; some of which were aggressively pursuing efforts to extend its use in new venues by military means.

For the first time in its history, excluding the time of the Civil War, the Nation suffered major fractures in the resolve and singleness of purpose within its population. Support of the national effort in these missions was not universal. In fact, a small segment of the population actively and aggressively opposed the efforts and demonstrated publicly against them. One might try to attribute the fracture to the fact that the nation was not in jeopardy. But that was clearly not the case, something important had happened, was happening, in the relationship between the nation, its leaders and its citizens. Acts by some of our citizens, in the opposition movement, undeniably bordered on treason as it had been defined in earlier days. And, although it was overt and widely publicized by the media, the perpetrators were not charged and prosecuted. Circumstances that may be viewed by future generations as serious lapses in judgement, with serious, undesirable future implications. The sense of trust and respect that many of us felt for the activists of the times plunged to an all-time low as we were forced to view the despicable way they publicly treated members of our armed forces as they served, selflessly and bravely in foreign lands; and when they returned home from years of dedicated service, life threatening activities and the continuous agony of helplessly observing associates, friends and others being "blown away" in the Korean and Viet Nam conflicts.

In the 200 plus years that our Nation has existed, it and its people have achieved some of the goals envisioned by its founders. Its citizens have enjoyed freedoms that are unique in the annals of man. The high standard of living is unparalleled by that of any other people on earth. The Nation has risen to be one of the major economic and military powers in the world.

And yet, we often encounter expressions of concern as to the viability of the Nation's health, its ability to continue to survive at its present level of opulence and to continue to provide a basis for the affluence to which its citizens have become accustomed.

The concept that "great nations rise and fall" is not new. Recorded history is replete with stories of nations that have risen to great heights of economic and/or military superiority only to fall and be replaced **at the top** by others. The rise and fall of the Roman Empire is a well documented example. The rise of Great Britain to be a major colonial power and ruler of the high seas with its mighty navy for an extended period, to be followed by its release of control over most of its colonies and its decline as a naval power; the rise of Nazi Germany to its zenith of military power and its subsequent collapse as a result of its defeat by the allies in World War II are others. Paul Kennedy has documented much of this aspect of the history of the world from the year 1500 to 2000 in his book, "The Rise and Fall of the Great Powers". (Random House, 1987)

Many nations and peoples have had their **time in the sun**, only to suffer the plummet back into a condition of relative obscurity. The lesson of history points to the probability that **our time at the top** will end, as have the others. The question, not if it will happen? but when? Individual and national interests of present and future generations of Americans and earthlings should provide a strong incentive for us to work together to seek ways to:

1.  Assess our present situation in the most objective, thoughtful way possible, utilizing all of the knowledge, ability and skills available to us.
2.  Identify areas where we have erred, where a total change in program direction may be desirable, and\or where we can improve the effectiveness of our present course of action.
3.  Identify the natural, human and financial resources available for use in meeting our needs.
4.  Develop new programs that are designed to meet realistic goals for mitigating the needs, in which actual progress can and will be measured against the program plan; and which can be **accomplished within the limits of our available resources**.
5.  Demand effective program management. Those programs that are accomplishing the desired result will be retained. Those programs with marginal benefit-to-cost ratios, will be carefully considered for possible redirection or cancellation. Those that are obviously not effective will be discontinued.

These proposed management techniques are not new. They have been proven to be highly effective. That fact, seems to have been lost to masses of the new generation of management people; especially that group trained in the Masters of Business Administration and Masters of Public Administration factories in some of our colleges and universities. Where they are cloned to pursue the tenets of overrated department heads; theorists only, who have limited, if any, hands-on management experience with which to prove that the concepts inculcated into the skulls of their students will effectively work!

Our oratory related to events of the last 200 years, has been merged with similar rhetoric of our expectations for events of the next 200 years. Of course, the pictures that were painted were of continued freedom, prosperity and success of our democratic form of government. Did you consciously react to those comments, or not?

Such a scenario may be possible. Whether it is probable is another question. My spontaneous reaction to such comments has been one of sadness. My intuitive feeling is that our system is not working that well. That, in fact, barring substantial change in our collective approach to nurturing and preserving our form of government, we may well find ourselves at or near the lower part of the cyclic curve, during the lifetime of even those who are senior citizens today. Those thoughts continually torment me. They have been a primary motivational force in my writing this book; to bring some of these concerns to your attention, to seek your perspective on them and to seek your help in doing what we can, together, to improve the outlook for this and succeeding generations.

I can probably make the statement that, "Some parts of our government are not working well," without substantially raising your level of aggravation. That is the general, non-definitive type of judgement statement that we have become accustomed to in today's passive environment. Our leadership in and out of government, insists on talking **around** situations and problems. We allow those in control of our institutions to shadow-box or completely evade the tough issues being encountered! We do not insist that they and others with whom they interface in their work, identify the **real** problems, seek **real** solutions that speak to the **real** needs for short-term remedies that are consistent with well thought out, long-term goals, and that will challenge our people and our nation to be the best it can be!

Let me test your "irritability factor" further by stating my concerns a bit more strongly, "Many parts of our government system are not working!"

Now that your thinking has been somewhat conditioned, by those statements, let me state the problem in a way that accurately reflects my fears and concerns. "Few, if any, of our Federal, state or local government systems are working as they were intended; as they must if we are to preserve a continuing adequate standard of living for ourselves; and as they must if our nation is to maintain its ranking stature, respect and power in the family of nations of the world! We are living on **borrowed time** as a **chosen people**.

I appreciate that that is strong language. In many circles it would surely provoke the response, "If you don't like it here in the good old U.S.A., you should go somewhere else." That response misses the point. I did not say that it cannot work! I said that we are not effectively exploiting its capabilities and potential. Properly translated, administered and executed, our democratic system, as pictured by those visionary colonists who provided it's foundation, may well prove to be the best method by which people can govern themselves; in both times of war and peace.

If it is used constructively, the knowledge that the system, our country and we are heading for troubled times, raises a number of questions:

1. What is your perspective of the situation? Is our system of government working? It is important that you do not misunderstand that question. The thrust of the question **is not**, "Is it working for you?" You may be sitting on top of the world; however, your good fortune and mine are directly related to the continued prosperity of our country. The question posed involves the effectiveness of operation of the entire system.
2. If you perceive that it is not working as it should, "What is the nature of the problem? problems? To what extent might it be problems with the system? or the result of human failure?"
3. Is it possible from your perception, that the system could be made to accomplish the vision of our forefathers? The one that we and future generations seek?
4. How do we go about making needed improvements. What buttons do we push? Who are the action parties? How do we activate and motivate them?
5. **Is my/your active participation necessary? Can you have an impact? Will you have an impact? Will you accept my share of the responsibility?**

It is important that we fully explore the implications and the importance of some of these questions and the spontaneous, knee-jerk answers that many of us might give to them. Is our system working? The honest answer of most persons probably is, "I don't know, I really haven't thought that much about it." There are good reasons for such a response. The details of all the activities in which our government is involved are so vast, so complicated and so confusing that the average person will have to work at understanding them, analyzing them, developing a position and then projecting his/her beliefs into the public arena. That average person cannot easily devote the time to get into all of that. He/she is faced with the difficult, time-consuming, all-important effort of providing the necessities of life for themselves and their dependents. How will they find the time to become knowledgeable about all of the many issues and opportunities facing society. Many will have trouble understanding the need for them to spend, their valuable time on such seemingly irrelevant issues; issues that do not jeopardize their immediate situation or have an obvious, adverse impact on their achieving their goals.

Of course, we select and pay massive numbers of people to operate and manage our governments—the collective business needs of the people. It would be nice—a reasonable expectation—to depend upon them to do this job for us. That is, after all, what they are paid to do! But, alas! that proves to be not possible. We find that many of the problems we must correct are the result of their ineptitude, inability, or unwillingness to do the job that must be done.

If there are significant existing problems, or if such problems are evolving within our society; someone must step up and lead the effort to preserve the freedoms and quality of life that we cherish. **They**, those who are in command, are not the answer! They are, often unknowingly so, the cause of the problem. It is you or me, or no one!

It is important that you give careful consideration to the question raised in item 3 above. Establish a position of your own on that issue. But please try to maintain enough flexibility in your position to allow you to change your mind later.

Much of what we will be discussing and thinking about in subsequent pages will provide new insight and possibly affect your ultimate answer to that question.

Your position on the issue raised in item 5 is also important. If your tendency is to conclude, in response to it, that your participation is not necessary; that you cannot have an impact, positive or negative; and that, as a result you'll **sit this one out**,—don't despair—you will have lots of company. Many others will share that view at this point. Suffice it to say, here, that **you really do not have a choice as to whether or not you will have an impact on what happens**. You will have an impact one way or the other. If you subscribe to the philosophy so prevalent within our society, that one person cannot make a difference, and as a result you do not wish to get involved; you become a member of that group of citizens we often respectfully (?) refer to as the **silent majority.** You relinquish control of the decision-making process to others whose views you may not share; and whose actions may result in serious misdirection of our programs. Your lack of participation has a negative impact upon the effectiveness of our government, since your ideas and ideals will not be factored into the decisions reached.

If you actively and conscientiously participate in the system; your input represents a positive influence; especially if you take the time and make the effort to assure that yours is a studied contribution that reflects your position in life, responds to what you perceive to be the needs of your community and state and your understanding of **what is best for the Nation.**

The fact that not all citizen contributions measure up to that criteria poses serious problems that we will discuss as we proceed. It is unfortunate, but true, that to a large extent, we the people, for what ever reason, are willing to prostitute our ballots; basing our decisions and actions at the polls upon narrow issues, which in the short-term may seem to be compatible with our individual needs but which in the short-term and long-term may, in fact, be detrimental to the national, as well as our individual interests. Much of the misdirection that occurs at the polls is probably due to a lack of understanding of what our system demands of its citizens. The institutions that exist in our society today; the schools, media, etc.; that could and should extol to our citizens the importance of their studied, effective participation in the process seem to accept little, if any, responsibility for doing so.

The deficiencies of our public school systems is well recognized in our society. The children, and the nation are short-changed by the inadequate education provided in the basic, three R's (Reading, wRiting and aRithmetic); in preparation for college, and in the basic sciences. It fails to responsibly meet the public's need for basic education in the history of our country, and of the world. It falls short in the teaching of civics, defined broadly as basic knowledge of our governments' structure, how it is supposed to work, and the individual's responsibilities, if it and we are to succeed in its effective implementation and operation. The importance of such knowledge to our people seems to have been lost to the decision-makers that establish the curricula, programs and graduation requirements for that system.

# CHAPTER 4

That from these honored dead
we take increased devotion
to that cause for which they gave
the last full measure of devotion
—that we here highly resolve
that these dead
shall not have died in vain
—that this nation, under God
shall have a new birth of freedom
and that government of the people,
by the people, for the people
shall not perish from the earth.

Abraham Lincoln
November 19, 1863

If we are to use the ideas and concepts of the Constitution in our own approach to citizenship, we must have knowledge of its contents.

As we proceed with a review of some of the important features of our Constitution, keep in mind, that the observations made here, are those of the author. Yours may be different in some instances. For you, your perception is the most important.

We must start with the Preamble. It sets the stage for our further consideration and better understanding of the entire document.

In Webster's Dictionary, Preamble is defined as follows:

1. An introductory portion; preface; specif., the introductory part of a statute, which states the reasons and intent of the law.
2. An introductory fact or circumstance.

The Preamble to our Constitution contains a special message from those who wrote it, to those who would follow them and whose responsibility it would be to provide continuing stewardship of the system for the nation. That message:

# PREAMBLE
# TO THE
# CONSTITUTION

WE THE PEOPLE, of the United States
in order to form a more perfect Union,
establish justice,
provide for the common defense,
promote the general welfare
and secure the blessings of liberty
to ourselves and our posterity,
do ordain and establish this Constitution
for the United States of America.

The Preamble indicates clearly that: (1) the Constitution is being written by, (2) the new government is being established by and for, and (3) it is to remain in the control of "We The People"; the citizens of the United States of America. It then enumerates goals and benefits that they expect to achieve for the nation and its citizens. The fact that the Preamble and the Constitution that follows speaks to a limited number of items, is thought by many to accurately speak to their intent. Interference and intrusion of the Federal government into the rights and affairs of the states, the people, and of lesser institutions was to be avoided.

They clearly sought an arrangement that would accommodate harmonious relationships between the states. They recognized the need for an effective system of justice, one that, by definition, would be fair to all and at the same time would be compatible with other priority needs. An effective arrangement for protecting the Nation and its people from outside predators enjoyed a high priority with them. They spoke to the concept of promoting "the general welfare", an important notion that can be and is defined in widely diverse ways by citizens of our Nation, today.

Whether or not the definition of "general welfare" being pursued and implemented by actions of our government, especially the Legislative Branch, is in agreement with public opinion or represents the best interests of the Nation, short- and long-term, is an important question that you need to carefully consider. Finally, they spoke of their desire to "secure the blessings of liberty" for themselves and future generations.

Our individual ability to accurately determine how well our government is functioning; to diagnose the problem areas; to identify possible remedies; and finally to mark our ballots to best address the needs identified, requires that we understand the provisions in our Constitution. That is, we must have an understanding of how it is supposed to work.

The first three Articles of the Constitution establish the organizational form and operational plan of our government:

The government shall consist of three major components; the Legislative, Executive and Judicial branches. Additional information contained in these articles relates to the staffing, personnel qualifications and the selection processes, the division of responsibility between the three branches, limitations that would be imposed on the states by Federal authority and identification of limits applicable to Federal intervention in the activities and business matters of the states and individuals.

In the following discussion of Constitutional highlights, statements enclosed in parentheses represent comments of the author.

# ARTICLE I
## *The Legislative Branch*

All Legislative (law-making activity) Powers granted by the Constitution are vested in the Congress of the United States. The Congress is to consist of two separate entities; the Senate and the House of Representatives.

All members of the House of Representatives shall be chosen every two years. To be eligible to become a member of the House a person must have attained the age of twenty-five years and have been a citizen of the United States for at least seven years.

The number of representatives for each state will be determined by the number of persons in that state. Each state shall have at least, one representative. The number of representatives shall not exceed one for every thirty thousand persons.

The Senate of the United States will be composed of two Senators from each state. Each Senator to be elected for a term of six years. The total number of Senators will be divided, as evenly as is possible, into three classes. Election of the Senators in each class to be staggered so that approximately one-third of them will be elected every two years. Each Senator will have one vote. To meet eligibility requirements to become a Senator, a person must have attained the age of thirty years and been a citizen of the United States for at least nine years.

The Vice-President of the United States will serve as the President of the Senate but he does not have a vote on issues there, unless the Senators are equally divided on an issue, in which case, his vote will break the tie.

The Senate has the sole power to try all impeachments. When they are sitting for that purpose, they shall be on oath or affirmation. (affirmation—a solemn declaration made under the penalties of perjury, by a person who conscientiously declines to take an oath) When the President of the United States is tried the Chief Justice of the Supreme Court will preside. Conviction requires the concurrence of two-thirds of the members present. Judgements in impeachment cases will not extend beyond,

(1) removal from office, and
(2) disqualification to occupy any office of honor, trust or profit under the United States.

The party convicted shall, however, be liable and subject to indictment, trial, judgement and punishment according to the law.

Article I, as amended by Amendment No. 20, specifies how Senators will be elected. It also:

— Specifies rule making provisions and rules for operation of the House and the Senate.
— Defines a quorum.
— Specifies that the houses may compel attendance of absent members, "in such manner, and under such penalties as each House may provide". (An interesting provision, that demonstrates keen insight by the writers and one that is used, on occasion, in modern times.)
— Gives each House the responsibility of determining the rules for punishing its members for disorderly behavior and for expelling a member, if two-thirds of the members concur in such action.
— Requires each House to keep a journal of its proceedings. Provides for the omission of items which must be kept secret. The yeas and nays of the members will be entered in the journal, if one-fifth of the members so desire.

— The Senators and Representatives will receive compensation for their services, as ascertained by law; to be paid out of the Treasury of the United States.

— Senators and Representatives shall in all cases, except treason, felony and breach of the peace, be privileged (immune) from arrest during their attendance at sessions of their respective houses and in going to, or returning from the same.

— Senators and Representatives "shall not be questioned in any other place" (held accountable or liable) for things said in any speech or debate in either house. *(A provision that probably is necessary to allow transaction of the necessary business to be conducted there. It is, however, one that is, in the minds of many people greatly abused by some of the more boisterous, insensitive, self-righteous members, especially when they are performing in front of the American people via use of the mass media.)*

— Provides that all bills for raising revenue shall originate in the House of Representatives; "but the Senate may propose or concur with amendments as with other bills".

— Describes rules for approval of all bills by the two houses and the President, for presidential veto and possible "override" by a two-thirds vote by both houses of Congress.

— Gives Congress the power to lay and collect taxes, to pay debts, to provide for the common defense and general welfare of the United States; to borrow money on the credit of the United States, to regulate commerce with foreign nations and among the several states and to establish uniform rules for naturalization. To establish post offices, Tribunals (courts) inferior to the Supreme Court, a patent system, etc. To raise and support armies, a navy, etc. and to declare war.

— Establishes a number of rules governing the relationship of the Federal government to the states, states to other states, etc.

## ARTICLE II
### *The Executive Branch*

The executive power shall be vested in the President of the United States. He, together with the Vice-President, elected for the same term, will serve for a term of four years.

The rules and process for electing the President and the Vice-President as set forth in Article II, and the 12th Amendment are complex. However, in general terms, their election is based on the votes of citizens in all of the states. As contrasted with the election of Senators by ballots of eligible voters, **only** in the state they represent; and of the members of the House of Representatives who are elected by voters, **only** from that portion (district) of the state that they will represent.

To be eligible for the office of President of the United States, a person must be 35 years of age and shall have been a resident of the United States for fourteen years. The President shall be compensated for his services; the amount of the compensation cannot be increased or decreased during the period for which he has been elected. "He shall not receive within that period any other emolument (wages) from the United States, or any of them."

Before entering into office, he shall take the following oath or affirmation:

> "I do solemnly swear (or affirm) that I will faithfully execute the office of the President of the United States, and will to the best of my ability, preserve, protect and defend the Constitution of the United States."

The President is the Commander-in-Chief of the armed forces of the United States. He has certain management authority and responsibility over the Departments of the Executive Branch. He has the power to grant reprieves and pardons for offenses against the United States, except in the case of impeachment.

With the advice and consent of the Senate, the President, "shall appoint ambassadors, other public ministers and consuls, judges of the Supreme Court and all other officers of the United States, whose appointments are not herein established by law". *(This provision raises some interesting questions as it has been applied on occasion. For example, that of a Democratic Senate majority, to a Republican President's (George Bush) nominees for high-level Executive and Judicial branch positions. The control, criteria or censorship mandated by that Senate probably went far beyond the intent of the writers of the Constitution. That Senate's action denied the country of the services of capable applicants, merely because their personal opinions or philosophies on some issues differed from those of a few long-time, established, powerful members of the Senate. A surprising circumstance, when in a braggadocio mode, we are told and some believe that a major strength of our system is that it provides the means for persons of widely diverse backgrounds, levels of knowledge, experience and opinions to come together, resolve differences and establish positions that contribute to the strength of our nation. We are led to believe that there are no deities, no Gods, in the system with which others must agree if they are to be allowed to participate and contribute their talents.*

*As is almost always the case, in situations where "cute ploys" are devised by foolish people who try to beat the system, counter-measures can be and often are developed and used to restore the balance of power or authority. This happened with the above situation. Although he had been in office for an extended time, President Bush continued to operate much of the Executive Branch with "acting" political appointees in management positions. Not the best modus operandi, but it provided a livable alternative. A good case, probably a Constitutionally sanctioned case, can be made for the fact that George Bushes election as president represented the mandate of a majority of all participants in the last election. Barring some illegal or otherwise totally unacceptable activity in the background of a candidate nominated for such a position, the President should be allowed to choose staff people that share his views and aspirations, and who will help to implement the programs that he promised.)*

The President, Vice-President and all civil officers of the United States shall be removed from office by impeachment for, and conviction of, treason, bribery, or other high crimes and misdemeanors."

The provisions of Article II were altered by Amendment 22 which was adopted on February 27, 1951. That Amendment limits the length of service of any President to a maximum of 2 terms, eight years. Under certain conditions, where a President serves the remaining portion of another's term, the maximum length of service is less than the eight year period.

# ARTICLE III
## *The Judicial Branch*

The Judicial Power of the United States shall be vested in one Supreme Court, and in such inferior courts as the Congress may from time to time ordain and establish.

The judges of both the Supreme Court and many inferior courts shall hold their offices during good behavior, that is, **they are appointed for their lifetime, barring some behavior that would require their removal from office.** The judges shall be compensated for their services; **the amount of**

**their compensation shall not be diminished during their time in office.** *(Inclusion of the two provisions in bold above, demonstrates the genius with which the writers of the Constitution understood some of the major threats it might be subjected to, and where such threats might originate. The simplicity with which they provided isolation and protection of the Judicial from overzealous members of the Legislative and the Executive Branches, demonstrates vision and managerial skill.*

*The reach of authority and power of the Judicial establishment is awesome.* "The Judicial Power shall extend to **all** cases, in law and equity, arising under this Constitution, . . ."

The Supreme Court will have original jurisdiction in cases involving ambassadors, other public ministers and consuls, and in which a state is a party. In other cases, the Supreme court will have Appellate jurisdiction.

# ARTICLE IV

Article IV contains a number of provisions that establish rules for Federal to state and state to state relationships.

"Full faith and credit shall be given to the public acts, records and judicial proceedings of every other state, . . ." The Congress has the responsibility and authority to "prescribe the manner in which such acts, records and proceedings shall be proved, and the effect thereof.

The citizens of one state shall be entitled to all of the privileges and immunities of citizens of the several states. A citizen charged with a crime in one state and who flees to another state, shall be delivered up to the state having jurisdiction, when so requested by that state.

Debts (service and labor) of a person incurred in one state, shall not be discharged by another state to which he/she might flee; but shall be delivered up on claim of the party to whom the debt may be due.

Provisions are included that govern the process for and prohibitions against the admission of a new state.

The Congress is given the power to, "dispose of and make all needful rules and regulations respecting the territory or other property belonging to the United States.

A caveat is included to the effect that, "nothing in this Constitution shall be so construed as to prejudice any claims of the United States, or of any particular state."

The United States shall guarantee to every state in the union a Republican form of government *(a form in which the sovereign power resides in a certain body of the people—the electorate—and is exercised by representatives elected by, and responsible to, them)*. The United States shall protect each state against invasion from without and against domestic violence (from within), when that state asks for help.

# ARTICLE V

Article V provides the rules and procedures to be followed in developing and implementing amendments to the Constitution.

# ARTICLE VI

Article VI provides for continuity of operation as the transition was made from operation of Government under the old Articles of Confederation to its operation under the new Constitution.

It provides that the Representatives, the Senators and all executive and judicial officers, both of the United States and of the several states, "shall be bound by oath or affirmation, to support this Constitution, but **no religious test shall ever be required as a qualification to any office or public trust under the United States.**" *(This requirement has an interesting possible application in the ongoing, intense, public debate on the issue of abortion. The legality or appropriateness of Senate interrogation of nominees for important executive and judicial positions, concerning the nominee's personal opinion on the abortion issue certainly should be called to question under this provision. The pro-life position is, for many, a matter of religious belief.)*

# ARTICLE VII

Article VII established the rules for ratification of the original Constitution. These conditions were fulfilled and the Constitution was ratified on September 17, 1787.

# THE AMENDMENTS

At the time this is written there are 26 Amendments to the Constitution. They have been added at propitious times, as evolving conditions made modification or clarification of some aspect of the Constitution seem necessary.

# THE BILL OF RIGHTS

The first ten Amendments are referred to separately as "The Bill of Rights". They were drawn up and adopted as a single unit in 1791, about four years after the ratification of the Constitution. Since many of these first ten Amendments will play an important role in some of our later discussions and because they are briefly stated in the document, they are repeated verbatim here.

## *Amendment No. 1*

"Congress shall make no law respecting an establishment of religion, or prohibiting the free exercise thereof; or abridging the freedom of speech, or to petition the government for a redress or grievances."

*(Although there are only 32 words in the first amendment, it's provisions have played a major role in the life of each citizen and of the Nation. It is not surprising that freedom of religious pursuits is prominently presented early in this Bill of Rights. Religious persecution, the inability to choose the religion of their choice was one of a fundamental reason the colonists had fled England. Isolation between the government and the church community enjoyed high priority with them. Extension of application of this amendment beyond what many perceive to be the original intent, continues to be a controversial issue in our society.*

*We can expect continuing widely diverse applications of the "free speech" provision. The intent of the writers of the Constitution was clear on this point. The people of the new Nation were expected to retain control over their government. If that was to happen, the citizens needed the protected right to speak out freely about any concerns they might have about the way it was working, or not working; about the effectiveness of those elected or selected to make it work and about changes, deletions or additions that would improve its operation.*

*It probably did not occur to them that the provision might be interpreted and used to prevent the elimination of cancerous growths in our society that are contributing to serious dimensions of moral decline. The cataclysmic decline in the ethics and morality in this nation must be recognized and addressed. Viewing the present condition with that of even ten years ago is worrisome. Many view what they believe to be inane interpretations of the "free speech" provision of the first Amendment as a major contributor to this decline. Some would accept an interpretation that allowed the creation of the kind of pornographic scum so prevalent in our society today. After all, we don't have to buy the material; and many of us don't for personal or family consumption. But as a taxpayer, I loathe the fact that I am forced to support activities of such sordid organizations and individuals. When my tax money is used to purchase such pornographic material for placement in school and public libraries; freely available to children of all ages, and to those older deviants who get their highs from the pictures and material in them—on their way to the commission of heinous, violent crimes against unsuspecting brothers and sisters in the larger societal sense.*

*Please recognize that the media would like to operate in an arena of no controls. Although they continue to exercise a smattering of control over the material they print or show on the tube, they have regularly and systematically allowed more and more suggestive? lewd material and sexually explicit performances. There are huge profits available to those who write, print and market pornographic material. They too, must gain great satisfaction out of the present interpretations of this amendment. Any organized effort to correct this situation, would certainly encounter great opposition. That should not stand in our way. The Constitution provides that course of action for the citizens when its officialdom is not responsive to their expressed needs and priorities.*

*Court rulings on this issue and others remain controversial with large segments of the population. Such court rulings are merely the opinions of the persons sitting on that court. That does not necessarily make the rulings right. But, Supreme Court rulings are the law of our land, until legislative or amendment actions correct the misdirection. As citizens, we accept their findings; but we don't have to agree with them.* **Our** *constitution provides the means for correcting the situation; put there by the founding fathers with the expectation that* **the people** *would use it when needed!*

*As an afterthought, can you imagine what would have happened to some malcontent of the times, who might have burned an American flag on the steps of Independence Hall while the writers of the Constitution were in town, about their business of creating our new Nation? It doesn't stretch the imagination too much to believe that he/she would have been charged with treason and dispensed with promptly and systematically.*

*Problems within the Judicial Branch of our government contribute greatly to some of the major problems we face. A cursory look at what we refer to as our "system of Justice" in this country can easily lead one to the conclusion that somewhere on the road to fulfillment of the national needs for a system of justice, the practitioners have become confused and disoriented; there is little about it that makes any practical sense.*

*For starters, I will be looking for something as we are going through this Constitution, that says that to be eligible for a judgeship on the Supreme or a lesser court a person must be trained as an attorney, and that applicants for the Supreme Court must be submitted to and approved by the American Bar Association. You, and I can hear it now! Their retort! the law and the business of the courts is too complicated for the layman to understand. They are, of course, partially right. Stated correctly, "the law, as they have nurtured its evolution over the years, is so complicated that no one understands it." Of what use is such a situation. How can a legal system fit the needs of the nation when the people can't understand the laws?)*

## Amendment No. 2

"A well-regulated militia being necessary to the security of the free state, the right of the people to keep and bear arms shall not be infringed." *(Never has the need for retention of this right, been greater than it is at this time. Our founders had good reason for including this amendment. Ownership and use of individually owned firearms played a major role in their recent victory. The ability to rapidly organize the population into an armed militia for the purpose of defending the country was an important issue with them.*

*There is a trend in our society today to associate serious crime with the fact that peace-loving, law-abiding people own firearms. It is wise to suspect that supporters of the elimination of guns ownership by the public may have other agendas that are not in the best interests of all the citizens and the Nation. It is not inconceivable that continued decay of our ethical and moral values and the competence of our system of justice will where the primary protection of the law-abiding citizen, his extended family and his property will depend upon his ability to defend himself. At the present time many people; good, law-abiding people find themselves to be prisoners in their own homes, and the system has been, in most cases, uninterested or totally ineffective in correcting the situation. If there is one thing that we can say with a high degree of accuracy; it is this, "it was not the intention of the writers of the Constitution, that it be used to benefit the criminal element—at the expense of law-abiding citizens.")*

## Amendment No. 3

"No soldier shall, in time of peace, be quartered in any house, without the consent of the owner; nor in time of war, but in a manner to be prescribed by law."

## Amendment No. 4

"The right of the people to be secure in their persons, houses, papers, and effects, against unreasonable searches and seizures, shall not be violated; and no warrants shall issue, but upon probable cause, supported by oath or affirmation, and particularly describing the place to be searched, and the persons or things to be seized."

*(The people should zealously guard this right against intrusion, especially against busy-body government officials and their employees. In matters of criminal law this amendment seems to enjoy considerable respect. However, it means little to local bureaucrats and the elected officials whose proper function it is to protect the interests of the citizens, who elected them.*

*In some communities, it has been the practice, for some time, for local officials to force their way into rental units when the tenants complain about uninhabitable conditions. In such cases the entry is usually authorized by some form of warrant. Of course, that activity costs money and the bureaucrats, always vigilant to identifying new ways to con money from the tax payer, diligently seek ways to force someone to pay the bill. In some communities they have passed laws that calls for inspections of all rentals units, once every year, whether they have a complaint or not. For this service??, they will bill all rental property owners at the rate of $15 per unit per year. A clever, unconstitutional way (by my standards), to force entry into personal property and to force those conscientious landlords, who keep their rentals in good condition, to pay the costs of forcing others to adequately maintain their units. These kinds of intrusions must be fought with zeal. Each such new action is but one more step in the loss of our control over our institutions.)*

## Amendment No. 5

"No person shall be held to answer for a capitol or other infamous crime unless on a presentment or indictment of a Grand Jury, except in cases arising in the land or naval forces, in time of war or public danger; nor shall any person be subject, for the same offence, to be twice put in jeopardy of life or limb; nor shall be compelled, in any criminal case, to be a witness against himself; nor be deprived of life, liberty or property without due process of law; nor shall private property be taken for public use, without just compensation."

## Amendment No. 6

"In all criminal prosecutions, the accused shall enjoy the right to a **speedy** and public trial, by an impartial jury of the state and district wherein the crime shall have been committed, which district shall have been previously ascertained by law, and to be informed of the nature and cause of the accusation; to be confronted with the witness against him; to have compulsory process for obtaining witnesses in his favor, and to have the assistance of counsel for his defense."

## Amendment No. 7

"In suits of common law, where the value in controversy shall exceed twenty dollars, the right of trial by jury shall be preserved, and no fact tried by a jury shall be otherwise reexamined in any court of the United States than according to the rules of common law."

*(It is interesting to note in the 6th and 7th amendments that emphasis is placed on the importance of the accused having the right to trial by a jury of his/her peers. After all, the whole thrust of this new government was that its future was being placed in the control and protection of its citizens. It is not difficult to understand their reasons for placing the fate of persons charged with unlawful acts in the hands of their peers. Such requirement was totally consistent with their perspective of where the power should be, even in those situations involving the Judicial Branch of the new government. It would seem that their intent was clear, it was not a proper function for the judicial system to make policy or laws. It was intended that the judicial **objectively** interpret the provisions of the Constitution; to judge the constitutionality of questioned;*

*1. statutes created by the Legislative, or*
*2. rules established or actions taken by the Executive, and finally*
*3. to provide a setting and a process whereby the "people" in their role as jurors could fairly judge the guilt or innocence of charged persons in criminal court or the question of equity in common-law cases.*

*So, tell me please, how did we ever get to the point where, with today's system, in many places throughout the country where the death penalty is the prescribed punishment for some major criminal violations; "guilty" decisions* by a jury of peers; those cases are **automatically** put into an appeal mode. The fate of the case is systematically taken away from "the people" and put into the hands of the legal profession. Where it is shuffled around in a nonsensical fashion, from court to court, judge to judge, prosecuting and defending attorneys ad-infinitum; for as long as 15 to 20 years—even in cases where there is absolutely no question but that the defendant is guilty. All of this requiring the continuing services of attorneys for the defendant, attorneys for the prosecution, judges and all of the other costs of the court plus incarceration costs for the defendant. Of course, the enormous expense of almost all of this is borne by the "good ole tax payer", you and me. Remembering that the Constitution, which should serve as the "Bible", so to speak, for our justice system: it is appropriate to examine the following quote from the 6th amendment of the Bill of Rights, "In all criminal prosecutions, the accused shall enjoy the right to a speedy and public trial, by an impartial jury of the state and district wherein the crime shall have been committed . . .". The intent of the writers of this document seems very clear. Any semblance between what they had in mind and what has evolved here eludes me! What about You?

Mind you, these people, these employees of ours, who are doing our work in this endless appeal process are not pikers. They can't get by on the $5.00, $10.00 or $15.00 per hour that the average citizen must subsist on. Fees of many of them start at $100 per hour! $400, $500, etc. per hour fees are not uncommon.)

## Amendment No. 8

"Excessive bail shall not be required, nor excessive fines imposed, nor cruel and unusual punishments inflicted."

(We can expect that your familiarity with the evolving interpretation of the term, "cruel and unusual punishments inflicted" will increase substantially in the immediate future, as more and more felons are released, unprosecuted, back into society; in many cases to continue to inflict their brand of cruelty and unusual punishment and their practice of crime upon the innocent, law-abiding class of citizens; because of "overcrowding" in our jails and prisons. This is a major problem in our society today. It will become more serious with passing time. As a Nation, we cannot continue to ignore it. Although it is about the only alternative being considered, the construction and staffing of more prisons is not an effective answer.)

## Amendment No. 9

"The enumeration in the Constitution of certain rights shall not be construed to deny or Disparage others retained by the people."

## Amendment No 10

"The powers not delegated to the United States by the Constitution, nor prohibited by it to the states are reserved to the states respectively, or to the people." *(It is meaningful that the last two amendments of this "Bill of Rights" deal once again with the idea that the powers of the Federal government and the states are limited and that the overriding authority and power resides with the people.)*

Although the remaining amendments, 11 though 26 contribute importantly to the totality of the Constitution, they will not be individually quoted or discussed here. Their provisions will have a lesser level of applicability to the issues we will be discussing. At some point, you should take the time to become familiar with them.

A few of the more interesting concepts included in them are summarized below:

| | |
|---|---|
| Amendment No. 13 | Forbids slavery. |
| Amendment No. 15 | Forbids denial of voting rights because of race, color. etc. |
| Amendment No. 18 | Bans manufacture, transportation or sale of intoxicating liquors. |
| Amendment No. 19 | Gives women the right to vote. |
| Amendment No. 20 | provides direction as to terms of the President and Vice President and selecting their successors, should that be necessary. |
| Amendment No. 21 | Repeals Amendment No. 18. |
| Amendment No. 22 | Limits the President to two terms. |
| Amendment No. 23 | Provides for the District of Columbia's participation in the electoral selection of the President and the Vice President. |
| Amendment No. 24 | rotects right of citizens to vote for national leaders even though they may have failed to pay any poll or other tax. |

| | |
|---|---|
| Amendment No. 25 | Provides rules for succession into the offices of President and Vice President. |
| Amendment No. 26 | Gives 18 year-old the right to vote. |

As we proceed with this discussion, it will be important that you stay closely in touch with the information presented in this chapter. Or, better yet, keep a copy of the actual Constitution document handy for reference.

Experience tells us that it is unwise for the electorate to passively and blindly allow the justice system to have a free hand in gerrymandering and manipulating the future of our country with slanted, non-literal interpretations that suffer from the interjection of the political beliefs and biases by the practitioners hired to do that work for us.

At the very least those people need to know that the people are watching what they do; and that they will get involved if that becomes necessary!

# CHAPTER 5

The concerns, ideas, ideals, hopes, visions, etc. of the author are presented here. Within that total context, we might hope that the people of the country could reach a consensus agreement as to the nature, scope and importance of at least some of the problems we face. But, in a democracy such as this, consensus never seems to be attainable. When everyone does not even agree that we have a problem; it surely is not possible to reach consensus agreement on the identification of a particular problem, alternative methods for seeking its resolution; calculation and examination of the cost versus benefit ratios of each alternate or a final decision as to the plan of action that will best accomplish our needed end-results.

Thankfully, those who developed the Constitution and other basic documents for our nation recognized that fact. In general, it was their intent that the majority opinion "of the **citizens**" of the country would rule. The government structure and guiding principles they established for our use were consistent with that concept. If you and I believe that our system of government can be made to work, we have to believe that there is a way to achieve majority opinion on complex, difficult issues.

For most of our history, that has been demonstrated to be possible; and effective. However, as a result of pivotal, misdirected, government actions during the past several decades, majority rule has been subordinated to the demands of the few. The population has been divided into a number of "special" groups; by race, by sex, by age, etc. by government action. The Legislative, Judicial and Executive Branches of government at all levels have caved in to self-serving, aggressive claims by members of these groups that they are victims of the majority of the population and of the system. Your government servants, and mine; the millions of people we hire and who are reimbursed with highly competitive salaries and perquisites, have foolishly awarded each member of those groups a vast array of special rights and remuneration. The losers of rights and finances, are, of course, the same group of honest, taxpaying citizens; who "pay the piper" for everything in our system. The recipients of such benefits know a good thing when the see it. We can not expect them to voluntarily give up "the good life", achieved at our expense. In my opinion, most of this social engineering of the country is not compliant with a literal interpretation of the Constitution. Is it with yours? If not, it is our duty to try to correct the problem.

These fractures divide our society into narrow minded, opinionated, intolerant groups; their members have no respect for any ideas or opinions but their own, they force themselves and their sometimes deviant, distracting, and disturbing actions into the environmental realm of others, and they exhibit contempt of the "rights" of others. Essentially, anything goes, as they singlemindedly pursue attainment of their own programs and goals. Motivation of our people to rise above this multitude of fractures, to strive for unanimity of interest and purpose may well be impossible in our present political environment. The resulting situation that we are forced to endure is unfortunate; **it brings out the worst in all of us**.

A primary tenet of our system is that serious, objective, honest consideration of the important issues we encounter in our life as a nation, can be resolved to a point of general acceptance by a majority of our citizens. Statesmanship is necessary in two arenas: on the one hand citizens' must be willing to subordinate some of their individual needs and goals to the needs of the nation. Secondly, the government must limit it's actions and demands upon the people to the minimum needed to achieve Constitutionally sanctioned government services. In our early history, government exhibited this second type of statesmanship quite well; and the system worked. But, as the elected and appointed officials and their bureaucrats have, over time, found it expedient to become our overlords, our "keepers", administrators of our resources, our finances and our souls; all of that has changed. Never has the intelligent use of the ballot been needed more. Of course, I wouldn't want to infer that you and I are less than true patriots in the ballots we cast. But! it is important for us to honestly differentiate between the ballots we often cast and the ones we would cast as true statesmen/women, who look beyond our immediate personal situations and cast the ballot that from our individual perspectives is "best for the nation"; ballots that look beyond single issues such as social security increases; abortion; labor union support; carte blanche, seemingly mindless support of any and all social spending; more or less taxes; etc.; etc. We recognize that these issues are important in many people's minds. However, our relationship, as humans, to the nature of the earth upon which we live and the complexity of the relationships between individuals, and of individuals to our public and private enterprises, is much too complex to respond correctly to such narrow, single-issue points of view. To achieve the degree of unanimity required, we must throw off the blinders and look at the broader picture.

Having spent over thirty years pursuing a professional engineering and management career; rearing two children, in partnership with my wife, Rosalee; and serving society as a volunteer adult scouter, Sunday school teacher, president of the Official Board, Lay Leader, Finance Chairman, of some quite large protestant churches, etc., I know of the demands that each of you have on your time. We simply do not have enough time to do everything that we would like to do; that we think we should do! Too often, that translates into our having no time to devote to the duties of citizenship.

Despite the fact that our citizens are preoccupied with day to day problems of substantial personal consequence, there are probably few, if any, that have not, at one time or another, felt some level of concern about the continued viability of our government. For large numbers of citizens the concern is driven by a fear of losing periodic government checks! All of us cherish the freedom and quality of life that we derive from our government!

The issues identified here are important. Agreement on a form of corrective action may be possible. Such effort and action is timely for today! Your reaction, be it passive or active, will determine important features of our country's future direction.

And so! what are some of these important issues of which we speak? For our purpose, they will be divided into two categories:

1.  Those which have been covered extensively in the media. These are issues that should be familiar to all citizens of voting age, to the point that their consideration should play a role in the ballot decisions each voter makes at the poles.
2.  Others that, for reasons not readily apparent, have eluded any significant level of interest or attention by the citizenry or the media. As a result, they are waiting to be discovered by concerned citizens.

As will become obvious as these issues are identified and discussed; their recognition, analysis, and development of plans and programs to deal with them, does not necessarily require a super human effort or ability. The lack of attention in some of these cases is probably due to oversight; in other cases, the perspective of those who gain personally from the status-quo may well result in intentional efforts to prevent exposure of potential problems to public attention and thoughtful analysis; which might lead to change.

That is, open discussion of such issues might violate covert, sacrosanct efforts to protect "sacred cows". However, open consideration of their influence and contribution, positive and negative, is important to any sincere, comprehensive examination of our society. They cannot be ignored if we are to succeed.

Many of our present activities and programs which utilize vast amounts of human and financial resources, continue to exist and receive financial support because of spontaneous, knee-jerk, unthinking actions by those in power. A well defined, final goal has not been established, against which on-going program performance can be measured. Quantification of results being achieved; and justification for the expenditure of resources being made are, therefore, not possible.

A nation or a world submerged in an abyss of such an illogical, irresponsible, management vacuum, has little chance for success. If our system is to be allowed to work properly, **WE WHO ARE RESPONSIBLE FOR MAKING IT DO SO MUST BE ABLE TO RECOGNIZE AND BE WILLING TO ACCEPT THE FACT THAT THE RESOURCES AVAILABLE TO US ARE LIMITED; THAT WE WILL NEVER BE ABLE TO DO EVERYTHING THAT NEEDS TO BE DONE OR THAT WE WOULD LIKE TO DO; THAT WE MUST IDENTIFY GOALS, ESTABLISH PRIORITIES AND MAKE PROGRAM CHOICES THAT WILL MATCH THE FINANCIAL, TIME AND HUMAN RESOURCE REQUIREMENTS TO THOSE AVAILABLE IN A WAY THAT WILL ACCOMPLISH THE MAXIMUM BENEFIT FOR THE PEOPLE AND FOR THE NATION.** The blind pursuit and continued funding of programs that are obviously not accomplishing the purposes for which they were originally intended is unforgivable when there are so many high priority needs for those resources; especially when we have the knowledge and ability to do what needs to be done.

The following items are representative of the kinds of issues included in the first category. They have received an appreciable amount of media coverage. They should, therefore, be viewed with some degree of familiarity by people of voting age in our country:

—Each of us must deal (struggle) on a continuing basis with the need to balance our personal income and expenses. Some will do so, in a formal, well documented way that forces compromise and that balances expenditures against income. Such personal and family plans and budgets are designed to assure some continuity of personal financial integrity and security.

Others, by default, mimic our public approach to the situation. They simply live "day to day" and put up with what ever the new day brings. Regardless of our individual approach to this endeavor, one thing rings "true and clear" to most of us. We are never able to obtain everything that we would like to have.

Our individual experience in the demanding need to maintain our own financial solvency, surely translates into some understanding and concern about the imposing financial problem that results from gross mismanagement of most government programs. Maintaining the financial integrity of our country is a responsibility shared by the Legislative and Executive Branches of our governments. The Federal debt has, at last, reached the point where even the members of those organizations recognize the issue as a major problem; one that they should address and develop corrective actions.

Our system is breaking down at this point. Those to whom we have entrusted the management of our affairs, simply do not possess and exhibit the necessary statesmanship and leadership abilities. A few short years ago, our country was the world leader in lending funds and resources to other nations. But! in the intervening period of time, our governments, Federal, state and local have been mismanaged to the point that we are now the world's largest debtor nation. That is, our debt to other nations exceeds that of any other nation in the world; and it continues to grow at an alarming rate.

As is usually the case with any issue we face, we can expect to encounter supposedly learned presentations in the media and elsewhere, suggesting that our growing multi-trillion dollar,

Federal debt is not a serious problem. We are left to individually sort things out and decide the issue for ourselves. It is important that we do so and not acquiesce to the inclination to take the easy way out; to pass the subject off as some one else's problem.

Consider, for example, that at the present time, we (you and I), must pay something over $250,000,000,000 (that is 250 billion dollars, just over $1000 for every resident of our country) per year in interest on the National debt amassed by past extravagances. We must do this before we start to pay for the necessary continuing current expenses of our government. And consider this, until recently, the Federal debt and that annual interest commitment has increased at a rapid rate. Payment of the annual interest expense will require greater and greater percentages of our annual national expenditures.

Personal experience, intuition and "common horse sense" tells us that it is a problem; a serious one! **Spending in excess of income is a problem for individuals and it is a problem for nations; even ours!**

—For those who understand the implications of the continuing, sizeable deficits in our "balance of trade" with other nations, that must also be a source of concern. During the past several years the dollar value of the items that the United States has imported (cars, electronic equipment, clothing, etc.) from other countries has exceeded the value of our exports by tens of billions of dollars. The cumulative effect of these annual deficits in the "balance of trade" has placed huge quantities of U. S. dollars in the hands of foreign nations and individuals.

Those dollars will be spent and invested in many ways and many places around the world. Many of them will find their way back into the U.S. economy, in a way that will result in increased foreign ownership of our real estate, our manufacturing and commerce, our transportation systems, etc. A measured loss of control of the destiny of our own country is sure to follow.

—The critical ineptness of our public school systems is a universally accepted fact; it has been for years. The aspect of this problem that is most widely discussed and accepted relates to the question of, "what our children **are not** learning", in our schools.

For some who have studied the problem in depth, "what they **are** teaching our children", in place of what they **should be** teaching them, is an even more serious problem. This situation is discussed in depth, and in a scholarly fashion by Allen Bloom in his book, "The Closing of the American Mind" (Simon and Schuster). As a member of the educational fraternity, Mr. Bloom wrote the book in their lingo. It is not easy for the lay person to read and comprehend. I suspect that in writing the book that way, at least part of his expectation was that, the educational establishment, when confronted with a respected insider's analysis and exposure of the serious problems in the system, would finally accede to the gravity of the problem, agree that major reform is needed, and to finally proceed to implement remedial action. But alas, the system is either brain dead or incompetent to the point that it is unable to react! Nothing happened! It seems obvious that improvement of the system will occur only if such action is forced by outside intervention.

Given the general agreement that this is a serious problem; it is incomprehensible that most parents of children in the system, those who have the most to lose, are not demanding that the effectiveness of these systems be improved! now! Instead, they and the general public cower in the presence of their "**elected**" school boards; tolerating ineptitude by that group and the teachers and administrators who are paid to educate our youngsters. Instead of banding together with others, and demanding improvement in the systems, those parents who really care about the issue, arrange for their children to be taught in private schools; at extra cost to themselves, and they forget about the total public situation. Unfortunately they, and we, cannot escape the dire consequences of this critical public problem. It's cascading, accumulating adverse impacts are ever present in the haunting, continuing deterioration of our society!

—And what of our system of medical services? Medical costs are rising at a rate that is unreasonable and beyond comprehension. Costs already exceed the purchasing power of large segments of our population. Medical insurance, a system by which our citizens have shared the risk of financing medical costs in the past, is rapidly being priced beyond the financial capability of most of those who have shared its past costs and benefits.

People who have spent decades of their lives training to serve the public in medical service work, are being forced to leave that work, because of factors beyond their control. The ridiculous attacks of and massive financial settlements assessed by our legal system, against individuals and segments of the medical system and its practitioners are, of course, legend. It is, also, no secret that they are very attractive and profitable to that small group of aggressive, fee-driven members of the legal community that solicit and transact that kind of work. Their success in "sucking" extensive amounts of the financial, life-blood out of the health-care system for themselves and for their clients jeopardizes the continued availability of a quality, affordable health care system for all of us.

The ludicrous, uninformed, onslaught being masterminded by elected persons and bureaucrats at all levels of government exacerbate the problem; and hasten the time when affordable medical benefits are no longer available for **any of us**.

As is the case with many of these problem issues, decisions are being driven by powerful, emotional forces that continue to become more deeply ingrained in the thinking and actions of our electorate, the politicians and the bureaucracy!

That we have fallen prey to the tentacles of this condition is understandable. It derives its strength from the most captivating and powerful of all of the instincts and character traits we share as humans; that of emotion. Simply stated, large numbers of our people are overwhelmed by the impact of what we will call "**the emotional plague**". The societal condition in which "**Emotional Idiocy**" dominates over reason, logic and intelligence in decision-making processes. We will refer to the societal condition that results as an "Era of Emotional Idiocy" (EEI). In such an environment, emotional considerations totally transcend everything else!

When leaders whose wisdom, honesty and ability we rely on for the development of effective policies and solutions and corrective action for our problems, suffer from the affects of the "emotional plague"; they fail us; and the nation. Crucial, national and international decisions by a "world power" that are dominated by emotional factors, as those in this country presently are, do not adequately serve the needs of any one. Public and private enterprises cannot function efficiently or effectively in an operating environment where important decision-makers are biased by the influence of the emotional plague; and where an aura of EEI prevails throughout society.

Intelligence, logic, reason, and negotiation; critical operational principles of any successful public or private enterprise are totally incompatible with a society operating in an "EEI" mode.

Lets pursue this a bit further. Normally, with emotional idiocy operational, our continuing analysis could proceed with no limits placed on the bases for our decisions. The assumption being that man has total control over his environment, and the universe. Of course, that is not reality. Human activities, what we can do and the way we do it, are limited by a set of fixed parameters. The sort of things that might be referred to, by some, as the **"laws of nature"**. Our understanding of these factors represents what we know about "the Master's Plan" for relationships between earthly creatures, their interaction and their relationship to the earth.

I remember a commercial that was once run extensively during an Olympic extravaganza. It showed a wide cross-section of earthly creatures, lying peacefully together; a picture of total harmony. There were lions, tigers, coyotes, foxes, wolves, etc. peacefully coexisting in an Eden-like setting with elands, zebras, sheep, and other animals that make up the food-chain for the carnivorous group. The deep, underlying concept apparently being conveyed by the genius of Madison Avenue was the desire for everyone and everything to live in harmony.

This presents a consummate example of the presence of "Emotional Idiocy". Never mind that, due to circumstances totally beyond our control, maturation of that dream situation is impossible. Under such conditions many of the animals in the picture would starve to death and become extinct. Some realities of the "real world" are difficult to accept emotionally. Watching carnivorous animals successfully hunt, chase, kill and eat other animals can be a traumatic, emotional experience for some. But that is the way it is in the "Grand Plan" that rules our universe. A plan developed by one, wiser and more visionary than we. A plan in which humans are cast to play a small role; and in which they are able to have some slight affect in the evolution of events that unfold with the passage of time.

In the "Master's Grand Plan", man has been given unique abilities and powers with which to rule his universe. To think, to learn, to analyze, to control, to communicate, etc. That is, to have some limited control over the evolution of our universe. We hasten to point out that the impacts of our actions are not always positive. The terribly destructive nature of errors in judgment seem to be lost to most of our people. We need only look to conditions in some third-world countries, where emasculation of the vegetation, erosion of top soil, over population, etc. are resulting in imposing conditions of hardship—malnutrition, starvation and death.

There is one television advertisement that has been shown many times with one of the Sunday talk-shows. I have seen it many times; and yet, its message always stuns me. It seems totally incomprehensible—impossible. The announcer tells us that—every second of every day there are three more mouths to feed on this earth!

The consequences of that are mind boggling—I revert to the use of my mathematics:

> 60 seconds in every minute—
> 60 min. in every hour          =     3,600 seconds/hour
> 24 hours in every day          =     86,400 seconds/day
> 365 days in every year         =     31,536,000 seconds/year
> 3 new mouths every second    =     94,608,000 new people/year

We will pursue this thought just one small step further. This does not imply that the increase will be 95,000,000 each year for each of the coming years. It will, in fact, be more than that. This activity fits into the pattern of a geometric progression in which the amount of increase, **increases, with each new year**!

We must continue on to other considerations. Please thoughtfully develop a priority list that presents your value judgment for some of the important assets of the earth; its creatures, minerals, institutions, etc. Consideration of the creatures part of that total picture could be helpful. For example, we might look at the relative value you would assign to humans, to fish, to birds, to large and small animals, etc. To further refine our thinking, we might limit ourselves to considering one human, one fish, one bird, etc. Of course, that will pose a problem. The question immediately pops up, which human? Are we talking about a close relative? Mom, dad, sister, brother; a distant relative? Uncle Joe, Aunt Mame, Cousin Jim? all of whom live far away, and who you have not seen in many years; someone on the other side of the U. S. that you don't know; the president of our country; the pope; someone in a far-away third world country; or who? It does make a difference to you! Doesn't it? That difference in value that develops in your mind results from emotional considerations. In a real-world, dispassionate setting; a human being is a human being; each essentially of equal value, and each of us a renewable resource. Although we represent a higher form of living organism, others can and will take our place when we are gone!

In a society commandeered by Emotional Idiocy, reason and logic are ignored in considerations that strive to establish the value of a human life. In such a society the education of our youth is of little benefit, if:

— That education is "politically correct", it only reinforces the trend toward emotional idiocy the student encounters elsewhere in their day to day activities,

— Society demands that emotional considerations control all situations! in which case a student who has been exposed and schooled in the true basics of knowledge and wisdom will not be allowed to contribute in making meaningful decisions.

In the "big picture" of universal considerations, the concept of renewability is important. That is, can an element or resource, once used, be regrown, renewed, or replaced within a reasonable time? All living creatures are renewable, as long as they are not allowed to go extinct. Forests, like all crops are renewable. On the other hand, many resources that are necessary for our continued habitation of the earth (en masse), are non-renewable! Once used up, they are gone—we cannot replenish the supply. Productive soils, most energy resources, etc., which are formed over millions of years are examples. That fact must have some impact on any viable priorities that we establish for the use and stewardship of all resources. Total utilization, or destruction of non-renewable resources will result in massive losses of creature life, *including humans.*

This line of reasoning leads to concepts that you may have trouble accepting. You will not be able to bring yourself to agree with it as long as passion and sentiment overpower intellect and reason in the decisions you make! Persons who are not infected with the **emotional plague**; who can subordinate temperamental, empathetic persuasion to logic and intelligence will be able to bring themselves to understand and agree with it! It is futile to struggle with the concept. It has been a major **positive** factor in what humanity has achieved and what it will continue to achieve in the future. It is not a matter of "if" each of us will one day depart from this earth; but "when". And we will be replaced by others who, if given a "proper" education and the opportunity to achieve; will in their turn serve as effective stewards of this nation and the earth.

Let me risk totally alienating you to this line of reasoning with an analogy. Let's approach the subject in this way. Have you been around where roses are grown? If you have, you will know that they are susceptible to attack by aphids, a small bug about the size of a pin head. Left to their own devices, aphids, reproduce in massive numbers and will soon inundate a host bush; and they will spread to other bushes in the vicinity. They systematically suck the sap out of the plant. Left uncontrolled they will ultimately destroy the source of their livelihood.

If you or I were able to gain a vantage point that would give us a panoramic view of the earth, that replicates the one we get of a rose bush; the similarity of the relationships—aphid to rose bush; human to the earth would be apparent to most. The existence of each creature, human and others, on earth creates some level of adverse impact; the accumulation of which, over time, has the potential for creating an environment that is no longer habitable!

The above concepts are important; if we are to successfully resolve the problems we face. Some will find it very difficult to accept them. Much more needs to be said about them; and it will be—later!

I don't want to be too hard on you; but it seems appropriate to "coin" a new term, here. Although it may be very demeaning to many, we can begin to understand the actual relationship of man to his universe if we recognize and become more comfortable with the similarity between him and his role to that of the aphids and the rose. We can acknowledge the similarities and the differences by reference to humans as "aphids erectus" *TM*.

What issues come to mind as we consider the second category of items? Those which have seemingly escaped attention, not just because they have been overlooked; but those which have intentionally been excluded from public debate because there are powerful interest groups who benefit from and are determined to protect the status quo. The mass media (which unfortunately sets much of the national agenda); our leadership; and vocal, minority segments of our population have knowingly suppressed discussion of such issues. As a result, these issues have not been allowed to compete effectively for attention in the ongoing public debate that establishes public policies and programs. The result! issues of major importance are ignored; and our human, natural, and financial resources are wasted on issues of myopic scale and importance:

—One item, which is significant in its own right, but which is even more consequential because of it's leverage and affect on a large array of other matters, pertains to man's relationship to the "laws of nature"; the rules of the universe and of our world. Rules that are absolute; over which we have no control, and which, if not adequately identified, understood, interpreted and respected; will have a profound impact upon the preservation of our own species.

Any discussion of the relationship between man, not just Americans, but all of humanity and the earth upon which we live may seem to be premature; a star wars type of consideration that is not yet a matter requiring our interest, concern or action.

Suffice it to say that careful scrutiny of our status today on the learning curve about the forces of nature and of our capabilities for its alteration and/or destruction, have identified some areas (the greenhouse affect and the affects of all-out nuclear war, for example) where there is some agreement that our activities may contribute to catastrophic damage to our planetary environment. Are we the dinosaurs of the year 3000 or 4000 A.D.? Will we create our own Armageddon?

In our society there are a number of well-intentioned groups that are vigorously speaking out and fighting for the preservation of the spotted owl, anadromous fish runs, wildlife habitat, etc., etc. Isn't it interesting that we recognize the possibility of extinction of those species, but demonstrate little or no interest, knowledge, or concern about the possibility that the human species faces similar hazards? The muffled voices of those who are speaking about this possibility, are heard by few people. The intellect that the subject demands is non-existent in today's public arena, where intelligent, experienced, the best-qualified applicants are passed over, in order to meet quotas established by the laws of clowns! It does not have to be this way. The solution to the situation is perfectly obvious. But! That does not infer that it will be corrected!

This largely by generations of Americans who take for granted the seeming ease and comfort with which we exist. Most have little or no knowledge, understanding or experience from which to develop a true perspective of just how fierce, intolerant and unrelenting is the nature of our universe and the earth that we call home. Most have not shared in experiences comparable to those of:

1. The early patriots as they spent long, cold; nights, days, weeks and months in the trenches and on the battle fields to secure freedom and a new system of government, or
2. The early settlers who as they traversed the Oregon and other trails westward, suffered the rigors of extremely hot and extremely

cold weather, of torrents of rain and heavy snow, wild animals and unfriendly natives, or for that matter

3. The millions of poor soles in many of the "third world" countries who, even today, are suffering malnutrition, disease and death because they lack the necessary fertile soil, climatic conditions and knowledge with which to provide the necessities of life.

It is so important to realize, and I am convinced that most of us do not, the thin thread by which we are able to survive here.

The potential for massive negative impacts, should we misjudge the importance of this issue, certainly dictates that it is better for us to be too early in our intellectual consideration of it than to be too late.

—Our governments, Federal and states, continue to support enormous amounts of medical research. What is the goal of that effort? Life expectancy has increased dramatically in the past few years. Given a measure of success in near-future efforts to find remedies for a number of cancers, heart problems and in the ongoing research to divulge the secrets of the gene structure and the significance of its various components to the events they might trigger during a lifetime, we could essentially expect to "live forever"! Is that what any of us really want for ourselves? Has anyone asked you that question? Activities in this area appear to be uncoordinated and totally out of control. Much of what is being done in the field, is being done just because it can be done! Not because doing it fits into some carefully crafted overall plan!

The short- and long-term goals seem to be undefined. The only time table that seems to exist, is to do everything, "as soon as possible". Are we really in that big of a hurry? Does all of this have to be done now, in our lifetimes? Can't we trust future generations with some of the responsibility? Can we afford to pursue such a chaotic approach to such an expensive effort?

Careful examination of the situation will reveal that the availability of massive amounts of "free" taxpayer money for these programs contributes to the problem. This being doled out, not on the basis of merit, but, instead, to friends and supporters as political-patronage payments by powerful members of the executive and legislative branches of governments!

By developing and presenting for use very expensive new procedures; medical research, as it exists in this country today; contributes significantly to the rapidly increasing medical costs for all of us. In an "Era of Emotional Idiocy" the reality is that all treatment procedures, regardless of how exotic and costly they may be, must be available for everyone—those who can pay, and those who cannot. Payment for the services to the multitude who cannot pay their own bills, is transferred in clever, covert, and I am convinced, unconstitutional ways to others; to the tax payer, to the premiums of those who have health insurance and to the hospital costs of those who pay for such services directly or through insurance coverage. And the escalation of costs in the medical field continues at an even more frightening rate! In a field of endeavor where effective management is absolutely necessary; we find that it is non-existent! The health care actions proposed by the Federal and state governments will only make the problem worse. Barring a more intelligent and responsive approach to the situation, the quality of health care in this nation will continue to deteriorate for all of us, regardless of our financial standing. The adverse impact of EEI on the issue must be recognized and dealt with.

—It is important to raise questions about the integrity and effectiveness of our legal system; our **system of justice**! Anyone who follows activities in that arena, has to shake their head in disbelief at what takes place there. Is this really what those who suffered through the early struggles of our country and the development and implementation of that original CONSTITUTION had in mind? I suspect not.

Where will our present approach to administering "justice" take us in future years? The continuing, aggressive intervention of "government", at all levels, into our private lives; the unwise, uncontested extension of the laws of our country into more and more of our personal activities; continuation of the "drift"? (probably more of a tidal wave) toward policies and practices designed not to determine guilt or innocence, but to accommodate the fancies and impose the views of the political and legal communities (legislators, bureaucrats, judges, lawyers, psychologists, psychiatrists and all of their related subordinates) upon the citizenry.

We are told that in 1992; 134,983 lawyers were paid $16.3 billion for their services in California alone! About $120,000 per lawyer, average. New York lawyers earned a second highest amount: $14.3 billion. Keeping in mind that your pay check and mine is the source of most of that money; does that make sense to you. Are you willing to passively continue on this path; recognizing that thousands of new lawyers are graduating each year and the cost to each of us, to pay for their schooling and to foot the bills of their work, can only go up! up! up!

One outgrowth of the present system is the rapidly growing, manpower intensive and very expensive problem of providing jail space and funding the ongoing incarceration costs of those who run afoul of our uncontrolled expansion of the legal "no—no's" created and enforced by our system. It has been reported that the staffing of this activity is the most rapidly growing employment area in this country. Does that really make sense? Is that the highest priority use we have for those human and financial resources? Where will continuation of present trends take us? What other options do we have? What are the relative merits of pursuing other alternatives? Emotional idiocy is involved here. "**What if**" it was replaced by intellectual analysis and the scientific method of problem solving?

—What are the unexplored issues related to the use of the death penalty in this country? The highly energized emotions that accompany any discussion of this subject, virtually eliminates any possibility for rational consideration of the pros and cons, alternatives, etc., of such action. There are important ramifications of our present practice that need to see the "light of day".

It seems so curious that the very difficult questions, "Who shall live? and Who shall die?", are not debated in the consideration of this matter. How many men, women and children are murdered each year by criminals who have killed before; sentenced to prison for "life" or less; who serve a small part of their sentence, and who are then released (by the system) to go back out into society and do "their thing"; again and again! Is there any question in your mind as to whether or not this system is working? If you think that it is, you owe it to society to make the argument so the rest of us can benefit from the logic and reason that brings you to that conclusion.

One of the prevalent, emotional arguments against the death penalty, is the abhorrent possibility that an innocent person will be executed for a crime he/she did not commit. I can understand that and I would be somewhat sympathetic to it, if we had another method that worked. But, in using the present system, we commit that grievous act of sentencing innocent people to death, hundreds of time each year! Are the lives of all of those people who die at the hands of released criminals that much less dear than the lives of those who kill them? Are the innocent children, women, and men who are victims of the present "system" any less deserving to live, than are those who take their lives? Incarceration in this emotion driven society is not the answer. The present approach is a cop-out! The people, their government and especially their "system of justice" will not let it work. There is one sure thing about all of this, criminals who are administered the death penalty do not return to kill additional innocent people! This situation deserves your careful consideration and follow-up action.

—Some of our citizens will be able to accept as constructive, a comprehensive discussion of the present-day affects, positive and negative, of organized labor to the problems we presently face. We can expect that others, those who presently benefit from its programs, will view any suggested changes with great suspicion. Organized labor has been a part of our society for a long time. It enjoys a great deal of respect and support in the minds of large numbers of our people. Everyone has some level of understanding of the substantial amount of influence it exerts over important economic and political issues. Influence that contributes directly to setting the course of our government's action; and that will impact our future ability to compete in the world economy. It is necessary that we carefully and objectively consider its impact upon our ability to survive as a nation!

—It is obvious to any astute observer of our society, that there are great fractures in the unity of the country today. To the point, in fact, that one wonders if it will ever again be possible to unify our citizenry, for support of any national interest, regardless of its importance to the survival of our way of life. How did this happen? What caused it? How deeply is it rooted in its adherents? Is it permanent? How can we best control it? Deal with it? Or eliminate it?

Legislative and Judicial branches of our governments seem totally oblivious to their individual and collective contributions to the origin and continued growth of this cancer in our society. They:

1. profess to continue to protect the individual rights of "the few" at the expense of the individual and collective rights of the masses and in total ignorance of the impact on the well-being of the nation, and

2. continue to "cave in" to new categories of people (victims?!.) demanding special rights and treatment at the expense of the rest of society. As we stand wringing our hands and helplessly and hopelessly watching the violence increase in regularity and savagery between the different categories of people, it is important to remember who created these discriminate categories, magnified the boundaries between them. Whose actions continue to aggravate the situation causing increased friction and hostilities between them.

—There is no question that individual rights, the bill of rights, were items of extreme importance to those who gave us our Constitution as it now exists. Freedom of speech, which in our time, can be and is translated into protection for all to speak out on any issue in nonlibellous ways. As the complexity of our institutions and processes has increased over the years, it has become exceedingly more difficult for the people to stay well informed; and as a result, to effectively carry out their responsibilities for maintaining a high level of performance and integrity of our institutions. The media could (should) play an important role in helping us in this area. Do they respond effectively to this need? On occasion, current events lead media organizations to ask the question, "How well are we doing our job. Almost without exception the question is asked of and discussed with other people in that same line of work. Of course, that is not the best place to seek truly objective, no-holds barred, constructive response. As a matter of fact, in that forum it is not even probable that the right questions will be asked! a circumstance that will severely limit the value of any such interrogation.

The influence and power of the mass media in our society is substantial. Biases of the institutions and of the "front line" performers, which should have no place in their electronic productions or hard copy, are readily apparent to the astute observer. Efforts at self-policing in the industry are seemingly non-existent.

—Finally, it seems necessary to raise the question, "Who is in charge in our country today"? Unfortunately, one believable answer is, "no one". A second answer, equally disturbing, is "everyone". These are questions and answers that certainly should stimulate our willingness to "get with it" and help do what is necessary to regain control. They both point to a nation in chaos with no mechanism in place to assure rational, effective government.

If, in fact, the government of our new nation was intended by the writers of our Constitution to be a democracy; a government "**Of the People, By the People and For the People**", to be guided into posterity by the document that they were developing; we can assume that each word in the document was chosen with great care. They certainly recognized the need for succeeding generations of "the people" to be able to understand it literally and to translate its provisions into action as society and its needs in the governmental arena changed. Thankfully, they succeeded in their efforts. We can understand what the Constitution says. It has generally served as an adequate foundation upon which to base decisions of significant moment during the two hundred plus years of its existence.

Of course, our Constitution goes beyond establishing our form of government as a democracy. It also specified that the President, Vice-President, Senators and members of the House of Representatives be elected by "the people"; an arrangement that is not required of a democracy, but which is consistent with a Republic form of government. Our form of government, as envisioned by our Constitution, is more accurately defined, as a democratic republic. For our purposes it is important to recognize this difference.

If it is to succeed in today's very complex, competitive national and international environment; any organization, public or private, must identify and employ the best qualified leadership, management, technical, professional, crafts-persons and all other workers. We will examine later, how well our system is fulfilling this requirement. Our question at this point, "Is the election process, as it is presently being used in our country fulfilling this requirement? Is it, in fact, providing us with the **best** qualified people available for these positions? Please consider all aspects of this question carefully. If you approach it objectively, the conclusion you reach may distress you. Each of us, and more importantly people around the world, seem to have intuitively attributed the seeming success of our system to the fact that we elect our government leaders. As the people in that block of countries that were under communist domination for the past several decades, threw off the restraints and repression of communism, their first and foremost demand was for the right to free elections of their leaders. It is important that **we, and they** interrogate honestly and objectively, the true effectiveness of the election process.

In view of the pain and suffering, the indignities and domination the colonists had experienced at the hands of the British; the terrible price they had paid to achieve victory over them; the dedication and zeal with which they worked to create the new Constitution and their vision of what this new Nation could be, we can forgive them for making the assumption that succeeding generations would be able, willing and dedicated to providing responsible stewardship for the system.

Their further assumption that the heirs to this responsibility would be wary of deviations that might threaten either the system or the people's control over it and that they (the people) would act swiftly and effectively to return activities to an acceptable norm, is also understandable. "Acceptable norm" to be defined, not by the Executive, Legislative or Judicial branches of the government, but by "the people", individually and by that group of qualified voters of each state and the nation. We can also understand that they may have overlooked the possibility that future generations of citizens would become complacent and soft, inattentive and neglectful of their responsibilities as stewards of the system and its benefits for future generations.

It is important to recognize that for many years, "we the people" have not been as diligent as we should have been in meeting these responsibilities of citizenship. Most of us have left to others, the interpretation of the Constitution and the decisions as to the application of its provisions to the on-going scene in our society. Rest assured that those to whom we have unknowingly delegated our responsibility in these matters recognize and covet the authority and power over others that they have gained through our inattention and carelessness. Don't be surprised or discouraged when our attempts to get back into the decision making loop are vigorously resisted. It is a well known axiom in the worlds of personal power and politics that, "advantage, once gained, is not easily, or willingly relinquished". It is important that we become aggressive in our pursuit of the "American Dream", we cannot sit back and passively accept other's interpretations and actions as the "only", "best", "most accurate", or "official" position. Recent events have confirmed ever so clearly, that personal biases and philosophies, with which many of us take serious exception, have been incorporated into our system through covert, questionable practices by those who will benefit from the change or through gross incompetence or negligence of those who are charged with managing the peoples' business and protecting their interests.

We can find these kinds of situations in all walks of life today; but they are especially commonplace in areas controlled by the elected, appointed and bureaucratic members of our government institutions; at all levels of government. When those institutions, large and small, reach the point that high levels of integrity, morality, ethics and quantity and quality of performance are not primary goals to which their leaders aspire; the situation is serious. We should not be surprised then, to subsequently find that these same attitudes and perspectives have trickled down to all levels of these organizations and that they ultimately dominate the lives and relationships of the total population: a condition that is well on its way to fruition. Toleration of such conduct can only lead to further decay and probable ultimate destruction of our society.

I grew up in a very fertile farming area in south-central Idaho; where conditions were especially adaptable to growing a wide of variety of row-crops and orchard items. In that environment, I learned first-hand about the "bad-apple syndrome". The problem is common to apples, potatoes and a number of other kinds of produce. It can be demonstrated by the following example. Take a large mass of good, ripe, firm apples; for example, a boxcar load. Place one or two apples in the car with soft, rotten spots on them. In a matter of time, the entire mass of what had been good fruit will be turned into a soft, gooey mass; a worthless mess. Some further examination of this situation is interesting. If our placing two "bad apples" in a boxcar of "good apples" resulted in ruining the whole parcel; no big deal! we will just reverse the process to get back to where we started. We'll put two good apples in this massive mess, and after a bit of time, we will get back our box car of good apples. Right? Okay? We'll do it! Put two good apples in and walk away for a while. What do we find when we come back? Is the process reversible? Do we find a carload of good apples? Unfortunately, it does not work that way! When we return we find that the two new, good apples have rotted and simply become a part of the total mess.

Of course, farmers and orchardists of those days were educated, intelligent people. Apples, potatoes, etc. that rot and must be thrown away do not augment the revenue they receive to pay expenses and contribute to their family's livelihood. Through experience and observations they learned of the delicate nature of some of their crops; and they protected the fragile ones from conditions that would destroy them!

What a blessing it would be, if we and our public officials of today shared some of the intelligence and discipline of those Idaho farmers! To the point that we recognized comparability of the fragility of our people and our institutions to those produce items! Thus shedding light on the devastation that results from so many of their actions; and pointing the way for immediate redirection of public policy and actions to constructive avenues!

Are you satisfied with the protection of person and property presently afforded to you; as contrasted to that afforded to the legions of repeat civil and criminal offenders? If you are satisfied, fine! If you are not, and it is probable that many are not, then individual and organized action directed toward achieving a more equitable balance of those rights between the law abiding and the law breaking segments of our society is necessary. The same officials, elected and appointed and in the bureaucracies, in all three branches of our Federal, state and local governments, those who have created the problem, have the ability to correct the situation; but! they will do so, only if we demand that it is done. Lack of what we, individually, consider to be proper response should trigger action for replacement of those who do not respond to the public's desires. Keep this clearly in mind, there are only so many rights. **Special rights given** to one person or class of persons are invariably **rights taken away from** another person or class.

Federal, state and local, elected officials, aided and abetted by an evolving, less than perfect system of justice, have systematically developed and put into place extensive systems designed solely to redistribute the rights and wealth of this nation. The process results in the confiscation of the rights and wealth of those who have claim to them, and reassigning them to others for any number of bogus reasons. This process preys upon the class of citizens who participate in our society, who are law abiding; who accept the responsibility for providing for themselves, their families and loved ones; who work to earn their own way and to hopefully provide some of the pleasures and luxuries that any surplus might provide them. They end up losers in both instances, rights and resources.

The basic concept at work here is one of ego and power of governmental employees demanding that they know better than we, how our resources should be allocated. That is, they inflict their own, largely corrupt, sense of ethics and values over our own in determining how **our** individual resources will be used. "BIG BROTHER GOVERNMENT", a concept that our Constitution was carefully designed to prevent.

The "rights taken away from us" and the "redistribution of our wealth" are not actions that are required by the Constitution. On the other hand, they probably do not violate its provisions.

That is, there is probably Constitutional "room" for the Legislative and Executive branches to enact such programs, **if that is what the people want**. If the people do not agree with such programs or proposals they have the right, in fact, the responsibility to make their desires known and to follow up in public, private and political arenas to see that the situation is corrected. Constitutionally we, the people, are not required to sit idly by and passively tolerate the taking of our resources to support charities personally preferred by our elected, appointed and salaried staff. We pay their wages to do **our** work; **the way we want it done!**

We do not have to look far to identify the existence of differences of opinion between the people and their public servants. Evidence is abundant, of situations in which the elected and appointed officials and the bureaucrats feel little need to heed the desires of the people when they differ from what they want to do.

It has been clear for at least the last decade that the majority of the people in the country are ardently opposed to new taxes. Polls show that to be the case. That premise is also supported by the results of the 1980, 1984 and 1988 elections of the president and vice-president; the only officials in our government who are elected by ballots of all of the voters from throughout the United States. The issue of "no new taxes" was a major, highly visible platform plank upon which the Democratic and Republican candidates differed in these elections. The "no new taxes" pledge of the winning republican candidates undeniably played a major role in their victories. Legislators at all levels of government are aware of the people's position on this issue, but it is difficult to identify even one instance where this has deterred them from enacting increases in spending! They take action to spend, without knowing what the action will cost; they completely ignore the question of where the funds will come from to pay the increased bills! When it is too late, the commitments have been made; they come groveling to the people for tax increases! And the people cave-in!

The arrogance is even more blatant in situations where the Federal Legislative Branch vote themselves and other senior members of the Executive and Judicial Branches substantial increases in pay and other benefits. This, in disregard of their clear understanding that such action is opposed by a large majority (possibly as much as 75 percent) of the voters of the country. This information is available to them at the time of their action, but they choose to ignore it. Our system cannot work properly with that kind of arrogance in place. The people, you and I, have a right to expect, in fact, to demand, more attentive, responsive performance by our pubic servants.

As we proceed with our review of the provisions of the Constitution, it is important that you develop some personal "feel" for your position on these and other similar current issues. Are you comfortable with what is happening? Are you uneasy, do you favor an effort to achieve some improvements? some increased control?

Don't accept, at face value, pronouncements by others, especially government officials, that your perception is wrong; that your preferred course of action is not possible. Never lose sight of the power of the ballot, your ballot, my ballot, our ballots when they are used properly, to achieve change and improvements that we believe are necessary. If, in fact, changes desired by a **majority of the people** are not possible; we can only conclude that our system of government is unworkable in its present form. That being the case, our alternatives in their proper order, are:

1. Force modification of the system through action of the incumbents in office. Lacking success at that, to
2. Replace those in elective positions who refuse to comply, or
3. Modify our system to make it responsive, or if all else fails
4. Change to a different form of government that will fit our needs.

The interpretation presented in this chapter is not that of a Constitutional scholar; whatever that might imply to you. It is, one citizens view. A studied perspective from which he considers candidates and issues and from which his ballots are ultimately marked.

It would be comforting to be able to look at what is transpiring around us and to conclude that all of these problems are in good hands. That conscientious, talented, knowledgeable, states-persons that understand the situation, recognize the gravity of the problems are working out and implementing solutions in a timely, effective way. Unfortunately, that is not what I observe as I follow the actions of different facets of our society on a daily, weekly or yearly basis. Let me repeat! The best (probably only) chance of success results from our actions; you and I have to get more involved!?

# CHAPTER 6

Earlier, we referred to the government that our ancestors created based upon the provisions of the Constitution as a democratic republic. What does that mean?

*DEMOCRATIC*

The word democracy originates from Greek roots, two words demos (meaning people), and kratein (which means to rule). Democracy;—rule by the people. Democratic concepts were used in governmental systems in ancient Greece between the years 600 and 400 B.C. in Athens and some of its other city-states.

The Romans experimented with democracy, but never fully accepted it as a complete system. With the collapse of the Roman Empire in the years between 300 and 400 A.D., the world entered a period of very limited governmental experimentation and development.

The next major thrust in the use of democratic principles in a documented, governmental environment came in the year 1215 A.D. when the Magna Carta (Great Charter) was approved for use by the government of England. Although the development and application of new democratic principles and improvements to its established concepts came slowly during the following 300 to 400 years, some of those contributions continue to be a part of our system. That should surprise no one, since most of the early colonists of our country were of English ancestry.

*REPUBLIC*

A republic is a form of government in which the citizens elect peers to manage their governmental affairs for them. The elected officials are then charged with the responsibility to manage the peoples' affairs; they are delegated the authority they need to do the job.

Again, the Romans were pioneers in the use of some concepts of this form of government, between about 500 B.C. and 25 B.C.

And so! the United States has not been the first to utilize many of the principles incorporated in our system of government. What is notable is that when founded in the 1770's; ours was the first and continues to be the only major country dedicated to total dependence on this form of government. Hence, the statements we encounter to the effect that ours is a "great experiment in self rule".

It is important to note that in terms of the time tables of governmental system evolution; development, reforms, decline and failure, time is not measured in weeks, months or years. As can be seen in looking over the dates in the above discussion, the evolution of governmental processes, their success or failure, has occurred over centuries. The fact that our system has seemed to work quite well(?) for about 200 years, in no way assures its success in the longer term.

There is a tendency for us to accept the term, "democratic republic" as an adequate, complete definition of our form of government. And then, we encounter in the media and elsewhere, references to the east-block portion of Germany as the GDR, the German Democratic Republic. Here was a country that depended on massive concrete walls and barbed wire fences to keep its citizens from fleeing to other parts of the world. It's form of government and the government's relationship to the people incorporated significant and obvious differences from ours; and yet the name is similar.

It becomes obvious that something additional is needed if we are to accurately and totally define the system we use. A nation choosing the democratic-republic form of government has available a number of options that may be adopted as complementary features which are compatible with a democratic-republic base system. The option selected for use greatly impacts the nature and quality of life of the citizens of the nation. Comparison of life in our own nation with that of the people in the GDR is, once again, an effective illustration.

As we prepare for discussion of our problems, symptoms, possible causes, alternative possible solutions, etc., it is important to recognize that the discussions will span a wide range of political, economic, personal and practical beliefs, held emotionally and intensely by citizens of our country. So much so, that it is almost impossible to generate searching, thoughtful, **objective** discussion of these matters. These are the kinds of issues that should be discussed by candidates for public office; but seldom are. The voters should demand that the candidates discuss them and state their position on each; but they do not. In fact, such an approach to campaigning today would undoubtedly work to the disadvantage of the candidate.

We want to do what we can to approach our discussion with an open mind; to maintain an aura of objectivity to the extent possible. We will not be pitting the position of Democratic party members against those of members of the Republican party; of the "left wing" against the "right wing"; the liberals against the conservatives; etc. On the other hand, it is not possible or desirable, to ignore these factions and their contributions to the "power plays" that ultimately determine the course of action that evolves for our nation.

An ideal approach to this discussion, would exist if all involved accepted the fact that no one special-interest group has all of the correct answers. The continuing, undivided acceptance and dedication of many of our citizens to all programs and candidates of a single party or other special-interest group will not, in the minds of many, serve the best interests of this nation. The best interests of the nation will ultimately depend upon our ability, as citizens to develop a forum where all ideas can freely surface, be objectively and intelligently considered. Where the best alternatives can be adopted, regardless of the affiliation of its original contributor. Our efforts must be **results oriented**.

Sadly, in most settings in our society today, individual citizens, communities and states have lost the willingness and the ability to work together in such a cooperative manner. What is more important, however, is the fact that at all levels of our public institutions, such objectivity, respect and statesmanship is even more lacking. Political, racial, sexual, age, etc. barriers have been established for the benefit of special interest groups. The platforms of each fragmented segment assume top priority in the minds and actions of its members. Consideration of what is best for the country is subordinated or ignored.

If our country is to succeed with this system of government, consideration of what is best for the nation simply cannot continue to be subrogated to so many trivial, relatively insignificant considerations, by those to whom its future is entrusted.

In some fairness to those we criticize, we must recognize our own significant contribution to the ineffectiveness of our system. What is the basis of our individual votes for candidates? What is the message we send to them with our ballots?

Do we carefully study the candidates and vote for the one that has demonstrated by his/her campaign, knowledge of the position and issues to be confronted in office? that has demonstrated an ability to "get the job done"? that has exhibited a level of enthusiasm and dedication for the job?

Or do our ballots support all members of one party? only those who are for or against abortion? only those who will support continued annual increases in Social Security payments? only those who support organized labor? etc.?. If we indicate that is all we expect of our elected officials, it is foolish to think that they will deliver more with their service!

It is a well known fact, in political circles, that "name recognition" is an important, positive factor in successful political campaigns. Persons who have been in public office for long periods of time; whose names have been in front of the public in the media, etc. have a big advantage, regardless of the quality or effectiveness of the service they have rendered. That does not say much for the quality of votes recorded! There is little that a qualified, potential new candidate can point to, that will encourage him/her to seek public office.

A few years ago, I ran for a relatively insignificant, nonpartisan political office. Although I found this to be an interesting experience, it was at the same time humiliating and distasteful. I came away from the experience believing that our election process and the effectiveness of our government would benefit greatly if all who participate in it; as voters, bureaucrats, etc.; would respond, at least once, to the opportunity to run for office.

At the time I announced my candidacy, a friend who had experienced some success in having been elected to a similar nonpartisan position, came to me with advice he had received from veteran politicians, friends of his, who had demonstrated the ability to win elections for partisan positions at the state level. The advice can be summarized briefly, as follows:

— Become actively associated with the major political party that dominates the politics of the local area. Their support is almost a necessity if you are to win. (That posed a problem to me. The inept performance of the "in" members of that group was a major factor in my decision to run);

— You've got to develop a friendly, carefree approach to campaigning; smile! (you can learn this) frowns and looks of concern wont get the job for you;

— Learn to discuss the subject of your candidacy in a pleasant positive way, don't talk about problems, don't get into specifics on the issues;

— Selling yourself in terms of your ability, knowledge of the work you would be doing or changes you would seek, if elected; will not work to your advantage.

Although my observation of the local political scene, led me to believe that he was probably correct, my motivation and my concept of how the system should work were well established in my mind. I was not willing to prostitute my reputation or my campaign, just to get elected. I did not want to contribute to any further degradation of the system. I had good credentials for the job and I had ideas and plans for performing the work, if I was the successful candidate. I talked about these things in a friendly, energetic, concerned way during the campaign. With only three candidates for the office; I came in third in the balloting. Neither of the other two candidates had any experience in the kind of work involved in the position. They did play the game as it had been outlined to me at the beginning of the campaign.

At that same time a local, ranking member of that dominant political party in our area, had the temerity to publicly agree with the position taken on a local issue by a member of that **other** major party. In a very public way he was harassed and threatened with expulsion from his party.

Emotions are close to the surface on these issues. In an effort to maintain a level of neutrality and to present objective data, the following information has been taken from The World Book Encyclopedia, 1965 Edition. The credibility of this source is enhanced because it is respected by most people; and secondly because it was written decades ago, prior to the severe polarization of thinking and a level of intellectual decay in this country.

The following information is quoted from that World Book source, to help establish a common level of understanding on the general subject of Democracy; the kinds of Democracy (that is, the options, mentioned earlier); the responsibilities and challenges in a democracy:

—Start of Quote—
## *"Democracy"* [1]

*"Democracy means rule by the people. Abraham Lincoln defined democracy as **Government of the people, by the people, for the people.***

*The word democracy* usually refers to a form of government. But democracy is also a way of life. True democracy recognizes the rights of all men. It states that all persons are equal before the law. It refuses to allow the government to grant special favors because of a person's birth, wealth, race, or religion. Democracy provides freedom of speech, freedom of the press and freedom of religion. Finally, democracy permits citizens to peacefully oppose actions by their government.

The citizens of a democracy take part in government in two ways, directly and indirectly. People take part *directly* when they gather together to work out laws, plans, and programs. This is *pure democracy*. People take part in government *indirectly* when they elect representatives who act for them. The United States has this *representative*, or *republican*, form of democracy (see Republic). In such a large nation, it would be impossible to call all citizens together.

Representative government has a democratic spirit. All the people may not agree on a certain political issue or candidate for office. But democracy *depends* on the majority of the people deciding among issues and candidates. The people express their decisions by voting in free elections with secret ballots."

And what about those optional kinds of democracy previously mentioned?

## *"Kinds of Democracy"*

*"In addition to being a political system, democracy is an economic system and a social system. Economic and social democracy usually exist where political democracy is strong.*

---

[1]     The World Book Encyclopedia; 1965 Edition; Volume "D"; pp 104-106. Quoted material is italicized. Parts of it may be underlined for emphasis; to indicate that it may deserve your special attention as you think through these issues.

*Political Democracy is a system of government in which the people govern themselves. They may criticize the leaders of their government, and they can choose new ones in an election. Democratic government rests on public opinion.*

*A basic belief of political democracy is that people of different interests and backgrounds have different political opinions. Political democracy accepts these opinions. It allows their free expression. In an election, the majority of the people show what policies they want their government to follow. The people accept the choices made by the majority of the voters."*

When considered against a background of election results of several recent presidential-year elections, the information underlined above poses fascinating, and possibly important questions. For example, in the elections in 1980, 1984, and 1988 the nation elected a Republican president; and a House of Representatives with a majority of members of the Democratic party. In 1980 the republicans won a majority of the seats in the Senate; in 1984 and 1988 the Senate was also controlled by Democratic party majorities.

Neither of the major political parties have presented platforms that recognize the true gravity of the problems we face. Nor have they honestly proposed to deal with those problems in an effective way. That is not to say that there are not, pivotal differences in their program proposals; the pathway to our nation's future. Such differences pose the pertinent question: "What message do the people intend to communicate to those in office, by splitting the power in the Executive and Legislative Branches between the two major political parties?"

The importance of that question is enhanced by the presence of widespread polarization of thought; the strong appeal and acceptance of emotion driven responses to questions and problems that demand intelligent, reasoned answers; the absence of individual and corporate discipline; and the overt arrogant, contemptible refusal of those in control of our government to debate, compromise and enforce a level of performance that will allow the system to work. Which side of our split ballot, the vote for the President or the vote for our Senators and Representatives represents our true desires for our government?

Any movement by the voters to help clarify that issue would be of significant benefit. The expectation that a government system whose condition already borders on that of "rigor mortis" can overcome such indecision by the people, is unrealistic.

The split of power between the major political parties that we vote into existence, in the Executive and Legislative branches of government is a major contributing factor to its lack of effectiveness.

Continuing the quote:

*"A country with political democracy has at least two political parties, and may have many more. A dictatorship permits only one party. Under political democracy, parties represent the opinions of great numbers of people. The United States, Great Britain, and Canada each have two major parties. Other parties may appear from time to time. The "other side" always has the right to make its opinions known to the people."*

Conditions in our nation compare favorably with the definition of a political democracy.

*"**Economic Democracy** gives every person a chance to improve his economic standing. He may choose a job according to his likes and dislikes. He may change jobs if he wishes to. He may advance in his job as far as his abilities permit. A dictatorship forces many persons to do work that the government selects for them. They must accept wages that are set by the dictatorship.*

*Most economists believe that economic democracy grows out of political democracy. Voting and other democratic processes protect economic freedom. If a voter approves the economic ideas of a candidate for office, he can vote for that candidate in an election. There are also other ways in which the individual can influence economic affairs in a democracy. Any person can own stock in a company. As a stockholder,* he may help form the policies of the company. Individual workers may join labor unions. By cooperating with other employees in one factory or one industry, workers gain *bargaining* power. They can ask for higher wages and various benefits. See Labor.

Businessmen can also influence economic life in a democracy. The owner of a store may join businessmen's associations. The work of such groups can affect the economic life of an entire community. In the United States, the owner of a large corporation may support a lobbying action to gain greater benefits for his corporation or his industry (see Lobbying).

Economic democracy is also called free-enterprise. Under a free-enterprise system, a nation's means of production and distribution are privately owned. The government regulates economic activity. *But this regulation aims primarily to keep individuals and corporations from taking unfair advantage of each other.* See Free Enterprise System."

The success of our nation in achieving great wealth; economic, military, and intellectual leadership roles in the family of nations of the world; exceptional levels of freedom; and a standard of living for its citizens never before equaled in the history of our planet can be attributed, primarily to our ancestors effective application of the free-enterprise system. During this period, the limited regulation imposed upon the people met the criteria specified in the statement underlined above.

During the past two or three decades government at the Federal, state and local levels have unilaterally and aggressively invaded the privacy of individuals and organizations, large and small, with mandated new regulation, new social programs and new taxes. All of which represents more and more departure from the characteristics of the system that had served our needs so well.

Our citizens are able, somewhat, to follow day-to-day activities and events in our society through the media coverage. However, the ultimate impacts of the resultant redirection of our government from one type to another are left for the individual to sort out and confront. Given our present passion for short-term, bottom-line considerations, and the popularity of the "me-here-now" syndrome; (dominance of the concept—what are the benefits to *me? right here and right now?),* the strategic importance of today's actions upon our future well-being as individuals and as a country seldom enters into the decision-making loop. Citizens' passive acquiescence to the chicanery of those in power poses distressing questions in the minds of many thinking Americans.

"**Social Democracy** *is sometimes called social equality. A democratic nation tries to give all citizens equal rights under the law. All laws apply equally to all citizens regardless of their birth, wealth, race, religion, or sex. A dictatorship usually favors one class of people or one political party. Social democracy cannot exist under such conditions.*

*Social democracy helps people in a material way. It encourages both governmental and private efforts to gain equality for all. In the United States, the Social Security Act protects most workers against the risks of unemployment and old age. Other laws enable more and more persons to have better housing, medical care, and education. State and local governments support similar aid programs. At the same time, private organizations serve society in various ways. For example, the Ford Foundation spends millions of dollars every year to support programs of welfare, education, and international aid. Other organizations work to solve such problems as crime and juvenile delinquency.*

*The goal of social democracy is not perfect equality for all. Democracy recognizes that a person's way of life is determined by his background, his abilities, and his efforts. The goal is to assure everyone an opportunity to make full use of his abilities."*

A careful look at the continuing re-direction of our government, driven by those we have elected to office, demonstrates clearly that the tenets of the free-enterprise system that served our needs so well, for so long, are being cast adrift in favor of more socialistic conventions. It is also clear that there is a relatively high degree of incompatibility between **Economic Democracy** and **Social Democracy**.

Economic Democracy and the free-enterprize system draw some of their effectiveness from exploitation of the personal attribute of greed, a very influential individual, personal motivating instinct. Success under Economic Democracy and the free-enterprise system is also greatly enhanced by opportunities it affords for individual recognition and rewards for outstanding performance at all levels of the career ladder in labor, supervision and management activities. In the drift of our government systems away from Economic Democracy toward Social Democracy, the concept of creating opportunities for our citizens to provide for themselves has become totally lost in the rush to give people who are "down on their luck"—a free ride; free homes for the homeless; free, extended welfare for all who seek it; free health care and discounted medical insurance; farm aid; bailouts for savings and loans institutions, and huge banks; the housing industry; ad infinitum.

The motivating force behind much of the movement toward socialism lies with a small, influential segment of the population whose judgements are driven by emotional instincts that eclipse other aspects of their psyche. In part, the "drivers" of this change can be characterized as people who, themselves "have it made". They have resources and a relatively high level of personal security; conditions that, in themselves, provide evidence of the past success of our free-enterprise system in creating opportunities for personal achievement and success. They are able to help those less fortunate than themselves, without a great deal of personal sacrifice. Their ability and willingness to commit some of their own resources to help those who are less fortunate personifies the "American Way". However, they are not satisfied with that. Their response to their own emotional reaction to exposure to the problems of the needy intensifies their motivation to do more. With their standing in our communities and their access to and influence with elected and bureaucratic members of our government organizations, they are able to develop arrangements that force **all of us**, through taxation and other actions, to support **their** favorite charities; regardless of our individual financial ability to do so and regardless of our own personal priorities for charitable giving. It is not unusual for the accumulated financial burden of all such actions to ultimately force many in society who are, borderline cases; just able to "get by" without help; into that group that needs help. And the problem grows and becomes more and more unmanageable. The demarcation line between a system of Social Democracy and one of pure Socialism becomes vague. Whether or not that is important, depends upon what the majority of the U.S. electorate wants for their government, if they care at all.

The electorate must not allow our country to be led unknowingly into a different form of government. It would be helpful if the nation's "truth-in-labeling" laws reached into the political arena. The names used by our prevailing political parties may lead to some confusion. The name of the Democratic party might indicate to some that their candidates, programs and aims are more supportive of a democratic form of government than are candidates of the Republican party. Of course, that is not true. The philosophy of a democratic (rule by the people) form of government has never been raised as a partisan issue between the two major parties. They both support the democratic form of government. However, major differences come to light if we go one step further in the definition. The Republican party and its candidates are generally supportive of **economic democracy** concepts. The Democratic party and its people, on the other hand, champion **social democracy**. The democratic party, as it has evolved in our society today, champions more and more government control, interference with and intervention into individual and organizational sovereignty, increased government spending for unlimited new programs and increased funding for existing programs whether they are working or not. Unbridled, Democratic party, movement toward social democracy will lead to a form of government, that more nearly approximates socialism than it does democracy.

Truth in labeling" might well require that the democratic party be renamed to reflect its dedication to socialistic ideals. Members of most, but not all, chapters of the Democratic party in our nation today are more accurately Social Democrats.

Continuing the quote:

### *"Responsibilities in a Democracy"*

*"**Obligations to Citizenship.** Democratic laws and institutions do not guarantee that democracy will succeed. People must work constantly for*

democratic freedom. In many countries democracy has been lost because the citizens did not help to govern themselves by taking part in public affairs. Two conditions must exist if a person is to take part intelligently in his government. First, he must be informed. Second, he must act on his knowledge.

An informed citizen knows the important issues in his community, state or province and country. Only if he knows these issues can he intelligently choose one policy or candidate over another. He can obtain information through newspapers, magazines, books, radio and television.

After he has become informed, the citizen must act. He may help the political party of his choice. Or he may run for an elective office in his local government. A good citizen does more than vote every two years. He remains active between elections. The results of an election and the type of candidate who wins, depend on what citizens do during these periods. Many persons also work with groups that deal with community problems and are not connected with any political party. These groups include the Red Cross, the Boy Scouts and Girl Scouts, the Community Chest, and schools and hospitals."

### *"Obligations of Government"*

"The most important obligation of a government official in a democracy is to look upon public office as a trust. A dictator believes that his power is his as long as he can keep it by force. Under democracy, all political power comes from the people. A public official in a democracy receives his power for a limited time. He must use it honestly. He must work constantly for the growth of democracy.

The second major duty of a government official in a democracy is to do what is best for the most people. Even though he represents one political party, he must work for the common good after he takes office. The President of the United States is the leader of all the people—Democrats, Republicans, members of other parties, and nonvoters. It is not easy for an elected official to be completely neutral. But officials in a democracy must try to achieve both these ideals."

### *"The Role of Education"*

"A democracy needs educated citizens who can think for themselves. They must be able to make decisions on public issues and to vote intelligently. Education can strengthen democracy by teaching students **how** to think, rather than telling the student **what** to think. Children who learn to respect the views of others will, in later years, more easily respect different social and political opinions.

*In a dictatorship, the student is taught to accept without question the policies and decisions of the individual or group in power. He learns to ignore moral and human issues, if necessary, in obeying the orders of the rulers. He becomes a servant of the state.*

*A democracy tries to give every person a chance to receive the type of education that suits him best. A student who wants to study engineering can usually do so at the college of his choice, if he can pass the entrance examinations. Most schools also give scholarships to needy students of exceptional ability."*

### *"Challenges to Democracy"*

*"Most threats to democracy come from rival governmental systems, such as communism and fascism. Democracy may also be threatened by such internal problems as civic neglect and depression. History has shown that inefficiency may sometimes endanger democracy. A bureaucracy (class of government officials) may take over much of the work of governing, reducing the authority of the elected representatives of the people. Or a democracy may have so many political parties that no party can speak for the majority of the people.*

**Communism** works to destroy democracy. A dictator heads a communist government. He keeps himself in power by using force to crush opposition. A communist government usually takes over all means of production and distribution. The government controls the press, radio, television, and all other means of communication. Communists claim that they seek equality for all citizens. But people have no way to protect their rights under communism. The interests of the individual are less important than the interests of the communist government.

Communism began to threaten democracy after the second Russian Revolution of 1917. The revolution brought communism to power in Russia. Lenin and other communist leaders called for worldwide revolution to establish communism everywhere. But communism did not begin to challenge democracy seriously until after World War II. The communist government of Russia installed communist regimes in East Germany and in many countries of eastern Europe. Communists also worked to take over nations in Africa, Asia, and South America."

Remember that these words were written in the 1960's. Communism continued to pose major threats to democracy, until the late 1980's. In 1988 and 1989 it became apparent to many of the leaders of the East-European, communist bloc nations that Communism as a form of government was not meeting the needs of their people. Activities in Poland, driven by organized labor and the people; street demonstrations of the general populace, often led by students; and the emergence of an enlightened Russian leader, Mikhail Gorbachev, provided the opportunity for major changes in their governments. Benefits included greater freedom for the people and consideration of and possible implementation of new, more effective economic, production and distribution systems.

Continuing the quote:

*"**Fascism** teaches that the government, not the people, is the source of all power. According to fascist doctrine, the people are too ignorant and emotional to rule themselves."*

A critical look at the developing situation in our country today, certainly legitimizes the question, "Are they correct in this belief?"

*"Under fascism, a special group of leaders, supposedly superior in mental ability, governs the country. A dictator uses force to control the people. A fascist government usually does not own the nation's means of production and distribution. But it controls them completely. See Fascism.*

*Fascism became a threat to democracy after fascists seized power in Italy in 1922. Led by Benito Mussolini, they destroyed all other political parties in Italy. The Nazi party in Germany, led by Adolf Hitler, expanded the ideas of fascism. The Nazis took over the German government in 1933. They immediately began to persecute many persons for religious or political reasons. Nazism taught that the Germans were superior to all other peoples. See Nazism.*

***Civic Neglect.** Some historians believe that an exaggerated desire for easy living can be a serious threat for democracy. If the majority of persons concentrate too much on their houses, clothing, wealth, and property they may forget to perform their duties as citizens. Under these conditions, some historians say, democracy could die. A communist or fascist leader in a democratic country might use the right of free speech to win followers. He would conceal his real aim—to work for the overthrow of the government. If the people were not alert, they might not know their government was being destroyed."*

The intelligence and vision of the writers of this statement more than three decades ago is impressive; an indication of the high level of awareness and of the quality of their logical and analytical skills that entered into their thinking processes. These conditions are noteworthy, because they are so rarely encountered in our society today. Those people had an "eye to the future"; a concept presently uncharacteristic of most of our people, our leaders of commerce and industry and most importantly our government institutions at all levels.

"***Economic Depression*** *may also endanger democracy. Some economists and political scientists believe that communism or fascism can take over a government more easily if the country becomes economically weak. Communism or Fascism might become popular if many citizens might decide that communism or fascism could solve their individual problems.*"

* End of Quote *

Recent history has demonstrated the probable accuracy of this statement; not as it has played itself out in our society; but as it has evolved in the decisions by the people and governments of communist-bloc nations in eastern Europe to turn their backs on major components of their communistic forms of government. The trend, as these changes are identified and implemented, is for them to adopt new principles and procedures for their new governments similar to some of those that have been used in the democracies.

As citizens of the United States today, we continue to have the same three alternatives for participation in our government, that have been available since its inauguration over two hundred years ago.

1. Leave it to George, I don't have time.
2. Continue with token participation that is entirely "party" oriented; supporting all candidates, programs and positions on the issues of one or the other of the major political parties. In this scenario the citizen surrenders to others, his/her rights as a citizen to participate constructively in developing the future direction of our government and its programs. Don't lose sight of the fact that the "others" we speak of, have agendas of their own that they have not shared with you and that may not be in your best interests or those of the country.
3. We can get actively involved, personally, in the way that was envisioned by our forefathers when they established this form of government for us; placing a high priority on achieving the real, justifiable needs of our country, states and communities.

We have no guarantee that those alternatives will always be available to us. It has become painfully evident during the last decade or two that there are powerful factions at work within government and among our citizens that are quietly and covertly changing its form. Many of the people involved in forcing these changes are intuitively reacting to strong emotional instincts, with no consideration of the future impacts of their actions.

There are two major factions in our country today that are pursuing two very different visions of the future:

—Vision No. 1—

More and more government involvement, interference, costs and inefficiency. More "freebies", more "giveaways" to a rapidly increasing number of people. Success of the faction that supports this vision will inevitably result in a more socialistic form of future government in this country. Any and all social programs; welfare, housing assistance, medicaid, medicare, assured health care to all (free if need be), child care; more and more money for schools, etc., etc.; seem always to be at the top of their priority list. Although some members of the group will on occasion verbally express some concern about program costs and the problem of our national debt, their actions are not responsive to those concerns. Their actions speak so loudly that we cannot hear (or believe) what they say.

They seem not to worry about how they (we) will pay the bills. Their preferred solution has been to quietly add the costs resulting from their actions to the multi-trillion dollar national debt; to be left to our children and succeeding generations for payment and resolution. If they are forced "to the wall" on the issue of how to pay for their programs, their answer is "to cut defense spending and/or assess more taxes". Although most of them do not say so publicly, they must believe that, as a country, we can continue to accumulate national debt forever. It would be constructive to get that issue out on the table for discussion and debate.

A favorite ploy of our elected legislative people, especially when control of the Executive and Legislative Branches is split between the two parties, is to blame the President and his administration for the problem. You can easily check this out. You should do so. The voting record of all members of Congress is available. Simply review the record of your representatives and senators over the past several years. Their consistent support of, and vote for all budget and other money bills will indicate clearly that they are a part of the problem, and should be replaced. Of course, the Executive Branch must share the blame; but Congress, with its budget review and approval responsibilities, must serve as the final authority in protecting the financial integrity of the country.

The original functions of government, some of which are spoken to in our Constitution, such as national defense; maintenance and rebuilding of the infrastructure (highways and streets, water and sewer systems, other utilities); balancing the national budget; and repayment of the national debt are near the bottom of their priority list, if they have one!

Members of this faction are referred to as "liberals"; they are usually, but not always, members of the Democratic party. That party, organizationally, supports these views. They never saw a social program that they didn't like and support. Socialism is obviously their ultimate goal! They seem willing to overlook the fact that it has failed everywhere it has been tried. They also ignore fundamental questions about the fiscal vulnerability of the nation and our ability to pay!

The geneses of much of this thinking is found in the "Great Society" program envisioned and begun by President Lyndon B. Johnson (LBJ; 1963-1969). His fundamental concept was that a country as rich as ours could afford to do anything and everything it wanted to do. During his tenure in the office, the country was heavily involved in the very costly, (in financial, natural and human resources) Viet Nam War. His theme was that we need not let that fact affect our domestic spending, especially in the social arena.

When LBJ took office the Federal debt was about three hundred billion dollars[2]. The continued acceptance of his programs and his philosophy by those who would lead us, has led to its massive increase; over 2000 percent in the intervening years. Those who have followed in his foot steps in the Democratic party have continued support for all of the social programs envisioned in his time, increased the spending for each of them year after

[2]   STATISTICAL ABSTRACT of the United States; U.S. Dept. of Commerce; 1976; P 229

year, and religiously enacted and financed new embellishments and new programs of their own. The staggering, ever-escalating costs of all of this poses major problems. One of the most serious being, that so many who find themselves out of the main stream of society become comfortable and uninhibited enough living on the government dole that their motivation to provide for themselves is stilled. And generation after generation, with its magnification of numbers of persons expecting support; the costs become onerous. The tax load overpowers many, who then find themselves becoming dependent upon hand-outs! becoming part of the problem, rather than contributors to the solution.

—Vision No. 2—

Decreasing the size of government; its involvement, interference and costs. A concentrated effort to create opportunities for citizens to work; to earn their own way, thus making it possible for more of them to actively participate in making the "American Way of Life" come true, in their own lives and in the nation. A growing U. S. economy that provides more jobs, an increasing gross national product; which increases the "real" wealth in the nation and which will provide additional wealth for the citizens. It favors minimizing taxation of all kinds. It favors Economic Democracy and the Free-Enterprise system of government which allows the people and their needs to set the priorities for our production and distribution systems.

Members of this group usually are associated with the Republican party (GOP); and are usually referred to as conservatives.

It is interesting to note that this vision is, in many ways, compatible with the thinking of some highly respected past presidents who were elected as candidates of the *Democratic* party. For example, Franklin D. Roosevelt (FDR; 1933-1945), was thought of as a progressive when he envisioned and worked to establish his "New Deal" program. In many respects his programs represented the inauguration of enormous social spending in this country. And, the concept of deficit spending at the Federal level gained a degree of respectability during his time. Some parts of his New Deal were continued as quasi-permanent commitments of support for those in need. Some other parts were not; they were used as a temporary support system during the years of the "great" depression in the 1930's; and then discontinued when it was perceived that they were no longer needed.

FDR was quoted as saying, during his term in office, that, "For three long years I have been going up and down this country, preaching that government . . . costs too much. I shall not stop that preaching."

And, it seems probable that when president John F. Kennedy (JFK; 1961-1963) said, "And so my fellow Americans, ask not what your country can do for you, but ask what you can do for your country"; he did not have a "socialistic welfare state" in mind.

He is also quoted as saying that, "If government is to retain the confidence of the people, it must not spend more than can be justified on grounds of *national* need or spent with maximum efficiency."(underlining added for emphasis)

The differences in the two major visions being championed by the electorate are significant. That fact contributes to the confusion created when, through the election process, we split the control of the Executive and Legislative Branches. By doing so, we do not create an impossible situation. Our government has worked in the past with such division. However, more recently those in office, especially legislators, refuse to allow the system work. The kind of government that will prevail here and the destiny of the country and it's people are in the balance.

It is important that we clearly understand the importance and impact of our individual roles in this developing situation. To aid in that effort, we need to define the additional concepts involved; namely Socialism and The Free Enterprise system.

In general, additional information about the following concepts will be helpful:

1. **Social Democracy**, leading to **Socialism**. Social Democracy has been defined earlier. What about Socialism, what does it have to offer us? Is that what we really want?
2. **Economic Democracy** and the **Free Enterprise System**. What does this have to offer? Would we prefer to take our chances with it?

Which option do we prefer? Do we want it bad enough to work for it?

We will rely on the same "World Book Encyclopedia" source for this information:

—Start of Quote—
## *"SOCIALISM"*[3]

"*SO shul iz'm, is both a doctrine and a movement which seeks to place in the hands of the people, either directly or through their government, the ownership and control of the principle means of production and distribution. Ownership may be by national or local government, or by cooperatives. For example, the city ownership of an electric power plant is no less an example of socialism than is the ownership of railroads by a national government.*

*Democratic socialists insist that control must be democratic. They urge that socialized industries should be controlled by public corporations governed by directors representing both the consumers in general, and the workers who invested their labor in the particular industry. Cooperative associations, common in many parts of the world, are much like socialism, because they extend ownership to many members of the community.*

*Socialism is a much-abused term. It does not mean equal income for everyone, but it does imply more equality in income than is now common. It does not mean a collective ownership of personal belongings, such as shoes or toothbrushes. Instead, it proposes collective ownership of the principal means of production and distribution. Nor does it mean political dictatorship, although some dictatorships have practiced it. Socialism is an economic system, not a political one. Many persons believe in both democracy, a political idea, and socialism, an economic one. They are called democratic socialists.*"

### *"The World-wide socialist Movement."*

"*Most persons think of Karl Marx (1818-1883) as the founder of modern socialist principles. But other persons had advanced socialist ideas at an earlier period. The term **socialist** was first used in its modern sense in Great Britain in 1827. A few years later it was used in both France and Great Britain to describe the social ideals of Francois Marie Charles Fourier, Comte de Saint-Simon, and Robert Owen. Louis Blanc (1811-1882) worked to have the French adopt many socialist principles during the late 1840's. In 1861, the first socialist party was founded in Germany. The movement rapidly gained strength and spread to other countries. World War I resulted in a temporary setback in socialist strength in most countries. But in Russia, socialists took part in the revolution which deposed the czar, and in the later revolution which overthrew the Kerensky government.*

---

[3]   The World Book Encyclopedia; 1965 Edition; Volume "S"; PP 461-462.

*Moderate socialists soon lost any influence they might have had in the new Communist government, which claimed to follow the principles of Karl Marx. See Communism; Russia (History).*

*After World War I, socialism picked up new strength in many countries. It continued to grow through the 1920's and 1930's. The Fascist governments in Italy, Germany, Spain, and other countries during this period had the destruction of the socialist movement as one of their major purposes. Fascist dictatorships reached a peak in World War II. Socialist groups emerged from World War II with renewed strength and increased membership. Today, almost every country of Europe and North and South America, as well as some countries of Asia, has socialist political organizations. Some of these organizations have great strength.*

### "Socialism and Communism."

*"There has been a long history in the development of differences between socialism and communism. Today the major communist parties maintain that socialism has already been achieved in Russia. In their definition, socialism is a step on the road to communism. They defend dictatorship and the denial of all civil liberties. They still hold to Lenin's teaching that first the dictatorship and then the state itself will wither away once capitalism has been abolished. See Government.*

*Democratic socialists say that the present economic system in Russia could best be described as state capitalism, that there is none of the democracy of control which is essential to socialism, and that obviously neither the dictatorship nor the state is withering away. Socialists oppose dictatorship and the abolition of civil liberties, and seek to bring about a peaceful transition to the new society. Socialists and communists disagree bitterly, and have seldom been able to work together.*

*In the United States, the Socialist party was organized in the 1890's. By 1904 its membership had increased to more than 400,000. By 1912 the socialist vote approached 900,000. Socialist votes increased to about 920,000 in 1920. By 1924, when the socialists supported the Progressive candidate for President, Robert M. LaFollette, their voting strength was probably about a million. Since then, Socialist votes have varied greatly in number. The number of persons who accept socialist principles may have gradually increased, but if this is true, these persons have generally voted with one of the major parties. In the 1948 national elections, the Socialist vote was 139,521. The Socialist vote fell to 20,189 in 1952 and to 2,192 in 1956.*

*The Socialist party platforms have commonly included demands for (1) the socialization and democratic control of natural resources, money, banking and credit, and monopolies and semi-monopolies; (2) better protection for workers and their families, such as higher wages and shorter hours, health and accident insurance, and old-age and mothers' pensions; (3) the extension of free public education; and (4) various political changes, including the direct election of the President and Vice President, and some device by which, in case of deadlock between Congress and the President, an appeal can be taken to the voters.*

*The Socialist party has advanced many proposals for political reforms. Most of these are designed to make the national government more flexible to the will of the people. Since the Civil War, the United States has adopted much social legislation and established many controls over industry. But the major parties have avoided the term* **socialism** *for fear of arousing possible prejudice."*

*Socialists claim that socialism holds the answer to many problems of modern industrial society, such as unemployment, poverty, business cycles, and conflicts between capital and labor. But it is also clear that socialization is likely to bring new problems with it.*

*The Tennessee Valley Authority might be considered an example of modern socialist practice, although the Socialist party would make various changes in its administration. This vast enterprise is controlled by a board of experts who have been freed from political influence. The citizens of local communities in the region carry on much of the detailed administration. This gives the undertaking a certain democratic character (see Tennessee Valley Authority). But the Socialist party would like to see consumers and workers take more direct part in the management of the Authority than they are now able to do."*

In the 1960's, when the above was written and printed in the Encyclopedia, the Tennessee Valley Authority was considered to be a very successful enterprize. But alas, for many of the same reasons that socialism has failed around the world, it no longer enjoys such a reputation.

Social Democracy and Socialism are competing in our society today with the Free Enterprise System under which our country and we have gained and enjoyed most of our economic success. Our unequaled standard of living can be attributed largely to the past success of the Free Enterprise Economic System we have used:

1. It provided an opportunity for citizens to succeed,
2. It created an environment in which success was recognized and considered desirable,

3. It motivated citizens to achieve, and
4. It provided compensation levels which correlated with the degree to which the individual contribution benefited society.

It is impossible for us to determine the true contribution of the Free Enterprize system to our high standard of living. We are unable to separate it's contribution from the illusive contribution that results from the multi-trillion dollars that our expenditures have exceeded our income in recent years.

Quoted from the same World Book Encyclopedia source:

### *"Free Enterprise System"*[4]

*"FREE ENTERPRISE SYSTEM. The people of the United States and Canada live and make their living under an economic system called a free enterprise system. So do the people of many other countries.*

*Most of us consider this economic system a basic part of our way of life. We wish to see it maintained and strengthened, partly because we have fared so well under it, and partly because we feel that all of our other freedoms may depend upon freedom of enterprise.*

*Strangely enough, many of us could not describe what is meant by **free enterprise system** Nor could we explain exactly how it differs from other economic systems. This article presents a brief picture of the free enterprise system—what it is, how it developed, and how it works.*

***What is Free Enterprise?*** *A free enterprise system is one in which (1) the means of production are privately owned and controlled, (2) each person is free to make his own decisions in economic life, and (3) each man's income is roughly in proportion to what his labor and other resources produce.*

*We can gain some understanding of the free enterprise system by studying how and why it developed. The system is first found in somewhat complete form in Great Britain and America in the late 1700's and early 1800's. Free enterprise did not develop in these countries as a result of a deliberate plan. Rather it came in "by the back door" when **mercantilism**, the existing form of economic organization, broke down. Mercantilism was a set of economic policies directed to the goal of making a nation stronger than its rivals. These policies meant that the government had to exercise considerable control over*

---

4    The World Book Encyclopedia; 1965 Edition; Volume "F"; pp 424-426.

the economic life of the people of the country and its colonies. The government decided what its citizens should consume, what they should produce, where and at what wages they should work, and where they should invest their money. We all know of the restrictions which Great Britain placed on the economic life of its American colonies. These restrictions were part of the mercantilist policy. The discontent they produced, particularly in the American colonies, helped lead to the Revolutionary War in America.

In Great Britain, too, this system of controls became more and more openly violated. For example, historians estimate that, at one time in the 1700's, more than one of every four persons who lived near the coasts of Great Britain took part in some form of smuggling. Most of the smuggling involved bringing in goods from France that mercantilist policy said should not be permitted to enter the country. Unpopular mercantilist laws were gradually modified or repealed, such as one making it a crime to wear anything made of colored calico. Gradually but surely the economic life of Great Britain was freed from the excessive controls of mercantilism.

Free enterprise came into existence as a reaction against government control of economic life. Adam Smith, a Scottish philosopher and economist, presented the free enterprise idea in positive form in **The Wealth of Nations**, which was published in 1776. The book greatly aided the development of free enterprise. In it, Smith demonstrated that the interests of the nation are best served by permitting each person to make his own decisions and follow his own self-interest in economic life. This is the central idea of the free enterprise system.

**How Does the System Work?** You may ask, "But how does an economic system work if it leaves everyone free to do as he pleases?" Let us start our answer to this question by finding out what problems of organization **any** kind of economic organization must solve. Economic life consists of producing, exchanging, and consuming goods and services. This process can go on only after certain decisions have been made. The **critical decisions** are: (1) **What** is going to be produced? (2) **Who** is going to do each of the jobs involved in producing the desired goods? (3) **How much** of the things produced is each person going to receive?

The task of an economic system is to see that the **what**, the **who**, and the **how much** are answered."

"Consumer Sovereignty. In a free enterprise economy, the consumer makes the **what** decision. Through the way the consumer spends his dollars, he determines what is going to be produced and in what amounts. When he wants more cars and fewer horse-drawn carriages, he casts more of his dollar "votes" for cars and fewer for carriages. But how and why do the people who are responsible for the production of goods understand and act on his decisions?"

"*Profits and Losses. The vote-counters in a free-enterprise system are the many, many firms that produce goods and services. They are the farms, the factories, the stores, the public utilities, and other producers. The men and women who run these firms are anxious to follow the consumer's wishes because the more votes for a product, or* **good***, the more dollars (profits) for the firms producing that good. In the same way, the penalty for not following the wishes of the consumer, or for producing something for which few votes were cast, is that the firm will lose money.*

*It is the desire for profits and the fear of losses which lead the managers of producing firms to do the consumers's bidding. A business can make a profit only by producing something that the consumers want and consider useful, and so production for profits becomes just one way of getting production for use. Profits and losses perform an important function in a free enterprise economy.*

**Freedom of Job Choice.** *The managers of firms can not produce goods without help. To begin with, they need the help of workers. If the workers are free to work wherever they wish—or not at all—what reason is there to suppose that they will want to work at the job of producing cars rather than carriages?*

*In other words, how is the* **who** *decision handled under free enterprise? The answer lies in the fact that the workers, like the managers, are guided by self-interest. They wish to make higher wages and avoid wage cuts. The firms producing automobiles are able to pay higher wages because they have received the most dollar "votes" with which to pay workers. The high wages in the automobile industry and the low wages in the carriage industry are signals, and workers follow these signals because it is in their own self interest to do so.*

"*Private Property. But it takes more than the labor of human beings to produce goods in a modern, industrialized society. It takes land, coal, oil, buildings, tools, and machinery as well. What assurance is there that these non-human resources will do what consumers wish them to?*

*The answer lies in one of the distinguishing features of free enterprise:* **private ownership of the means of production.** *Each piece of land, each building, each factory is owned by some person or group of persons. The owners of these resources receive incomes from selling the services of their resources to the producing firms. The firms making cars will be able to offer a higher return to the owners of the resources than will the firms producing carriages. Thus resources will move into the car industry and out of the carriage industry. Self-interest, made effective by the device of private property, will lead to the use of even the nonhuman resources in the way that the consumer wishes them used. Many people feel that under* **public ownership** *of the means of production, there would not be the same* incentive to put the means of production into the uses preferred by consumers. These people believe that the consumer would be the loser.

**Dividing the Pie.** The final question is the **how much** question, or the question of dividing the things produced among the people in the consuming group. On what basis is this division made under free enterprise? In the first place, each unit of each good—each car, each loaf of bread,—goes to the person who is willing to pay the most for it. Other things being equal, the person who is willing to pay the most for the product is the one who wants it most, and who get the most satisfaction out of using or consuming it. To see the importance of this, just imagine the situation that would exist if a box office manager selected names at random from the telephone directory and gave away all the tickets to an important baseball game, instead of selling them to people who really wanted them. The same situation might occur if a famous hobbyist gave his valuable collection to the first person he met on the street, rather than to someone who would value it.

The total amount of goods any person will be able to buy will depend on the prices of the goods and on the size of his income.

In general, the size of each person's income depends on how productive his resources are. For example, the more productive the labor of a worker, the more firms will be willing to pay for his labor, and the higher his income will be. By distributing income in this way, each person is given an incentive to put his resources into those uses where they will be most productive—where they will contribute the most to satisfying consumer wants. This way of distributing income is essential to the free enterprise system because it provides the **incentive** needed to get people to satisfy consumers' wants. At the same time, this way of distributing income always produces an **unequal** distribution of income because no two individuals have exactly equal resources. This fact can lead to serious problems if the people of the society are not willing to accept substantial amount of inequality in the distribution of the total income.

**The Role of Competition.** Competition is needed to make the free enterprise system work. The exact meaning of **competition** is still a subject for dispute among economists and others. We shall say that competition exists whenever each person—each businessman, each worker, each buyer, each seller—can get ahead only by offering more product for less money. One of the most important problems confronting a free enterprise society is how to make sure that each person can get ahead only by offering more for less.

This problem is made more difficult because some persons consider competition an undesirable way of life. And many of us dislike facing strong competition in our own economic activities.

*The government has an important role to play in a free enterprise society, particularly in maintaining the conditions, such as competition, necessary to make the system work.*

**The Future of Free Enterprise.** *The great point of strength of free enterprise, and the factor which promises well for the future of the system, the American people have reached a level of economic well-being never before equaled in the history of the world. They are better fed and better clothed, and enjoy more luxuries, than people of any other country. Free people, making free decisions in economic life, and using some of the world's richest natural resources, have produced an amazing record of economic progress.*

*Perhaps the greatest danger to the free enterprise system comes from the threat of war. Even if nations hostile to free enterprise do not defeat free-enterprisers in war, the strains and stresses of war make it difficult for **any** kind of economic system to work efficiently. In times of emergency, people may be tempted to make radical changes in the economic system, even though there is no proof that any other system is better suited to either war or peace than free enterprise.*

*Free enterprise also is threatened by problems from within. As the system works, it shows some obvious faults. Its tendency to fluctuate from prosperity to depression is one of the more important problems of the system. The existence of poverty in the midst of plenty is another. However, problems of this kind can be reduced. The future of free enterprise depends chiefly on whether the majority of us will be willing to accept the features that make the system work, and vigilant in maintaining the conditions necessary for it to work properly.*

* End Of Quote *

In summary, this chapter has provided what might be considered a minimum of definitions of terms and background information needed to qualify us for effectively discharging our responsibilities for citizenship in this nation.

It helps us understand in some detail the characteristics of a Democratic Republic form of government; the differences between Economic Democracy and Social Democracy forms, the extent to which each of them are incorporated into our present system. It helps us understand the division of thought and support for incompatible, competing systems of government in our country: Socialism with its mothering instincts that appeal to many—the government will take care of all of your needs; and Communism and Fascism with their dictatorial, militaristic limitations and control over everyone vying to replace the Democratic Republic form of government that we profess to have. It describes the free enterprise economic system, it's origin, how it works, its advantages, and the challenges it faces from other systems.

It is clear that there are many optional forms of government that a country may choose. They are not all equal in the benefits that accrue to the citizens. Historically, the experience of others demonstrates clearly the weaknesses of many combinations of the available options. Their inability to successfully do the job. We must not leave the selection of the one that will dominate our society to chance! We must be alert to electorate inattention or passivity to evolutionary changes that might dictate a form that is not compatible with our needs. This is an important decision that deserves the considered, unemotional, intelligent, attention of all of us!

# CHAPTER 7

★★★★★★★★★★★★★★★★★★★★★★★★★★★★★★★★★★★★★★★★★★★★★★★★★★★★★★★★★★★★★★

**Democracy is based upon the conviction that
there are extraordinary possibilities
in ordinary people**

**Harry Emerson Fosdick**

★★★★★★★★★★★★★★★★★★★★★★★★★★★★★★★★★★★★★★★★★★★★★★★★★★★★★★★★★★★★★★

In discussing the two major concepts that are competing for domination of our system of government, we referred to them as "Visions". That title is probably more generous than is deserved. "Vision" in its broadest sense, would imply that those who promote and support its implementation, have a clear picture of some future desirable condition that they aspire to for the country. Their day-to-day, week-to-week activities would then be consciously and carefully directed toward the ultimate achievement of that result. It is unfortunate, but seemingly true, that the future consequences of today's activities in our private sector and especially in our government organizations receive little, if any, consideration as decisions are made that guide our destiny. The emotional response, as well as that driven by greed, lead to spontaneous decisions that fit comfortably into our "me-here-now" environment; with its, "I am important, what I want is what matters, and it is vital that I have it right now". Too bad! We have a right to expect more of ourselves than that.

It is not as if we are traveling in uncharted seas. There was a time, not that long ago, when our **Democratic Republic** and the **Free Enterprise System** were serving our needs quite well. Well enough, at least, that any openly debated proposal to relinquish them in favor of some alternative government system, would surely have been rejected. Debated openly and honestly, it probably would be rejected today also. But, of course, it is not happening that way. That such an attack has been generated and has been (is) slowly eating away at the system, eroding its effectiveness and its ability to produce and deliver the quantity and quality of services and products we need, at prices the people can afford, seems not to be widely recognized.

Like many forms of cancer; early detection, diagnosis and treatment of such a malady may be critical to achieving a successful cure.

The **Social Democracy** and **Socialism** into which we are drifting are not new. They have been tried in many countries, in some for long periods of time. In general they have been found to be woefully inadequate in their ability to deliver what they promise to the people. They have been found to be unrelenting in their demand for more and more taxes to support their ever increasing number of new social programs and the continuing, persistent increased demands for resources for their existing social programs. They have proven to be flagrantly inefficient and ineffective in their management of the government operation. They have failed to provide the most basic economic needs of the people, in quantities needed and at prices they can afford.

Many countries are retreating from their experiences with these and similar systems, to move toward a form of Economic Democracy with more emphasis on a market-driven, free enterprise economic system . . . with characteristics similar to those that worked for us at one time. Isn't it interesting that, at a time when so many others have come to publicly recognize that their socialistic economic systems are not working, and that change is needed, they are moving to adopt some methods that have seemed to work for us. At the same time we are quietly, unthinkingly, and probably unintentionally, moving further away from what worked for us, and toward practices and concepts that did not work for them,—or for anyone else. Is there any reason to believe that we can succeed with a system that has been a universal failure in all of its previous applications?

The recent history of Sweden can serve as an example in considering where our present drift toward Social Democracy and Socialism might lead us. For most of the past 100 years the Social Democratic party has established the policy direction to be taken in governing Sweden. In the early 1990's when this was written, that party had ruled Sweden and crafted its fortunes for 46 of the last 52 years. On occasion they found it necessary to form a coalition with the small Communist party in the country to obtain the necessary majority.

Allow yourself to react personally to the stringent economic conditions their citizens have experienced and to the limitations they have tolerated in many of the personal freedoms that we take for granted. Are such conditions really worthy of our pursuit? Are they what you want? Do they represent an improvement over what we have experienced?

There are, of course, a multitude of sources of information on this subject. You may wish to explore it in more depth. The following discussion draws from a collection of news clips and other media coverage of the subject.

The direction taken in governing Sweden over these many years, has resulted from three major decisions made by the Social Democratic party at critical turning points in its history:

1. In the early 1900's, the party decided to support and utilize a concept of evolutionary rather than revolutionary change.
2. Later, in the 1930's, it developed, supported and began implementation of a policy of privately-owned rather than state-owned industry.
3. In the 1950's, it decided to build and implement a generous welfare state.

By the late 1980's, the leadership of the Social Democrats and most of the people in the country, began to realize that the system that had evolved from those decisions was not working; they recognize that their problems were serious and that corrective action was necessary! This brought them to acknowledge the need for a fourth major turning point in the evolution of their "vision":

4. At this crossroad, the party and the people recognized that the welfare state with its insatiable appetite for funding and costly and ineffective government administration could not be allowed to continue to grow forever. They also became aware of the serious need for changes in their economic system. They looked to implement changes that would make it more responsive to the marketplace.

The Swedish people were the most highly taxed people in the world. Tax revenue, country wide, equaled almost 60 percent of the gross domestic product, as compared to about 30 percent in the United States. Their top marginal tax rate was 72 percent; a reduction to 55 percent was proposed.

The government had regularly assigned people to specific hospitals and day care centers, both of which had been run by the government. Some softening in this assignment practice seemed appropriate. They looked to privatization of some of these types of services, to increase availability and efficiency.

The Swedish people started this adventure as idealists. They had exhibited unlimited faith in the ability of government to solve all of the nation's social ills. (Sound familiar?) They were now beginning to recognize that government is not "the answer". It too, has its limitations. With the passage of time, they had seen dwindling benefits from the staggering, increases in tax burden they were forced to pay.

The following quotation from an article written by Mr. Steven Greenhouse in late 1989 for the New York Times News Service, will help us better understand the situation in Sweden:

—Start of Quote—

"There are waiting lists of a year or more to obtain coronary by-passes, hip replacements and cataract operations.

Many parents cannot find places for their children in day-care centers.

A lot of parents complain that their school books are falling apart, . . . , Ceilings have fallen down in some schools.

For years, conservatives argued that high taxes slowed economic growth by pushing Sweden's entrepreneurs to emigrate to Britain and by encouraging people to work less.

Since people who earn $35,000 a year fall into the 72 percent tax bracket, many workers prefer compensatory time-and-a-half to extra pay, for working overtime.

"This helps explain why the average Swede works just 31 hours a week, the lowest in the industrialized world. It also helps explain the long lines for medical operations.

Since more than half of any wage increase goes to taxes, Sweden's powerful unions feel compelled to demand hefty pay raises.

**Inflation rate soars**

Many economists say these wage pressures are one reason that Sweden's inflation rate consistently exceeds those of most industrialized nations."

—End of Quote—

A November 1990 article stated that interest rates in Sweden were hovering at the 17 percent level; wages were increasing at the rate of 13 percent; inflation, rate of increase of prices, was running about 11 percent.

The developing situation in New Zealand, represents another informative case. The following quote from the July 16, 1990 issue of "Insight" magazine poses some interesting similarities and stark differences between their situation and our own.

—Start of quote—

"We're not driven by some mad philosophical conviction", says Roger Douglas, a former finance minister and the architect of New Zealand's restructuring program. "But for 40 to 50 years we weren't following policies that were in the interests of the nation." Instead successive governments, both liberal and conservative, were following a Kremlinesque plan: Protect non-competitive industries with subsidies and tariffs, pay for this luxury with astronomical taxes, and cosset [To treat as a pet, to fondle, to pamper] the public with a social welfare net so cushy it is a pleasure to fall into it.

It was a recipe for disaster. When the current Labor government came to power in 1984, inflation averaged more than 10 percent, growth was the slowest in the Organization for Economic Cooperation and Development, and the national debt was crushing. The new government set about to revitalize the economy with a zeal of a born-again free marketer, transforming one of the world's most regulated economies into one of it's least.

There was, in fact, almost nothing the government did not have its finger in. Apart from the major utilities—Wellington [the capital of New Zealand] presided over an empire that included Radio New Zealand, Television New Zealand, the tourist hotel corporation, steel, oil, banks, coal, irrigation, and a film production company. Much of this has been sold or is about to be."

—End of Quote—

As the New Zealand tale unfolds, we discover a familiar story. Government was involved in everything. It did nothing well! In fact the inefficiencies and ineptitude was slowly and surely paralyzing the country. One interesting parallel between their situation and ours, that we can all relate to, is discussed in the following quote from the same source.

—Start of Quote—

"Certainly no private company could do worse by the public than the government had. Take the case of the Post Office, of which Telecom [their telephone system] was a part: Three businesses in one—banking, the mail and the phone system. At its height the postal megalith was twice as large (in staff) as any private corporation in the country and less than half as efficient. In 1985, the government reported that the postal savings bank lost fully half of its market share in the decade to 1986, even while increasing its spending by 75 percent."

—End of Quote—

The situations in New Zealand and our country are similar in several ways:

1. The relentless pursuit of new and larger social programs;
2. The demonstrated inability of big government, any government to do anything efficiently or effectively;
3. The inattention to the developing economic crisis in the country; and
4. The continual meddling of government in business affairs and activities.

In New Zealand (N.Z.) the government actually owned and tried to operate most businesses. In our country, governments at all levels have developed even more sinister modes of involvement; they simply legislate taxes; employee protection; employee benefits such as holidays and family leave, mandatory health care and/or insurance; guaranteed insurance on deposits in financial institutions; and legions of unnecessary and undesirable rules and regulations governing a wide diversity of operating relationships and control of business activity, public and private. In the case of government ownership of the activities in New Zealand, the government could be held accountable for the inefficiencies, ineffectiveness, and failures it caused. By contrast, our U. S. government is never held accountable in our country, for failures of private enterprises caused by an overload of red tape and irrational demands foisted off on the business community by government.

The situations in the two countries are similar, in that, large segments of both populations are dependent upon huge, government-financed, give-away, social programs; and they, the benefactors, are comfortable with those conditions! Changes that are being made in New Zealand, face a great deal of opposition from the general population, just as they would, if implemented here.

Action was initiated in New Zealand when their National Debt reached a level that was 75 percent of its Gross National Product. In our country, in 1988, our National Debt was 55 percent of our Gross National Product; up 20 percent from 35 percent in 1980.

The growth of the GNP in our country slows down or speeds up in direct relationship to the health of the economy. It will surely react in a convulsive manner with activities such as the savings and loan bailouts; bank bailouts; losses by Housing and Urban Development and the Federal Housing Administration; costs of foreign policy military operation; etc. Each of the above debt-impact centers represent failures of major components of our government—in all branches and at all levels.

The GNP will also react to changes in the level of our national debt. Funds required to pay the interest on the national debt get the highest priority. What remains can be used for other needs.

Doesn't it seem reasonable to expect that given such a pathetic record of failure and such a staggering burden of uncontrolled debt, that those we pay handsomely to manage *our business* would react with some intelligence, some sense of understanding and concern; and move to decrease spending to the bare necessities? Is that happening? Of course not! Foolish spending continues for anything and everything. And, the national debt continues to grow in zany, uncontrolled patterns!

Contrast this with the New Zealand example. Their government leaders recognized the gravity of the problem and initiated action to correct the situation in the face of much public opposition.

In making comparisons between these two countries, it is important to remember that the annual Gross National Product of New Zealand in 1988 was about $38.5 billion; less than one percent of that of the United States (just under $5.0 trillion). The average annual per capita income there was about $1150; compared to $16,000 plus in the U.S.

Just what are some of the things they are doing there? and what level of pain or sacrifice will the citizens of that small country be confronting in the action to regain command of its "out of control" government spending?

New Zealand moved to reduce government spending by $350 million in the first year of the program and $1.35 billion the following year. Actions considered in their plan included: scrapping of compulsory unionism in recognition of its contribution to their problems; a 25 percent decrease in a single man's unemployment benefit from about $80 to $60 per week; cancellation of a 25 percent increase that had been promised to elderly beneficiaries starting in April 1991; cuts in educational spending including cancellation of plans to build a new law school; and cuts in defense spending. Medical costs, including prescription drugs, in New Zealand, had increased about 50 percent. Welfare payments increased from about $500 million in 1988 to over $1,750 million by 1990! They would have ballooned to

$3,000 million by 1993 if nothing had been done! Sadly, we see no similar demonstration of such statesmanship in our country. Hopes we might have had for such a miracle were dashed when after several months of negotiations in the summer and fall of 1990 between high level members of our Legislative and Executive Branches, between the Social Democrats and the Republicans the agreement that was finally reached was totally non-responsive to the need or to the public demand. In our country great strides could be made in cutting our annual deficit problem by simply instituting a program that would freeze the level of spending on existing programs for a limited number of years. But, even that is not a satisfactory approach, especially to the Social Democrats. The contribution of organized labor to our problems, good or bad, is never discussed or debated here. One of our Sacred Cows! Incumbent politicians can usually count on a lot of votes from this source, if they "behave" in a way that pacifies union members.

We come to understand that the party platforms here, are not that different; that neither of the parties nor the individuals who lead them, are willing to do the job that must be done! We can only expect further inattention to our problems and continuing deterioration of our financial and social conditions!

Poland is another classic example of the failure of Socialism. The total collapse of the economy there has resulted in serious unrest in the country for several years. Solidarity, an organization of unionized labor, with Lech Walesa as one of its most visible and effective leaders, played a major role in convincing the ruling Communists to step aside. Tadeusz Mazowiecki, a Solidarity leader was elected premier of the country in September of 1989.

Ineffective management of the government and excessive borrowing, mostly from western nations left the country with a foreign debt of almost $40 billion dollars, fourth largest of all countries in the world. The country's budget deficit had increased to where it is about one-third of the government's total spending each year. *In the third quarter of 1989 prices more than doubled,* with an increase of 107.3 percent. Huge numbers of the Polish people were totally dependent upon "free meals" provided by the Red Cross and the Polish Committee for Social Assistance.

The new government, under Mazowiecki, faced many serious problems. Getting the budget deficit under control was a high priority. The effort targeted the huge payments being made to unprofitable and inefficient state owned and operated industries that produced coal, steel and many other goods *at a loss.* Although they are opposed by many of the older citizens, with their bent toward communist and socialist beliefs and methods, the new government favored development and implementation of new, market-oriented, economic policies and practices.

The cause and effect of the situation in Poland at that time is graphically portrayed in the following quotation from an article written by John Tagiable, for the New York Times News Service in late 1989.

—Start of Quote—

"The big smokestack enterprises, built in the fever of communist industrialization in the early postwar period, are a case that clearly illustrate the malaise of the Polish economy.

Like other Polish Companies, Nowa Huta, with about 10,000 steel workers, is a paternalistic operation, not only offering a monthly wage but distributing housing, providing medical care, running theaters and movie houses, and arranging summer holidays for workers and their families, regardless of the enterprise's profits. In the absence of a system of unemployment payments, workers are not laid off, even if their jobs are totally unproductive."

—End of Quote—

Most of us have some understanding of the hardships suffered by the Polish people. Television news coverage of that country during those years, showed the long lines of people waiting to buy even the most basic of foods; and the essentially bare shelves that greeted them in most of their markets.

Another example. The people of East Germany had been ruled for decades by an authoritarian government; and they had depended upon a democratic-socialist economic system during that period. They too suffered massive shortages of goods and services.

The examples that we have used are different in one important way. In the cases of Sweden and New Zealand the people "did it to themselves". They voted the Democratic Socialist party into power, with knowledge of the program contents and what it would mean to them and to the country. In Poland, and in East Germany, the people had it "done to them", by their authoritarian, communist governments. The economic system of the country was chosen by the leadership of that government. Regardless of enormous differences in their forms of government, their democratic-socialism economic systems which had much in common failed the test of any successful economic system; to meet the needs of the people for goods and services.

What is important here is the demonstration that their mis- management problems of continuing and expanding levels of undisciplined spending; income limited to an amount far short of that required to pay for the expenditures they approved; and public demands that "government" do more and more, socially and economically; simply provides another level of evidence that governments are extremely ineffectively and inefficient in all that they do.

In the example cases, in our own situation, and elsewhere around the world a critical examination will produce convincing evidence that "big" government simply does not work. Spiraling costs of social programs designed to do everything for everyone, impossible red tape, and ineffective utilization of resources *always* result in impossible financial demands and ultimate failure. The odds for success in government enterprises will be enhanced by limiting the number of activities they are involved in, and in keeping them small—"lean and mean". Elected and bureaucratic government officials are not chosen for their ability to do the job before them. They are leaders of and participants in that irrational notion that has gained credibility in our society that says that workers and especially managers can do their job without any knowledge or experience in the field they are working in! What a sham!

Once again, the wisdom of those who wrote our U. S. Constitution becomes obvious. They summarized, in Section 8 of Article I, their perspective as to what the responsibilities of the Congress should be. By omission of many additional duties and responsibilities that they could have listed there, we can assume that they intended to set boundaries as to how deeply involved that body should get into the peoples' business.

To this point, we have reasoned that our own self interest, and that of future generations of Americans are the primary reasons that we should aggressively identify, diagnose and develop cures for major problems confronting us. However, in these times of such widespread volatility and change in the governments of the world, there are other important reasons. In its purer form, prior to the 1970's and 1980's, and the big push in our country for social reform, our Democratic Republic form of government and the free-enterprise economic system demonstrated a unique ability to provide a proper balance between programs and resources and to serve the needs of the people quite well. True, it was not perfect, but its effectiveness outstripped what might have been considered to be second-best at the time.

If our government is now allowed to fail, it will be important to realize that the failure does not necessarily mean that the system is at fault. We must recognize the possibility that failure resulted from faulty implementation by a nation of people and their leaders who became distracted or disinterested. A nation of people, who somehow became enchanted with the idea that they were a "chosen" people; set aside in a near-garden-of-Eden setting; given freedom to control the circumstances of their own existence, showered with unique benefits that contributed to a quality-of-life unequaled anywhere else; and freedom to roam the expanses of the earth and beyond.

Any post-mortem analysis of the failure will provide information, too late to be useful to us; but, it may be useful to other nations who are just beginning to implement the system. In that analysis, with its advantage of the more perfect vision afforded by hind-sight, factors that contributed to the demise of our "empire" will be identified and the contribution of each to the ultimate failure can be established. This increased knowledge will surely reflect adversely upon those of us who sat idly by and allowed this to happen. It will become readily apparent that many (most) of these contributory factors were visible to us, if only we had taken the time and made the effort to understand and solve the problems that confronted us. At that point in time, awareness of the relative importance of intellectual decay and complacency to the total failure, will be of little usefulness to us!

Hope springs eternal, at least in the hearts of some Americans. In this case we find ourselves hoping—believing—that there is a way to awaken the sleeping-dead among us to the perils we face, as individuals and as a nation. To effectively issue a call to arms to those who might care enough to join the struggle for survival, to preserve our way of life. We have to believe! We have to try! Should we fail to accomplish these ends and our empire collapses, our efforts will not have been entirely in vain. We will have, at least, documented for future generations that not all people living in the United States in the late 1900's and early 2000's were as stupid as is implied by their seemingly, uncaring disregard of symptoms of critical, life threatening problems; and the accompanying failure to institute timely, aggressive, corrective efforts to protect this way of life for ourselves and for them. Future generations will realize, that there were citizens who were aware of the precarious nature of conditions in the United States of America during our time. Individuals who tried to marshall the people to a meaningful effort of corrective action. That is part of what this book is all about!

That block of countries with whom the free world has experienced the costly "Cold War" over the past several decades, are being confronted with undeniable evidence that such international discord and distrust is counter-productive. Pursuit of that confrontational posture over the past several decades has resulted in great waste of natural, financial and human resources. It has overtaxed their economic systems, and our own, and led to significant hardships and sacrifices for their people to bear. This recognition is leading to decisions for major reforms in government and economic systems elsewhere. The "Cold War" mind-set is fading. For the first time, in modern history, we may be embracing an opportunity to devote the bulk of the time and resources of the nation and the world to peaceful purposes.

As the many unbelievable and unpredictable changes began to occur in that region of Eastern Europe and Asia, it became immediately obvious that certain practices prevalent in our own U. S. society would influence, in a major way, the character of the reform movement that developed over there. Their public protests mirrored demonstrations that have been nurtured and developed to the point of almost being an art-form in this country. Of course, we profess to having a democratic society, where the will of the majority prevails and decisions are accepted by all. However, with weak spines, our officials and justice system cave-in to the demands of the small, special-interest groups who protest. And, the theory of democracy, governance that meets the needs and the desires of the majority gets lost in the process. The country and the majority of its citizens become pawns of small, special-interest, splinter groups of people who are allowed to press ahead with programs that interest and benefit them; at the expense of the rest of us. The term "civil rights" has taken on an image of majesty and undeniability in these events. The civil rights of the demonstrators, that is! The rights, civil or otherwise, of the rest of us, are ignored. Demonstrators are betting that the passive, "silent", majority will not react to protect their rights. They are usually correct in that assumption. If the establishment participates at all, it will usually be in the form of police whose primary mission is to protect the demonstrators.

**How does that strike you? You and I pay for the police to protect the demonstrators, from us; at a time when they are bent on destroying rules, regulations, systems and procedures that we advocate!**

Protection of the property and person of the law-abiding, majority are of little concern. Of course, the mass media, especially television, is always johnny-on-the-spot; right there with emotionally charged presentations, usually biased in the direction of whatever cause may be the issue of the day. And the insurgents receive free national and beyond publicity for their cause.

People of the world have witnessed these demonstrations, either as students in this country or as partakers of the media coverage. Without exception, demonstrations have been used as the device for challenging the totalitarian governments of eastern Europe. With two exceptions, Romania and China, the leaders succumbed to the demands of the crowds without inflicting loss of life. In Romania the government resisted for a time, with some loss of life, but it fell when the military ultimately refused to continue to support the regime in power.

In China the government resisted and ultimately prevailed. The magnitude of the loss of life of citizens is unknown to the outside world, but is thought to be quite large. Not unexpectedly, the condemnation of the Chinese government was immediate, wide spread, and strong in this country. Emotions reigned supreme,—again! If there was any thoughtful analysis of the "China" situation in the United States, it was not obvious. No one spoke out publicly to point out that, like all disagreements, there are at least two defensible sides to any problem.

To thoughtful people, the arrogance of an upstart nation, 200 years old, challenging and criticizing actions of a nation that has existed for thousands of years and that is 20 times its size; must seem a bit out of place. Especially when present conditions here demonstrate so clearly that those offering all of the advice, to China and numerous other foreign countries obviously don't have all of the answers. In fact, it is important for everyone, here and there, to recognize that we, in the U. S. have not yet proven that our government and economic systems will work. To the contrary, we may be at an advanced stage of proving that, as applied in our country, they will not work.

Our national view, and that of many of our citizens, is naturally biased by the fact that China is ruled by a totalitarian regime. It is true that the standard of living there does not equal ours. And their citizens do not enjoy all of the freedoms experienced by citizens of the United States. Not-withstanding those facts, the leadership of China has done a "fair" job of providing the necessities for its people. Its leadership has recognized opportunities to improve the performance of their government and economic systems. They have been, and are continuing to do so, moving in an evolutionary, as contrasted to revolutionary, manner toward a more democratic society and free-market economy.

Keep in mind that the government of China is responsible for the well-being of about 5,000,000,000 people; twenty to twenty-five percent of all the people currently alive on the earth. That is an awesome responsibility. It has been indicated that there may have been as many as 200,000 people in the Tiananmen Square during the demonstrations. Although that is a lot of people, for every person demonstrating in the Square, there were 25,000 citizens of China not represented there. The 0.004 percent of the Chinese people that demonstrated was insignificant to the point that they did not represent even a dependable "sample" of the total population. They were intent upon destroying the existing government. As is usually the case in these situations, they had no viable plan for meeting the needs of this huge population had the government capitulated to them.

All "feeling" persons were repulsed, by what happened at Tiananmen Square; at the loss of life. Only the passage of time, will provide the perspective for an objective, historical panorama of what happened there. For those who suffer the "emotional Plague" the choice of what should have occurred is easy and clear. That does not make it right! An intellectual case can be made that the government's action represented the best of the options available to the Chinese leaders, when long-term interests of the country are factored into the equation. The alternatives available to them were limited by the demonstrators themselves to: government capitulation to demonstrator's demands, or the action that was ultimately taken. Had the leadership succumbed to the demonstrator's demands and a dysfunctional government resulted for an extended period, the loss of life and degree of hardship for the Chinese people could have been much greater for an extended period of time. Real-time, emotion-based decisions; the folly of many of today's demonstrators, students and others like them, their academic impresarios, large numbers of our government officials and some of our citizens; are a luxury that important national and international leaders cannot blindly embrace in responsibly serving their country's needs.

The world has yet to see the results of allowing this mob-rule, demonstration-oriented abstraction play itself out to an ultimate conclusion. Such actions, in our country and elsewhere, have been allowed to bring down the establishment or to achieve benefits for the demonstrators that they could not have gained through the democratic process.

We will begin to develop some comparisons of the effectiveness of the two courses of action quite soon. Those foreign nations that gave in to the demonstrator's demands, must now deal with the more difficult "what now?" question. Their path to recovery is strewn with obstacles. Development of new, democratic, responsive, and effective governments will take time. There is no assurance of their successful identification, recruitment and election of able, as contrasted to popular, inept, new leaders the first time or two around. When all of that is successfully accomplished, and the new leadership and procedures are in place, a more severe test of the people will begin. Major benefits of the new government and economic systems will not be immediate, or for that matter, certain to follow. Success will be contingent upon a great deal of dedication, cooperation, work and patience by all of the people. Additional sacrifices will be required of the people. Demonstrations during this period of time will only delay the process. Without the support, *real support*, of the people, no leadership group can succeed in such a difficult task!

It will be interesting to see if the students and other demonstrators will display the discipline, patience, intelligence and character necessary to join with the leadership and the general population to achieve goals common to all of them. Will they be willing to pitch in and help achieve the best, most effective solutions? Chances are that some will; and some will not! Discipline and patience (intelligence?) have not been in evidence as a discernible part of their psyche.

In considering this general subject, it should be recognized, that there are pockets of counter-culture; individuals who inhabit (slink in) the hallowed halls of our educational institutions. They are intimately aware of the unique nature of their positions to influence the destiny of the country, not as part of the "establishment" which supposedly responds to the wishes of the majority, but in response to whatever "offbeat" organization and/or personal crusade they may subscribe to. By successfully planting the seeds of their counter culture ideas and ideals in the young, active, fertile minds of some of the students with which they are entrusted, your children and mine, they are able to magnify their own influence on the course of national and world events. In this role they become active, covert, anonymous entrepreneurs fashioning their own kind of society outside of, and, in spite of, the intent and direction of the recognized and accepted national goals and programs of the majority; without any negative personal recognition or peril to themselves. That, is reserved for those pawns who dutifully carry their banners into the public arena.

There is absolutely no reason to believe that we have a monopoly on this activity in this country. After all, masses of young people from countries all over the world have come to our institutions of higher education, over the years, seeking what was at one time, a preeminent education, unequaled by institutions elsewhere. It is interesting that so many foreign nations continue to send so many of their young people to this country for an educational experience. They seem to discount the recognized, present plight of our public educational system, the reluctance to teach youth what they go to school to learn, and abundance of evidence that the student's minds are being shaped by teaching them what to think, as contrasted to the preferred action of teaching them how to think. The latter, then leaves it up to the student to go out into the world; study and experience what it has to offer and to then make up their own minds on all of the questions and issues they encounter. Foreign nations that continue to finance educations for large numbers of their college-age citizens in the United States must be aware that continuation of that practice results in importation of revolutionary ideas and cultures into their midst.

We can logically assume that many foreign students trained in this country, over the years, have entered the educational systems in their own countries. As respected staff or leaders of those institutions, they are actively institutionalizing there what they learned here.

On the other hand, it *is not* obvious that there are other pockets of personable, dedicated, effective individuals in our institutions who are as passionately devoted to teaching the countermanding principles and values of the "establishment". The need for young people, and all of us, to work together for common goals and to contribute in positive ways to making our institutions and our system work properly. The notion that our country and the world will be what *we* make it is sobering but true. *Every* person's contribution, will have some impact—positive or negative!

The universal demand by successful demonstrators in the eastern-block countries, for open democratic elections has presented a second major indication that reform movements would model their actions after some of what they had seen happening in our country.

This leads to interesting and in some ways frightening questions with respect to what they might do next. Would it, in fact, be desirable for them to do all things the same way we have done/are doing them? Have we done everything right? or have we stubbed our toes along the way? Are there things that we should have done differently? should be doing differently? Any objective look at the situation in our country today would convince most *literate* persons that those questions should be answered "yes", and "yes".

This brings us to the recognition that we, the citizens of the United States, who would gain the most from such action, have not objectively and conscientiously analyzed our own actions, procedures, programs, etc., over the years, to determine the degree to which they are, individually contributing in positive or negative ways to deliver the results we desire, at reasonable, acceptable costs.

In this nation which did more than any other to develop "closed loop", scientific methods for solving difficult problems, we seem to be unwilling to use those techniques for solving problems in our own non-scientific activities. "Feedback" from actions taken, its identification and quantification; and then directed, measured, corrective response to it are important factors in the successful utilization of that system to solve complex problems.

What is feedback?

As a small boy, living in southern Idaho, my family was very poor. Our circumstances were in many ways similar to those faced by the Joads in John Steinbeck's book, The Grapes of Wrath. We had fled the ravages inflicted upon northeastern Nebraska by the great depression in the 1930's. My parents, two younger brothers, my maternal grandparents, a large German Shepherd dog named Laddie and I, along with everything we owned left Lynch, Nebraska in early September of 1935 in a big Dodge truck that had seen much better days; and off we went! Our intended destination was the Couer d' Alene area of northern Idaho. The trip went slow but acceptably well for about two weeks. Then near the small town of Filer in south-central Idaho, we experienced a major problem. There, 500 miles from our destination, we encountered important feedback; the truck wouldn't start, we were out of gas. More important, however, was feedback to the effect that we were out of money. We camped, by the side of the road, in the truck and under tarps attached to it for several weeks until a local farmer, with a heart of gold, noticed our plight and offered to let us live in two small lean-to sheds on his nearby property. Given some work in the harvest fields of the area, our ability to catch fish in some streams in the area, to shoot game birds and rabbits, and to glean dry beans and potatoes from the fields after they had been harvested; we were able to survive.

We lived in these two small, buildings for a couple of years. They were papered on the inside with newspapers. There was no insulation and it often got very cold. The living area, as contrasted to the sleeping area, was heated by a pot-bellied stove. There was no heat in the sleeping area.

Feedback, that cannot be ignored forever, played an important role in our lives at that time. The sense of hunger, feedback that presses upon a person's other senses the fact that the body needs nourishment. A dreadful sensation, "feedback" that descended upon each of us, often in the middle of extremely cold nights, that a trip to the outside, unheated and unlit toilet, one hundred or so yards down the path toward the creek could not wait until morning.

Feedback assumed the role of the smell of scorching material or of the burning sensation on your backside as you stood by the heating stove trying to stay warm. Each communicating clearly and effectively the need for immediate response. It displayed itself in the form of a red-hot, going toward white-hot stove. Thereby, communicating the need to decrease the flue draft and to forego additional fuel or suffer the consequence of a "meltdown". A word familiar to most of us today, in another context.

Although feedback usually demands response in strong terms, that is not always the case. As a result of less demanding "feedback" to my parents and grandparents; to the effect that, we can "get by" here, all four of them lived out the rest of their lives quite comfortably in that small community.

Thankfully, the development of housing with lights and heating systems was left in the hands of practical people, scientists and engineers. The development of the nation had not yet been turned over to the politicians; bureaucrats; social workers; psychologists; psychiatrists; and "instant" managers turned out in massive numbers of questionable ability by Master of Business Administration and Masters in Public Administration factories at many institutions of higher learning. Instead, the problem solving system was allowed to work; and it did so effectively. Today, in most situations, the furnace or other source of heat for our buildings is located in the basement, the garage or some other out of the way place. Located in strategic places in the heated areas, and connected via low-voltage, electrical circuits to the heat source, are small devices called thermostats. The desired temperature settings are placed on the thermostats, and those temperatures are maintained in the heated areas by continuous and effective interaction (feedback and reaction to it) in the closed-loop control system between the two devices.

In the complication and sophistication that has become more and more a part of our everyday lives, the scientific method comes into play in many ways. It is often necessary for humans with their unique ability to reason and logically analyze alternatives and quantities of data, to serve as one link in a "feedback" loop.

Most of us drive automobiles. As a driver, we become an important part of a quite complex "closed-loop system". Our eyes and ears serve as sensors; they communicate information (feedback) to our brain where that information is analyzed and developed into signals to appropriate body elements to take any action required. You are going down a straight stretch of road at 65 miles per hour (MPH) and you come to a sign that indicates a sharp turn in the road ahead, the sign says 25 MPH. It is important that all parts of the closed-loop system function properly in a timely way. The feedback—eyes on the sign to brain, brain to the foot you brake with, eyes on speedometer to brain, etc. cannot be ignored, if you and your passengers wish to survive.

Some of the most sophisticated closed-loop control systems that presently exist are developed for and utilized in aviation and space exploration. During most of our time aloft in modern commercial airliners today, the plane is under the control of the automatic-pilot systems that control all aspects of its operation on a continuing basis; the rate of climb or descent, cruising altitude, speed, direction, etc.; all in response to instructions entered into the system by the flight crew at the beginning of or during the flight; and to feedback from a number of monitoring devices throughout the aircraft.

This brings to mind a story I recently heard on this subject. Maybe you can relate to it, as a result of some experience you have had in recent travels:

> A large group of people had just boarded their 747 airliner at the Washington, D.C., Dulles airport for a flight to Seattle Washington. As they settled back into their seats and tried to get as comfortable as they could, the engines were started, the plane was pushed back away from the loading area, and it taxied out to the end of the runway for take off. The engines burst into action; the plane lurched forward; and in a short time, it cleared the ground and was on its way. The expected flying time was about six hours. As Dulles was fading into the distance, behind the plane, a pleasant, resonant and calming voice came on over the speaker system in the passenger's cabin.
>
> "Good morning ladies and gentlemen, welcome to our flight 1234, this morning to the Seattle-Tacoma area. The management and staff of the **X Y Z** airline thank you for flying with us. This is your Captain speaking to you from the control tower at Dulles airport. You have the honor of flying on the first fully automated, coast to coast flight of a domestic airliner; have a nice flight; do not be concerned about the pioneering aspect of this flight because nothing can go wrong . . . can go wrong . . . can go wrong . . . can go wrong— . . ."

Space exploration was in its infancy when the practical difficulty, near impossibility, of being able to shoot a rocket and its payload directly to a rendezvous with some far away, rapidly moving, outer planet, became apparent. Guidance systems and other equipment carried on the space vehicles of early missions, provided ground, launch and flight crews feedback as to its trajectory and location at all times. That information was/is compared continuously with the programmed flight information and criteria that were established and programmed into computers prior to the launch; criteria that had to be met if the flight was to be successful. The dependability of the success of these missions increased greatly when the ground or flight crews were given the ability to react to this feedback-information and introduce route corrections into the system during the flight.

I suspect that the above provides more information about control systems and problem solving than you have felt you needed to know. To be candid, it has stretched my knowledge of the subject. I do not consider myself an expert in the field. It is included to make a point. In everything we do, we need to monitor the consequences of what we do. Did it achieve the desired results? If not what can we do differently? If it did, might we refine the process to make it more effective or less costly. As we achieve success, whatever the effort may be, it is important to monitor costs. Is solution of whatever the problem, worth what it costs to solve it? Or should those resources be utilized to accomplish higher priority needs?

For most of my adult life, I have worked as a leader and been an active participant in the Boy Scouts of America program. As a Scoutmaster for several years, my success was dependent upon the quality of leadership provided to the 50 to 60 boys in the Troop, by a select group of boy leaders. Each summer the entire Troop went to summer camp for one week. In addition, we took the boy leaders on a one week, high-adventure, activity to recognize their selfless service to the group. It also gave the adult leaders that went on the outing a way to relate in a special way with these boys who were rising to the top, in leadership and citizenship roles that would someday be important to our country. On several occasions this special outing took the form of an eight-day, 100 to 150 mile canoe trek down the McKenzie and Willamette Rivers in western Oregon. We traveled, two persons per canoe. We carried all of our camp gear and supplies for the entire trip with us. On one of these trips. David was my canoe partner. He was not as experienced in canoeing as were most of the rest of us, I ended up doing most of the steering from the rear seat of our canoe. If you have ever done much canoeing, you know that it is not just a matter of getting in and operating the paddles. Unless you know several special strokes with the paddles, it is difficult to go in a straight line from one point to another. If you paddle all the time with a straight stroke on the right side of the canoe, it tends to turn left, and vice versa.

I always carried my 35 millimeter camera with me on these outings. One sunny afternoon as we entered a long calm, straight stretch of the Willamette, I needed to put a new roll of film in the camera; this seemed like a good time and place to do it. I told David what I was going to do, and suggested that he would have to paddle a bit harder during that period to be sure that we would keep up with the other 11 canoes. With those instructions, I went to work changing the film. Although I had my head down, looking at what I was doing, I knew that David had stepped up his pace as I had suggested he would need to do. He was, in fact, working so hard at it, that at one point he splashed water on me, the camera, my film and some other items that I carried in a waterproof container in the back of the canoe. I cautioned him about that and went on cleaning up that problem and changing the film. When I finally had finished my project and looked up, to once again, do my part, I couldn't believe what I saw. The other canoes had disappeared around the next bend of the river. The wake of our canoe indicated that during the time I had been predisposed, we had made about two or three large circles in the water. Our only progress, down river being due to the drift with the current, which was almost non-existent at that point. David had done exactly what I had told him to do; no more, no less. He had put his head down and worked very hard paddling the canoe—he was so intent, in fact, in doing as he was told, that it never occurred to him to look up and check the direction he was going; to see if all of his effort was accomplishing the desired result! Now David at the time was probably 13 or 14 years old. I found it easy to forgive him for his lapse, unbecoming as it was to a "leader"; the sort of citizen that we hoped he would become. I also took the time to think about and learn from my part in the experience. Working hard, in itself, is not enough. We must have goals. We must decide where we want to go, where we want to be at some point in time in the future; even then, hard work will be effective, only if we look up occasionally, measure our progress toward our goal and make any adjustments in magnitude and direction of effort that seems necessary.

What a blessing it would be if everyone in this country could be a part of and learn from such an experience. How many of us have goals for *ourselves* that reach beyond today, this week or this month? And, how many of us have established goals in our minds for our country; where we would like it to be next year, ten years from now, even twenty years from now when our children and their children's inheritance will be what we have preserved for them, or in a worse case scenario, what we have done to them!

What about our country. How does all of this fit here. I know of no way that anyone or any organization, be it government or private enterprise, can be successful without setting goals; having some idea of where it aspires to be at some point of time in the future. And that is only the beginning. Success in such efforts then requires intelligent, thoughtful direction, analysis and redirection. With that and a great deal of dedication, perseverance, and hard work; success *may* result.

Do you see any of this taking place in your surroundings? In the Federal government, your state government, your county or your city government? If you can truthfully answer such questions in a positive vain, you are fortunate. My experience demonstrates that effective management by public officials is a rarity. We will be contemplating this issue in more detail as we proceed.

In past times, when managers were held responsible for setting and then meeting production goals of goods and/or services, it was recognized that, "If you don't know where you are going, it is easy to get there!"

My attempts to critically assess the effectiveness of management in the public and private activities that I encounter in today's environment; leads to great disappointment. The predominance of failed programs, failure to recognize that such programs are not working and the senseless pouring of massive amounts of additional resources; natural, human, and financial into them is very discouraging. Given the wide variety of high priority needs that exist for the limited resources we have; such incompetency, borders on criminality. We do not have to and we should not; settle for anything but the best qualified managers, supervisors and workers available in these activities; and we should demand that they do credible work on the job!

And what about the private enterprise side of our economy? Is it doing any better? That it is not, is only partially the fault of the system. Encumbered by unending government interference at all levels, by a philosophy that supposes that any organization can succeed when it is managed by committees—*no one* in charge, and by a business environment created by tax laws and other intervention that forces decisions to be based on "today's" "bottom line" and forecloses any management philosophy that looks to and considers future needs; the odds are stacked in favor of failure.

All of this seems especially pertinent at this time, because it raises this important question, "Have we in this country made only right (correct) moves in arriving at where our society is today?" Have we made any mistakes? Is the seemingly, unquestioning acceptance of "our way" by so many of the people involved in changing the form of government used in other parts of the world, well founded? That level of trust deserves some consideration on our part. Will such hasty, impulsive trust serve them well?

Have we, in fact, demonstrated beyond a shadow of a doubt that our form of democracy works? My answer, "probably not". What do you think? And what about the effectiveness of the "open election" process? Has it worked for us? Is it now working effectively for us? We can understand, when people in other nations fall victim to the aura of wealth, freedom, prosperity and affluence enjoyed by most citizens in this country. We shouldn't blame them for that! Most of our own citizens, who should know better if they are to be constructive and effective in fulfilling their citizenship responsibilities, fall victim to it also. How many times have you heard some do-gooder remark that, "In a country as prosperous as ours; this or that should not be allowed to happen"?

These are questions that will need to be carefully considered and answered by each of us individually. A general response might be to say that in the difficult formative years of our country, free elections seemed to have identified and placed into office, able, dedicated patriots for vital positions of responsibility in our government; and they usually enjoyed the patriotic support of the people. Although we could probably identify exceptions, the election process seemed to fit our needs quite well until the 1940's or 1950's. During the past several decades the demands upon our elected officials and the appointed bureaucracies have changed a great deal. At the same time the nature of the candidates from which our leaders must be selected has also changed substantially. In earlier years people on the ballot could be accurately classified as citizen-candidates. Their service was not always a full-time job. As a result, they entered the public arena with some experience and understanding of the "real world"; the one that confronts you and I daily! Where we must choose between the things we desire to have. Where priority lists for the use of all resources, are a must! And, they understood and reacted to a sense of statesmanship, placing the needs of the country in its proper perspective, ahead of personal benefits; as they served us. They did not view political service as a career.

In later years, public servants have become more oriented to the career-politician philosophy. In this situation the importance of the "national interest" has become subordinated to many things, including the "personal interest" of the servant and his/her compelling self-motivation to get reelected. Many of those who go into it as a career, do so early in life. They have no "real world" experience upon which to base important decisions they will be called upon to make on our behalf. If they do enter politics with some experience background, that experience becomes obsolete or forgotten after a few years and they lose touch with what is reality, outside of government. This new breed of politician is usually the product of our failing public education system. We can only guess at the impact of this factor upon what is taking place, but indications are that it is considerable. An unrelenting feature of this situation, is that these people believe that they are qualified for the positions they are assuming. They have been given grades and diplomas by the public school systems; actions which tend to assure them that they have been properly prepared to go out and perform satisfactorily in the work place. Of course, the young people believe that to be true; they have no way of judging otherwise, until they find themselves being tormented and pummeled by work-place expectations that they are unable to meet! I am haunted by a situation I observed on television some time ago: of a young girl walking away from her high school graduation exercises; confidently stating, "We are ready to take over!" Such shallow thinking and arrogance, left unchecked, can only lead to disaster! Experience provides many arguments for returning to the non-career, citizen-politician arrangement. Term limits, a concept that is sometimes considered at the Federal level and in many states could be one step in that direction.

In the above discussion there is a reference to do-gooders. It seems appropriate that we discuss that term briefly. The term probably means something different to every reader. My plea is that you not be offended by the use of the word here. Do-gooders come in many forms; one form provides an important foundation for effective operation of our society. They are the ones that have taken the time to understand the underlying causes of problems they encounter. They willingly and aggressively contribute their own time and resources to improve conditions for themselves, but more importantly for others, around them. Although they may discuss and promote with friends and the general public the need for help with their projects; they respect the rights of others to identify and support the charity or benefit program of their own choice.

This is contrasted to other types of do-gooders who are much less useful in this arena. One type, in particular, organizes themselves in small, splinter groups. They are not satisfied with the limited accomplishments of their own efforts to satisfy a particular need. They are determined to force the rest of us to support charitable causes that *they* deem most worthy. In so doing, they deny the rest of us the option of setting our own priorities and giving to the charity that we prefer!.

With the Socialist Democrats having control of our Federal and most of our state Legislative and Executive government organizations, this class of do-gooders have learned how to successfully force their agendas on the rest of us through enactment of laws by that group. During these same decades (1960 to 1990) many of our courts, and the system, have been politicized by the selection of judges who do not see their responsibility as simply that of interpreting the Constitution and bringing it to life in the debates of the day. They come to the judgeships with personal emotions, interests and agendas of their own and they feel free to react to all of this in the decisions they make. These actions are seldom challenged by the majority.

In our modern society the problem of this latter type of do-gooder is made even more troublesome by the intransigence of most people in that category to accept any but their own opinion or desire on an issue. Splinter groups of activists develop on both sides of an issue, neither side will budge in their position and for all practical purposes, our system simply is unable, or unwilling, to deal with the problem effectively. The abortion issue; old growth timber—to harvest or not?; the spotted owl versus the timber interests; etc. are examples of this kind of situation. And the controversy continues to fester. Emotionally charged demonstrations are held more frequently by both sides, the groups and the individuals in them become more hostile toward each other, law enforcement is expected to protect everyone from everyone else and the silent majority pays the bills. As is the case in so many situations, our collective preoccupation with erroneous definitions of "Civil Rights" for the individual thwarts enforcement of what laws prevail in the area.

# CHAPTER 8

> Fellow-citizens, we cannot escape history. We . . . will be remembered in spite of ourselves. No personal significance, or insignificance, can spare one or another of us. The fiery trial through which we pass, will light us down, in honor or dishonor, to the latest generation.
>
> **Abraham Lincoln**

The basic thrust of our inquiry here is one of curiosity, concern and apprehension about the health of our country. Is it and our way of life in jeopardy?

To many, the symptoms that present themselves are bold announcements that call for aggressive, effective corrective action. To others those same symptoms are invisible; they are accepted as not being troublesome; or they are simply ignored.

We have discussed the disappointment so many of us feel as a result of the numbing disregard for the serious deterioration of our situation by those we trust with our affairs-of-state. It is not as though they are unaware of the nature and gravity of our problems! It is obvious that they are.

In the mid 1980's the Congress passed and the President signed into law, the Gramm-Rudman (G.R.) Deficit Reduction Act. It is interesting and "telling", that our elected Representatives and Senators finally concluded that a special law was necessary to *force* them to do a job that was already, clearly enunciated as their responsibility! Primary duties and responsibilities that we, the people, had put them there to do. But! which individually and as groups they had been unwilling to execute. Their leaders, simply ignored reality, and the majority of the rest of them obediently followed their lead!

In retrospect, it is interesting that they, and we, thought that the mere existence of a new law would make any difference! During recent years the budgets had been out of balance by huge amounts; with the spending exceeding the income by hundreds of *billions* of dollars.

The new law was especially designed to *force* elected officials in the Federal Government to ultimately develop and pass into law each year, annual budget programs in which the spending and the income were balanced. In an attempt to limit the "shock" on the economy; the law established annual deficit limits of decreasing amounts over its first five years of operation. The intent being, that five years after its implementation, the budgets would be balanced. Further provisions of the law required that if the two Branches had not agreed upon a new budget that met the requirements by a date-certain each year, automatic spending cuts would go into affect, making across-the-board cuts of adequate amounts to achieve the balance needed. A few items in the budget were excepted from this process.

The United States Constitution clearly establishes the primary responsibility of the Legislative Branch to maintain and protect the financial integrity of the country. All Federal spending is the result of specific action by the two houses of that Branch, and the approval of the Executive Branch; via the President's signature. Ineptitude and irresponsibility of our elected officials and bureaucrats in both Branches of our Federal government, and by members of both parties there, has resulted in a "staggering burden" to be born by the people of the country; a Federal debt that exceeds five trillion dollars ($5,000,000,000,000). Amassed by huge annual deficits, this debt and interest payments on it, must be paid off by levies against the people for decades to come!

Lacking the intelligence and courage required to maintain viable financial arrangements for the country, these servants of ours apparently felt that the new G.R. law would cushion public reaction that might result from their taking the actions that were necessary. It would hopefully free them from responsibility for their excessive spending programs of the past. And, it would provide them with an excuse with their constituencies for not proceeding with a multitude of new social programs they had promised. Finally, they obviously hoped that it would diminish and divert public hostility when they found it necessary to extract new taxes that would probably be necessary!

As Director of the Office of Management and Budget in the Executive Branch of the Federal government during several years of the Reagan Administration, David Stockman was in the position of having to try to negotiate with the Legislative Branch, budget agreements that would best meet the needs of the country. President Reagan, who he served, was elected by a majority of about 55 percent of the voters in 1980, and by almost 60 percent in 1984. It is recognized that the nature of the campaigns run in recent national elections have left something to be desired. However, in those two campaigns it was perfectly clear to the voting public that Ronald Reagan intended to work for less government; in terms of size, costs and intervention into the lives of the citizens; and that he would try to achieve a balanced budget. His intent, mode of operation and his priorities were surely more clear in the minds of the voters in the 1984 election, based on the events during his first term. His majority in that election increased by about 5 percent over what it was in 1980. If, in fact, ours is a government, "of the people, by the people and for the people", it would seem that his vision of government, its priorities and programs, would be treated with some respect in government circles. That the programs and budget proposals developed in his Executive Branch would be received with some respect by other persons and organizations sharing that responsibility with him. People, whose mandate resided in the fact that they were elected to office by the voters of *only one state* or *only a portion of one state*. But! something was obscenely wrong! That did not happen. Ego and power-mongering got in the way. In the words of the Kings and Queens in the Legislative Branch, the Reagan budgets were Dead on Arrival, (DOA) when sent to congress for consideration. Not unexpectedly, these pronouncements were made before they had studied the documents. They did not know exactly what they contained. Their differences on matters of politics, spending, intervention in personal lives, and social spending were so intense and so predictable that they could and did shoot from the hip. The fact that such action would put them at variance with 55 to 60 percent of the American voters, seemed to be of no consequence to them. In a kind or respectful vain we might refer to their actions as arrogance, an absence of effective leadership, or individual and group incompetence. In a more serious vain, it should be obvious even to them that our system of government was not designed to work that way; in fact, it cannot possibly work with such disrespect for their peers in the system, and/or the system! The fact that they might not understand that, raises serious questions as to their qualifications for the positions they hold! If they did understand; their neglect of and disregard for the situation, raises more serious questions of resolve and patriotism.

Shortly after he left the government service in the mid 1980's, Mr. Stockman published a book entitled, "The Triumph of Politics", in which he discusses the impracticality of trying to implement the Graham-Rudman law. He predicted that the law would never be successful in reducing the massive Federal budget deficits by any significant amount; that the law would not work. History has proven that prediction to be correct.

He further predicted that as a result of the realization that the law would not work, it would be repealed or radically amended. He was intimately familiar with all of the "games" and insidious and deceitful practices that are part of the normal operation in our Capital; but even he, seemed unaware of the degree to which illegal and unethical practices had come to dominate activities there. He assumed that our government would not flagrantly and arrogantly disobey it's own law! He was wrong. The law did not do the job! It was not allowed to do so. But! neither was it repealed or amended. Although some agreements were forged between the Executive and Legislative Branches to limit spending in some areas, deficit limits required by the law have simply been ignored.

At the same time, the costs of the Savings and Loan bailout continued to grow, tens and hundreds of *billions* of dollars each time it was revisited. It is conceivable that the banking industry may need a similar massive infusion of financial assistance from the taxpayer. Federal programs are in deep financial trouble everywhere; society is gaining little real benefit from their enormous sacrifice of tax money.

Most state governments are in deep trouble; facing annual deficits that reach into the tens of *billions* of dollars. But, most states are bound by their constitutions to balance their budgets each year. Thankfully, they are not given the luxury of deficit spending, and with one or two exceptions they have adhered to that requirement. Major cities in the country have faced or are facing bankruptcy. Acceptable solutions to their problems are almost non-existent! It is important to note that some of the trouble faced by the states and cities is not of their own doing. They are, instead, results of additional, unconscionable Federal actions. It would seem logical for us to hope (expect?) that the serious financial problems we face at the federal level, would result in severe limits in spending at that level. But! alas, that has not happened! Instead, the Feds have simply continued their spending ways; extensions of existing Federal social programs; and creation of numerous new programs, many of which pass the responsibility for payment of costs for implementation and funding down to local governments! The flood of social legislation with generous benefits to "the people" continues without the need for the perpetrators to fund them. That triviality is left to the people's elected representatives at the state, county and local levels. Such actions have come to be known as **"unfunded mandates"**.

Prime examples of such actions are proposals for extended child care arrangements, and health care for everyone, regardless of ability to pay. There are no dependable estimates of the annual and total costs of these new programs, but it is known that they will be in the tens and hundreds of *BILLIONS* of dollars. There is no apparent intent, on the Feds part, to provide new funding to offset these massive costs.

Each elected official and all of the high-level, bureaucratic managers in the public service, are sworn into office by oath similar to that established by Article I; Section 1 of the Constitution, for the President:

> "I do solemnly swear (or affirm) that I will faithfully execute the office of the President of the United States, and will to the best of my ability, preserve, protect and defend the Constitution of the United States".

Given such a commitment, it seems logical for us to expect that the *legitimate needs of the nation*, would enjoy a *top* priority in the policy development and performance of persons, so sworn! Of course, there will be differences of opinion in the minds of the many elected officials, bureaucrats, and all of the people as to what constitutes the highest priority items to be included in our list of legitimate needs. It is not unreasonable to expect that those differences will be negotiated into a program that legally does the job.

A question that looms grotesquely before us: "does the continued gross mismanagement of the people's business result from incompetence? does it represent a lack of character and statesmanship?, or is it the result of a combination of these factors?"

If incompetence is indeed a factor, the people seem not to have followed through in their thinking to determine whether the problems result from ineptitude of the individuals? from incompetence and misdirection by their leadership? or from the fact that the system of government we are trying to use simply is not adequate to meet our needs?

Why is the public so accepting of this situation? The statement that illiteracy is commonplace in this country, today, does not generate any argument. The plight of those who cannot read, is emotionally and sympathetically characterized in the mass media as a blight upon our society. We accept that situation as one of the causes of the problems we face.

Having done that, however, it is important to point out that the appeal to emotion and sympathy, have been, and are being, grossly overworked in the explosion of media presentations of all sorts of sob-story, emotional problems in our country and in the world. The empathetic response of real Americans, good people who care about a lot of things, is simply overloaded. And, they respond financially; willingly and under duress of tax codes, beyond their ability to do so; despite the absence of any evidence that their sacrifices result in any significant, lasting benefits. The Era of Emotional Idiocy increases its grip on people and its control over our society. The case for employing effective, intellectual methods withers, unable to gain attention through the tears and deep emotional concerns and expressions of those suffering the emotional plague.

The situation with illiteracy is no exception. Tears and emotional distress will only attract the attention of the multitude of psychiatrists, psychologists, etc. (manipulators of the mind) and the hordes of social workers in our society today. Problems such as this represent significant economic opportunities for these groups, especially when "easy government money" is involved! A hard look at the contrast of our society today, as compared to what it was in the 1940's or 1950's; prior to the explosion of the graduation of such operatives, will properly raise questions as to what, if any, positive contributions their services have made, over time. Indications of negative impacts are everywhere.

Illiteracy, when viewed from an emotional and/or sympathetic perspective tends to be a "black and white" issue. People who cannot read are illiterate. All others are literate! But alas! it is not that simple! Important, consequential, differences exist in the levels of literacy within that wide spectrum between the illiterate, (those who cannot read); and those who are truly literate in theoretical and *practical* senses. Please note that literacy as defined here is not measured just by the amount and type of formal schooling a person is exposed to. To the contrary, it is not difficult to develop a thesis that in many fields of endeavor increased exposure to the offerings of our present day, public educational systems, decreases the functional ability of people to contribute constructively to our society.

Exposure to the media offerings of our time would seem to indicate that the decay of competency, morality and ethical behavior is widespread in our society. It's grip on the members and leadership of the counter-culture is obvious. But what is the extent of its penetration into the ranks of the silent majority?

Some major tools of the political domain and of other enterprises in scoping, diagnosing and solving diverse problems involving people and social issues can be of help to us in looking for answers to that question.

Public opinion polls and "studies and reports" done by reliable persons and organizations are examples of these tools. But! in our time, they must be used with great skepticism and care. The authenticity, reliability, and value of many such sources have been corrupted by ineptitude or by cunning misdirection in their development. Legions of special interest groups have discovered the unquestioned authority that can be gleaned from commissioning and using studies, polls, etc. that will falsely demonstrate the validity of points that benefit their causes. There is an old saying that, "Liars can't figure but figures can lie". It is common place, especially in the public sector to award "study contracts" to so called "experts", with a tacit understanding, between the parties, when the contract is initiated, as to the results and recommendations that will flow from the effort.

For example, elected officials and their bureaucrats find it beneficial to award such contracts when they want to increase their own pay, perks or other remuneration. The results of such a study are never in doubt. I have never known of one that failed to recommend the increase in stipend that the benefactors wanted. The logic of such a situation is quite simple. Such positive findings are "good business" for the contractor. Contract results and recommendation that did not support the wishes ("needs?") of the client, would surely limit the opportunities for that contractor to obtain future jobs for that client. Clients would not be willing to take a chance on such a contractor, especially when there are other "dependable" bidders for their work. The use of "outside contractors" is especially attractive to elected officials because it implies an additional aura of objectivity in the process. Public acceptance of increased cost proposals is enhanced; public condemnation of "self serving" actions, such as voting pay raises for yourself, is usually cushioned.

If you live in a medium sized or larger city, you will surely encounter an even "cuter", more sinister and sophisticated ploy by public officials. Many local city and county, fathers and mothers have adopted the presently popular "big time", nation-wide approach to selecting new people for top bureaucratic jobs. The underlying theory, seems to be that we who live in an area are not smart enough to do the job for ourselves! In yet another scheme, ad hoc or standing committees of citizens are selected; by the manager, of course; to recommend courses of action in matters of pay, capital improvements, zoning matters, etc. If you examine closely how this is done in your area, you will quickly learn that knowledge or experience in the particular field are not obvious selection criteria when naming the members of the many groups. You will find that appointments are, once again, made that will unflinchingly support management proposals. The extent to which they are successful at achieving this goal is apparent from the fact that decisions of the groups are almost always unanimous.

It is not unusual for state governments to use this scheme. A few years ago, the citizens of the state of Washington voted for, the establishment and use of such an appointed committee to set salaries for top state officials. It sounds like such a good idea! And it might be; if the membership consisted of knowledgeable, responsible people. But, in appointing the members, the governor is not exactly a disinterested participant. The results, in Washington, have been disastrous. The actions of the committee have been so unreasonable as to embarrass even the beneficiaries of their actions. It is important to recognize the sophistication of these schemes. They effectively take the voter out of the critical path. Most voters will not understand the interaction through the organization well enough to be able to identify the elected official or officials whose replacement could correct the problem.

If you are encountering these ruses in the operation of your government enterprises, chances are good that a review of the roster of people who have served you in these positions over the years, will show that they are all products of the factories in our system of higher education that award Master Degrees in either Business Administration or in Public Administration. These cute and clever ploys seem, almost always, to be a part of that curricula. They represent proven tactics for limiting or eliminating citizen contribution and control of their own public business.

A brief examination of one other form of misinformation that is regularly foisted off on the public as being factual, may be helpful. Our society is being slowly but surely transformed in the images of numerous, very intense and dedicated, small groups of activists. Their causes, which are usually self serving, are routinely "sold" to the public in the name of some great humanitarian conviction; for example equal opportunity, human rights, helping the homeless, and the most effective of all—today! "they are doing it for the children!" Such honorable motivation never seems to be questioned.

Such activity is a vital part of the continuing, organized attack upon our society. Special-interest, special-privileged groups have been created and coddled by the actions of our "public servants" over the last several decades. Those seeking special privileges and benefits in the "equal" opportunity and "civil rights" arenas are especially clever in its use.

An example:

The media reported on the results of a study commissioned by a group of university women, who it seems have little patience with the fact that we don't all think alike. Especially, that all girls and women in this country still have not shed some of the god-given characteristics, views, emotions and maternal instincts that allow men to be men; women to be women, and for each of us to be individuals with our own likes and dislikes, talents, interests and dreams. They seem driven to transform all females in our country to be monotonous, narrow-minded, sexless, greed-driven clones of themselves. They seem driven to convert our society with its history of rich diversity of thought, action and future dreams into some dull, limited, unisex, predictable, illiterate, aberration of their own design.

The study was awarded to a contractor that specialized in research on women's problems, one that was, of course, associated with an institution of higher learning. It is unclear, but it doesn't take a great deal of imagination to guess that the lady who managed the contract effort, may very well have been a member of the contracting organization, and thoroughly familiar with its expectations from the study.

These arrangements, when viewed critically, do little to assure us of objectivity. The findings were predictable; they were totally compatible with the biases of the contracting organization; and they will serve them well in advancing their assault on the rest of us. We aren't told the source of the considerable funding for the study. It is not unreasonable to assume that taxpayer money was involved. You and I probably paid for it.

The study claims that boys receive more attention and are given more praise and helpful criticism than are girls. Grasping at straws? Of course! Anything goes! Proof is not offered to support the finding. My experience is that if such were the case, the boys would be complaining about being picked on. The burden of proof that any significant benefit flows from such "favoritism"? is ignored. That there is some sort of nationwide conspiracy in this regard seems very unlikely. If such conditions do exist in isolated situations, it does not follow that the quality of education received by either the boys or the girls suffers because of it. There is a principle, ever present in these situations; it is not a requirement for data from the discovery process to support the conclusions. In fact, conclusions are often stated, "ad lib", with no requirement that there be any logical, conclusive evidence to support them.

The study recognizes that groups such as their own have been successful in increasing girls' exposure to mathematics, at least through the twelfth grade. But it complains that the girls still avoid careers in mathematics and science. Of the students who study calculus and physics in high school, a larger percentage of the boys went on to study engineering and science in college. Isn't it interesting, that groups such as this feel free (compelled) to intervene in the lives of young people and deny them the right to make crucial career decisions that they, in their own time made freely. Even the most foolish among us realize the importance of matching personal careers to our personal interests. Enjoying our work contributes so much to the enjoyment of life. Although we have not demanded much from those who serve us as university and college faculty, it would seem that even they would realize that fact and respect it in dealing with the students. That they feel free to use the public educational system and funding to make our young people, your children and mine, "pawns" in achieving their foolish, ill conceived, tawdry goals is offensive and should be stopped.

The study claims that girls are restricted from courses offered to boys. As proof of the statement, we are told that arrangements for girls who become pregnant often (but not always) result in those girls not having access to some courses. One simple solution to such a problem, if it exists, is to not provide *any* special arrangements for children (girls) who become pregnant or who have babies. In accepting the responsibility of educating our children, the public has not overtly accepted the responsibility of rearing the childrens' illegitimate families.

Like so much of the material that comes out of today's institutions of higher learning and the staff in them, this study effort is presented in a pseudo, high-intellect orientation and setting that greatly belies its value to society. It contributes nothing of tangible value toward resolution of any real problem we face. The intent is, of course, to intimidate we lesser mortals. If that is allowed to happen and the material is not recognized outside of the women's movement as the "fluff" that it is, further adverse impacts will follow. Efforts such as this and their follow-up, contribute in a "grass roots" way to the evolution and continuation of our "Era of Emotional Idiocy".

The results of the study will surely be presented, by members of the movement, cloaked in an aura of being a serious, objective work. We can only hope that it will not be accepted by the politicians, in their usual blind rush to fix non-problems with more laws, more money and more and more intervention into our private lives and into the process; intervention already so massive that it has choked up the system and prevents it from working.

There is no doubt that our public education system is dysfunctional. And it needs to be fixed. But this effort like all others that are generated by people within the system, or by politicians, deals with minutia; with self-serving, narrow-minded proposals that will only exacerbate the deteriorating situation!

The actors in this activity are a part of the counter-culture environment that exists in our system of higher education that we discussed earlier. Question: Is this what we expect of our *public* schools and the *public servants* in them? Are you willing to continue to silently and obediently pay the massive, continually increasing costs of such activities? Or should we demand that this sort of insurrection isolate itself from the intimate contact that occurs between student and faculty in our public education setting?

There are some interesting ironies about this situation:

1.  One media article on the subject told us that the results of this study was presented to 1800 delegates at a recent four-day convention of the group in a nearby city. Which raises questions. Is such attendance considered to be "business" activity for the participants? Are they reimbursed for their travel, lodging and food? Are they considered to be in a work status while they are at the convention; and therefore, they draw salary while there? How, and by whom, are such activities judged to be necessary business expenses? Are such expenses partially or totally funded by your tax money and mine? If we are paying for it, what are we getting for our money? Are the goals of the organization compatible with those of our higher education system? Who is accountable for auditing and controlling this sort of possible breach of expectation and faith?

2.  Since this convention was of a national organization, we can expect that the 1800 delegates were from all parts of the United States and beyond. The costs of transportation were certainly significant. As were the costs of room and board!

    Most members of the middle class, those who pay the bill for so much of this kind of foolishness in the public arena, do not feel that they can afford the expense of staying at luxurious four and five star hotels and motels when they are paying their own travel costs. Is there any logical reason why those working and traveling on our business and at our expense should not be subject to cost controls that are compatible with our ability to pay?

    Lets recognize that the use of top quality facilities, as was the case for this convention, is not unusual. As a matter of fact, the costs of travel, room and board for public business are mushrooming to staggering levels.

3.  The expense of this kind of event is obvious. And, of course, this is only one of thousands of such activities of questionable value

that take place each year; at the public's expense. Why is it that the national media reports the propaganda of such groups so obediently and faithfully; never questioning the usefulness of the effort, its impact upon society, or the costs and benefits that accrue from it?

This is a national media that for weeks on end will do everything it can to focus the national attention and agenda upon the travels of individuals such as John Sununu, the White House, Chief of Staff or other members of a Republican Cabinet. Such media crusades are not driven by political interests in Washington, D.C. Members of the entrenched power structure there are not at all interested in risking disclosures in this area of activity, lest it draw attention to their own activities.

Neither is the media responding, to a loud, grassroots demand to know more about such activities.

We are all interested in keeping costs down; and travel by these people is costly. On the other hand, we understand that major government policy makers, such as they, are lightning rods that attract the attention of malcontents, the depraved, or even terrorists. And, they may become targets of such individuals or groups. It has been our practice to provide special consideration and protection to them while they are serving us in these positions. To expect them to use public transportation, especially "air" would not only increase their exposure to harm, it would also endanger those members of the public who might be traveling with them. There would seem to be little, if any, logic to support a position that such special consideration is no longer needed. The threat to them, if it is changing at all, is increasing.

So how can we explain the media actions? One perspective is that they treat the liberals and the counter-culture with kid gloves; without questions because the objectives of those groups are in harmony with those of the media.

On the other hand, John Sununu, and others of his ilk, are considered to be conservatives. They march to a different drummer. In their positions of power and authority in the Administration, they represent a threat to achievement of liberal programs and objectives.

Before leaving this subject, it seems prudent to recognize that the above comments will surely be subject to criticism by many, as being chauvinistic and biased. And from the perspective of a realist, it is understood that nothing can be said to change that position in the minds of the "hard core" reformist. Each reader will react to the information in unique ways and will need to deal with it differently.

Let me deal with the issue in this way: As an early observer of the "women's" movement, I looked forward with anticipation to what I thought would surely be a thoughtful, constructive, positive contribution by the increased involvement of our female population in all of our activities. I have always been impressed by the contribution of the two women who have been most prominent in my life; my mother and my wife of almost 50 years. They have shared many noble traits. It was my thought that society could gain a great deal from an infusion of such ideas, ideals, hopes, dreams and personal dedication to family and humanity.

I can best characterize my reaction to what has happened, is happening, and to the kinds of activities discussed above as being one of deep disappointment. The movement has been taken over by relatively small factions, that are often loud-mouthed, reckless, and of questionable real intelligence. If they have realistic goals that presume to be good for all the women of our nation and for the nation itself; that is not obvious. Most of you have probably seen and smiled at the bumper sticker that says, "The best man for the job is a woman". The implication seems to be that we can solve all of our problems by simply turning everything over to women. If only it was that simple! I find myself focusing attention on some of those activities in our society that have been dominated by women in the past decade or two; our public schools, Savings and Loan Institutions, Banks, the abortion issue, etc. Is more of that the promise they project for all of us and the nation? If so, that is not a very hopeful, compelling, future expectation to strive for. The "real" women of the nation are sold short by such a prospect! They, and we, as individuals and as a nation, can do better! Much better! It is imperative that we do so.

What contributions might we realistically expect from an intellectually honest, intelligent, patriotic, effective, *caring* women's movement? Lets consider some examples:

> David Frost's recent interview of Margaret Thatcher of Great Britain provided insight into what is probably a premier example. Mrs. Thatcher will surely go down in history as one of the great persons of this century and possibly of all time.

She took over as Prime Minister of Great Britain at a time of great anxiety, concern, and need in that nation. She took over, never trying to find advantage because she was a woman. She did not make it a point to surround herself with other women. She had the presence of mind, intelligence and the character to realize that the problems she faced required the best qualified persons available to her; and she surrounded herself with those people. She never asked for favors and she didn't give any. She plunged into seemingly insurmountable, serious problems and gained a meaningful measure of progress in their resolution. She demonstrated an ability to deal *intellectually* with problems of great *emotional* consequence.

The second example that comes to mind is vastly different from the first. At first glance, the people involved would seem to have nothing in common. Sammantha Smith was a 12 year old New England school girl. She was deeply concerned about the evolving international relationship between the United States and the Soviet Union. Each of these super powers had inventories of atomic bombs capable of annihilating humanity from the face of the earth several times over. She worried that those in charge might lose control of the situation. At first glance, her approach to the problem would seem to reflect a great deal of innocence. On second glance, we can see in her approach some vision and a lot of faith. She wrote to the leaders of the Soviet Union expressed her concern, and implored them not to expose us all to the horrors of atomic war. Unexpectedly, she received a response, part of which was an invitation to visit the Soviet Union. She accepted, she spent an extended period there, and proved to be an outstanding ambassador of the American people and an effective spokes person for our nation.

Her approach to this situation was consistent with our heritage. It was honest, intelligent and caring. It was not fostered by greed. It was not dedicated to improving the welfare and dominance of just women. It was, instead, focused on improving the welfare of all of humanity. It expressed faith in mankind and in our societal systems. It respected the rights of others to nurture and promote ideas, concepts, and beliefs that were vastly different from her own.

The striking nature of these two brief examples, can be emphasized by comparing them to the following experience:

> Not long ago I had the occasion to go into the library of an elementary school not far from where I live. There, in a glass encased showcase that extended from floor to ceiling and that was about six feet wide, was an attractive display designed to champion the case *for* **"WOMEN'S RIGHTS"**. It included pictures and quotations that are regularly used to advocate and hawk that warped concept. About 350 children attend that school; and for lack of better information, we can assume that half of them are girls and half are boys. Total staff at the school, at the time was about 25 people. Of that total, only 3 men were employed there, as teachers. All others including the principle and the janitorial staff were women. This situation raised several questions in my mind:
>
> 1.  Whose idea was this? It surely was approved by the principle! Why?
> 2.  Who was the message directed toward? (It had to be the children.)
> 3.  We can assume that the message(s) of the display somehow contributed to accomplishment of the mission (goals) that the school staff has set for itself. What is that mission? What are their goals?
> 4.  What impact did the principle and the staff hope for in the fertile, impressionable minds of the young boys in the school? The young girls?
> 5.  Are those "hoped for" impacts consistent with the expectations of the parents of the children? Of the conventional establishment and majority of the citizens of the city? the state? the country?
> 6.  It is obvious that the display had to be viewed by many parents of children going to school there. Do they all agree that exposure to such information is a positive, constructive experience for their children? Is it their desire that their children be molded into clones of any counter-culture persons and groups they encounter; that they be taught what to think? Or, would they prefer that their minds be

developed in ways that will stimulate and prepare them to objectively and intelligently view the "world around them", and to then make their own decisions, based on the facts before them?

7. Why do parents sit idly by and allow such things to happen? Are they "intimidated" by the system? Are they afraid to fight the system? If that is the case, that is too bad, because they are probably the only ones that can correct the situation!

The convention and its participants discussed above represents a relatively small sample, of the total activity in our nation by minorities and by women that is self-serving for their own cause and destructive toward society and the nation as a whole. Comprehensive coverage of that subject could be the theme of another book by itself. What is important, at this point, is to contemplate what might happen in our society, if just a fraction of the hundreds of thousands of persons who are presently bent upon improving their own condition at the expense of the country and others, would be reborn into citizens with perspectives and dedication beyond themselves; so that they cherished and aspired to some of the ideals of Mrs. Thatcher, Sammantha, and others like them. To contribute in a positive rather than negative way to our national agenda.

So! we recognize the limitations of public opinion polls and "studies". That does not mean that all such information available to us is unusable. Some of it can be used, if the sources are carefully screened and if the user recognizes the limitations of the product and its source. In fact, it is often necessary that we use such material that is timely and applicable to large, sophisticated problems facing us. Such is the case with a study recently made and reported in a book by James Patterson and Peter Kim entitled, "The Day America Told the Truth—What People Really Believe About Everything That Really Matters."[5] The poll is said to have a margin of error of two to four percent.

Information in the book relates that the truth is that "we Americans" lie, cheat and slap our consciences silly, if we have one. The survey shows that we mold our moral rules to fit our idle whims. Such a characterization of our society is not totally unexpected! However, the extent of ethical and moral decay reported surely surprised most people who read it.

---

5　　Prentice Hall Press, 15 Columbia Circle; N.Y., N.Y.; © 1991

In its further revelations the book concludes that, we make up our own rules and laws. We choose which laws of God we believe. There is absolutely no moral consensus in this country—as there was in the 1950s and 1960s." Eighty-six percent of those polled admitted to *regularly* lying to their parents, about 75 percent to friends and siblings and a slightly lesser percentage to their lover, boss or child. These statistics on lying are beyond my comprehension. If true, they portend a level of folly in our people that exceeds any I have imagined. It is understandable, I suppose, that people would lie if cornered in some difficult, extemporaneous, embarrassing situation. What is unbelievable is that so many might make lying a way of life.

Especially so, when viewed from the perspective of Harry's Theorem (truth) No. 1:

IF YOU TELL THE TRUTH; YOU DON'T HAVE TO REMEMBER WHAT YOU SAY!

Compliance with that concept simplifies life, reduces stress and *it makes you feel good.*

Careful examination will demonstrate that the alternative is totally non-competitive. There is the old saying that, "one lie leads to one or many more." One lie forces a person to remember in detail what he/she said. Subsequent statements and activities must be carefully crafted to adapt to and further the course projected by the falsehood. This presents impossibly difficult situations; the stress can be intolerable and eventually mistakes are made that force the truth to come out after all. Why would intelligent, thinking persons knowingly subject themselves to such needless torture?

Who are our heros? Who do we look up to? In a compilation of the ten most admirable occupations listed in the study, Catholic priest is listed number seven below firemen, paramedics, farmers, pharmacists, grade school teachers and mail carriers; in that order. Pastors and leaders of other denominations are not on the list.

In a list of the ten sleaziest ways to make a living, local politician and congressmen are numbers 6 and 7; preceded in the list by drug dealer, organized-crime boss, TV evangelist, prostitute, and street peddler; in that order, and just below car salesman which is number 8.

It will not surprise most of us to learn that Americans have lost faith in the institution of marriage. Nearly 50 percent of those polled said there is no reason ever to get married. This has to be a result of and at the same time a major contributing factor to the continuing moral and ethical decay of our society. The pity is that the present direction of our governments will only make this situation worse.

According to the study, religion plays almost no role in shaping most lives. A surprising finding, at a time when the membership in, contributions to and participation in the activities of the churches by so many of our citizens would seem to indicate differently. Our understanding of this seeming dichotomy may be facilitated if we make the assumption that the term "religion" was interpreted by people responding to the poll to be synonymous with "the church today".

We can then focus on that narrow issue by posing one very simple question. "What does this church; any church; but, especially established, mainline churches, stand for today?" To many of us, the thoughtful, correct answer is, "Not Much!" Although there are some exceptions, primarily in the independent, breakaway factions, the church universal does not speak out in intelligent and forceful ways on important ethical and moral issues as they once did to their membership and to society as a whole!

In the mainline, protestant denominations with which I am most familiar; consideration (worship) of maintaining membership, more money and worldly goods are now given priority over those tenets of the written word and the pursuit of the good, faithful, productive life that once provided a strong attraction to many of us to be a part of that church.

For example, the casual surrender by church officialdom; to groups of neo-theorists, spurred on by ambitious, aggressive, arrogant members of the women's movement; to the baseless revision of church doctrine and literature will properly generate questions in the minds of the masses, as to how valid and relevant the basic foundations of the church we once treasured really were? Are?

The results of this study as reported in the book, does not lead to great optimism that we will be able to revitalize the interest of the people in matters of public policy, citizenship and active participation in the political process. The ranking of politicians in the study demonstrates some of the disdain that is felt for them and the quality of work they are doing for us. The study demonstrated that idealism is not high on the lists of American's dreams. A majority of the respondents to the poll identified their personal weight as the thing they would most like to change. Given the opportunity to alter one thing about their lives, nearly two-thirds would opt to be wealthier.

The study findings are frightening to any thoughtful, caring citizen who truly understands and appreciates the benefits we enjoy as citizens of this country; and the jeopardy that will surely result to all of that, with continuation of this decay and indifference to the unquestioned need for effective administration and management of the business of this country.

It is not my intent to preach any sermons in this book. But, it does seem important for us to recognize that the decay of our ethical and moral values is not because we lack proven, cornerstone documentation of fundamental ideals in this respect.

The fact that literal translation of important historical documents such as the Bible, the Constitution, etc. comes under question in much of our society today, is yet another contribution of that elite, pseudo-intellectual contingent in our society.

Results of the study would intimate that our knowledge of, reliance on, and trust in biblical guidance has diminished. That is obviously true. However, one does not have to be a student of the bible to be aware of some of the supreme counsel provided there. For example,

## THE TEN COMMANDMENTS
From the BOOK OF EXODUS; Chapter 20; Verses 1 through 17

1. You shall have no gods before me. (Contemporary question: Is there such a thing as "right" or "wrong?")
2. You shall not make any sculptured image, or any likeness of anything that is in heaven above, or on the earth beneath or that is in the water under the earth.
3. You shall not use the name of the Lord your God in vain; for the Lord will not hold him guiltless that takes his name in vain.
4. Remember the sabbath day, to keep it holy. Six days you shall labor and do all your work, but the seventh day is the sabbath of the Lord your God. In it you shall do no work, you, nor any member of your family and household, nor any person living with you. For in six days the Lord made the heaven and earth, the sea and all that is in them, and rested the seventh day. Therefore, the Lord blessed the seventh day and made it holy.
5. Honor your father and your mother: so that your days may be many in the land that the Lord your God gives you.
6. You shall not kill.
7. You shall not commit adultery.

8. You shall not steal.
9. You shall not wrongly accuse your neighbor.
10. You shall not covet (envy) your neighbor nor desire to have his house, his wife, his servants, his animals, nor anything that is his.

Or consider:

### THE GOLDEN RULE
From the BOOK OF MATTHEW; Chapter 7, verse 12

"So whatever you wish that men would do to you, do so to them"

We often paraphrase this as follows:

"Do unto others as you would have them do unto you".

Please take the time to reread the above items; in a careful, thoughtful way. The Bible continues to be the best selling book of all time. It does not necessarily follow that it is the most read book. Our lack of familiarity with its contents probably results from the same awe and intimidation that inhibits our relationship to and understanding of our Constitution.

It is unfortunate that this may be the case. There is a more positive, accurate way to view such documents and the impact they can have on our quality of life. Living a life in compliance with the commandments will not lead to a dour, idle, unexciting and uninteresting existence. To the contrary, compliance will steer a person away from the multitude of temptations, indiscretions and mistakes in life that lead to unnecessary, heavy, sometimes unbearable burdens of worry, guilt and sorrow.

If the biblical, religious approach to achieving a good life does not appeal to you, let me suggest another approach that may be more your style! Its application in our society is especially timely and practical. One of the all-consuming concerns of our times is the seemingly impossible task of challenging our children during their formative years; keeping them interested in life and the world around them; rearing and educating them to provide the quality of citizen that is needed if we are to sustain our complex, sophisticated and beneficial society and way of life.

In my many years of adult service to the Boy Scout movement, I have worked intimately with hundreds of boys, age 8 through 18. During the latter 1960's, the 1970's, and the 1980's; the boys, other adult leaders and

I walked through "mine fields" together on a day to day, week to week, and year to year basis. Each of those participants have been continually exposed to the same concerns, problems, and temptations that led so many of their peers to quit school, to run away, to live on the street, into criminal activities, into alcohol and drugs, and in general to "blow" their opportunity for a full, exciting, and productive life. Against such a background, the record of achievement of "my boys" is impressive. Of course, it would be nice if I could take personal credit for this success. But, I can not. The results are largely attributable to our belief in and our effective execution of the program of the Boy Scouts of America. The program relies heavily upon what we refer to as "Scout Spirit". Scout Spirit is a way of life; life lived in accordance with a simple, unassuming creed embodied in the Scout Law, the Scout Oath, the Scout Motto, and the Scout Slogan. Application of these tenets to define "an American Spirit", is entirely feasible. The lives of citizens who adopt and live by such a creed would be vastly more satisfactory, pleasant, and productive. They and the nation would benefit greatly.

The Scout Law consists of twelve points:

*THE SCOUT LAW*

A Scout is:

TRUSTWORTHY.     A Scout tells the truth. He keeps his promises. Honesty is part of his code of conduct. People can depend upon him.

LOYAL.     A Scout is true to his family, Scout leaders, friends, school and nation.

HELPFUL.     A Scout is concerned about other people. He does things willingly for others without pay or reward.

FRIENDLY.     A Scout is a friend to all. He is a brother to other Scouts. He seeks to understand others. He respects those with ideas and customs other than his own.

COURTEOUS.

A Scout is polite to everyone regardless of age or position. He knows good manners make it easier for people to get along together.

KIND.

A Scout understands there is strength in being gentle. He treats others as he wants to be treated. He does not hurt or kill harmless things without reason.

OBEDIENT.

A Scout follows the rules of his family, school, and troop. He obeys the laws of his community and country. If he thinks these rules are unfair, he tries to have changed in an orderly manner rather than disobey them.

CHEERFUL.

A Scout looks for the bright side of things. He cheerfully does tasks that come his way. He tries to make others happy.

THRIFTY.

A Scout works to pay his way and to help others. He saves for unseen needs. He protects and conserves natural resources. He carefully uses time and property.

BRAVE.

A Scout can face danger even if he is afraid. He has the courage to stand for what he thinks is right even if others laugh at or threaten him.

CLEAN.

A Scout keeps his body and mind fit and clean. He goes around with those who believe in living by these same ideals. He helps keep his home and community clean.

REVERENT.

A Scout is reverent toward God. He is faithful in his religious duties. He respects the beliefs of others.

It is interesting that the Scout Oath is often compared with, "THE OATH OF THE YOUNG MAN OF ATHENS". The Athenian Oath was taken by each young man of Athens when he became 17 years of age. That oath has much "food for thought" as it might apply to our times:

### THE OATH OF THE YOUNG MAN OF ATHENS

"We will never bring disgrace on this our city, by an act of dishonesty or cowardice.

We will fight for the ideals and Sacred Things of the city both alone and with many.

We will revere and obey the City's laws, and will do our best to incite a like reverence and respect in those above us who are prone to annul them or set them at naught.

We will strive increasingly to quicken the public's sense of civic duty.

Thus in all these ways we will transmit this city, not only less, but greater, and more beautiful than it was transmitted to us."

### THE SCOUT OATH OR PROMISE

On my honor I will do my best
To do my duty to God and my country
and to obey the Scout Law;
To help other people at all times;
To keep myself physically strong
mentally awake and morally straight.

### THE SCOUT MOTTO

BE PREPARED—(Translated to mean * * * for anything that you may encounter; do not let yourself be surprised or overcome by what ever might happen.)

### THE SCOUT SLOGAN

DO A GOOD TURN DAILY—(Translated to mean * * * looking for chances to help throughout each day, then helping quietly, without boasting and without pay)

It is unfortunate, but true, that in some circles of society today, participation in this excellent program is not recognized for the great learning experiences and opportunities it provides to young men—in the making. This is especially true within the ranks of those boys in the age group that it serves. True to the nature of the American mind in so many other important areas of activity, boys learn to strut around exhibiting "macho" or "jock" attitudes that effectively isolate them from the realities of the world around them; the world that they must understand and meet head-on, if they are to achieve the health, happiness and prosperity that we wish for them.

Most parents are in a better position to understand the importance of the decisions that are made in a boys life at this young age. It has been demonstrated, over and over again, that parents understanding of the advantages of the program, their helping to sell it to the boys, and their continuing recognition of the boy's achievements and successes provide great motivation for them to be involved in it. The crowning benefits and value of the program to a family and all of its individual members will come with Mom and Dad's active support and assistance in providing leadership for the group! There is no better way for adults to become aware of; sensitive and responsive to their obligations for helping to develop the leadership and effective citizenship in the future leaders of our country.

And what of the boys?

The boys that enter the program come from all parts of our society; all races, all nationalities, all classes and all levels of economic standing. Some are short and some are tall; some are husky and others frail, some are rich and some are poor; some are introverts and others are extroverts; some are quiet and inactive and others are hyperactive and loud; some are agile and well coordinated, others are clumsy and have great difficulty doing many things; some come from stable, two-parent homes, some come from single-parent situations and unfortunately some come from even more unstable and heart rendering situations than even that.

And the magic of the program is that over many decades, it has demonstrated an ability to serve the needs of all of those categories of boys and to equalize to a very great extent their opportunities for success and happiness.

Boys, even those who do not stay with the program to achieve its highest rank—that of Eagle; will receive lasting benefits from their participation while they are members.

For over twenty-five years, I have served as the Chairman of Eagle Boards of Review, representing the National and local BSA organizations in visiting with and judging the qualifications of boys who have finished the long, tough journey to the top; boys who are candidates for the Eagle rank. In the several hundred boys that I have reviewed in this role, I have never encountered any two boys that were even remotely alike. And yet! each of them have been pleasant, outstanding individuals in their own way.

They are athletes, scholars, musicians, class presidents and other officers. They are usually involved in numerous activities in their schools, churches and communities. They often have paper routes or other employment endeavors with which to help finance their own activities, including future schooling, beyond grade 12. They have thought carefully about and made plans for their futures; whether it be attendance at trade schools to learn a skill or at college to prepare for careers in the professions or in the world of white collar employment.

They become doctors, lawyers, merchants and chiefs. They all share one trait, important to me and, I hope to them. I am honored to be their friend and to have played a part in their development. Because of them, I and many others who have shared in this task, will be able, someday, to go peacefully to our "everlasting reward", knowing that our lives have contributed something of lasting value to the future of our country.

All of this simply demonstrates, once again, that living in accordance with these tenets of a good life, biblical or non-biblical, is not inhibiting, confining, bothersome, irritating, or embarrassing. Why do people gamble their futures and those of their children and all of the rest of us on other approaches that have proven to be less effective or actually counter-productive to our best interests?

No! our problem is not that we do not have proper, positive principles by which to live our lives. What is more likely, is that individually, we have not fully recognized the extent of the changes in the "world in which we live". In simpler times a person could get by without well defined guidelines, strictures, and goals, similar to those outlined above. Today, in our daily lives, we encounter large numbers of false prophets with very convincing arguments that support their special interests and self-aggrandizing positions. Large portions of our present "intellectual"? community have "flaked off" into a world of make believe and emotional idiocy; leaving behind the world of practical realism.

It is not "implausible" to suspect that the amount of shallow (not based on fact), biased, misinformation presented to us in this country, today exceeds the amount of accurate, supportable, factual material available to us. It is not unreasonable to advise everyone, not to accept anything at face value. Be prepared to question all that you see and hear, and measure it against your own senses of what is right; ethically and morally. Senses that are continually being tested; and, if we are not careful, eroded to the norm of the masses. Gradually, over time, we can feel ourselves slipping into modes of thoughts and actions that make us uneasy; that do not meet the criteria that we have established for our own conduct. We must keep our guard up. In such situations it is helpful to have a fall-back philosophy, a statement of principles, against which to measure our response to what society offers us; or tries to force onto us! Response to this need, has always been a difficult individual problem. As is demonstrated, so clearly by the statistics reported in the study of "What America Really Believes"; today's search for respectable, honest, productive lives is made more difficult by the fact that the number of good examples and sources of support for such an effort are becoming more rare.

# CHAPTER 9

A democracy supposedly derives its strength
and character from the diversity of its
many voices, but the politicians in the
Capitol speak with only one voice, which
is the voice of the oligarchy that buys
airline tickets and television images.
Among the company of legislators in
Washington or Albany, N. Y. or Sacramento
Cal., I look in vain for a representation
of my own interests or opinions, and I
never hear the voice of scientist, the
teacher, the plumber, the police officer,
the farmer, the merchant. I hear instead
the voice of only one kind of functionary:
a full time politician, often a lawyer, who
spends most of his time raising campaign
funds and redistributing the national income
into venues convenient to his friends

Lewis H. Lapham[6]

It does not seem necessary to continue to submit proof that we have serious problems. Even the politicians and bureaucrats, whose actions and inaction over the years have caused the labyrinth of ineffective and inoperative rules, regulations, and processes that drive our system, publicly acknowledge that we face many serious problems. Their intent, incompetence and/or ineptitude is clearly displayed when we look for response to that acknowledgement. It never seems to occur to them that: (1) these problems might be caused by

---

[6]    Harper's Magazine; via the July 1991 Reader's Digest Magazine.

actions they have taken in the past; (2) that a major first step in resolution would be to look carefully at what has resulted and what is occurring, good and not so good, as a result of those past actions; and (3) then to repeal or amend those pieces of legislation that are not contributing positive results, are not accomplishing all that was expected of them, or all that they might accomplish if they were properly focused. Instead, they ignore the option of recognizing and correcting past mistakes and continue to pass new legislation that simply makes the situation worse!

I am one of those millions of Americans who have been taught that we should respect those that serve us in elected and appointed positions of high responsibility. That we should address them as "honorable" senator or representative, so and so in our relationship with them. I will honor that practice in other correspondence and contacts with them. But, it is obvious, as we view the failed efforts of so many others who have respected this protocol and tried to spawn corrective action in this arena that another approach is probably necessary. David Stockman's 1990 book, "The Triumph of Politics", is a classic example. It seems not to have been able to penetrate the wall of arrogance and disdain that surrounds the institutions and their inhabitants. I am unable to identify any specific corrective actions or improvements made by the Washington establishment that resemble credible reactions to any of the pathetic, somber, serious revelations in his book.

And so we find ourselves between the proverbial rock and a hard spot! Do we stay with the protocol, mind our manners, so to speak! Or do we regretfully proceed, calling a "spade" a "spade"; doing what it seems must be done if our honest attempt to have a positive impact on the situation. Our success will depend upon our ability to capture the attention of and arouse the public to action; a staggering challenge! Our electronic and written media provides a continuing stream of information, in bits and pieces, that identifies the scope and gravity of the situation; with little consequence. Demands for responsible government, probably will not penetrate the cocoons that have formed around our centers of government power and the elected officials and bureaucrats that languish there, until the "silent majority", is aroused to the point that it demands reform loudly and clearly. There is little to indicate that we can succeed where so many others have failed. The argument is strong for "shucking off" the constraints of formality and deal with these issues and these people on a person to person basis; one of equality; peer to peer.

Having accordingly set the stage, we can continue the above discussion in an effective manner. There can be no doubt in anyone's mind that excessive

government spending is a problem of great moment. We all know that.
Those in Washington, D.C. are intimately aware of it; they have been for
years. So what do they do? Cut back in spending for existing programs and
refrain from passing new spending measures. Of course not! They continue,
unabated, to escalate spending on existing programs. And, they continue to
pass new bills that call for massive amounts of new spending.

They regularly proceed to enact these spending bills; without first,
obtaining reliable estimates of the costs involved; and without any
consideration of how the increased expenditures will be paid for.

The new Child Care legislation, enacted subsequent to the end of the
Desert Storm fracas is a typical example. Health Care for everyone is on
the horizon. These programs share the characteristic that they will be costly
beyond our comprehension. The silence in the hallowed halls of Washington,
is deafening when we "press" to hear "the rest of the story". How do those
"honorable" agents, put there and paid handsomely to manage our public
business; to protect and advance your best interests, and mine; plan to pay
these additional costs? Or do they simply plan to ignore that triviality, and
simply add these costs to the billions of others that make up the rapidly
growing, incomprehensibly massive national debt? The biggest charge
account of them all; one that is already grossly out of control. The national
deficit for the fiscal year (F.Y.) ending September 30, 1991 was estimated at
$282,000,000,000; and for the fiscal year ending on September 30, 1992
another $348 billion. All of this, and much more to come! to be added to
the national debt!

Remember that this was occurring at a time when our government was
operating under the provisions of a new, special law that they had enacted
and that the President had signed into law. Action that was, in itself, an
overt admission that they understood the gravity of their uncontrolled
spending "habit"; the size and rapid growth of the National debt; and that, as
individuals and as a group, they lacked the discipline, the political conviction
and the sense of duty to the country to take the necessary corrective action!
Coercion by a "phony" sword of Damocles hanging over their heads was
thought to be necessary!

Compliance with this law would compel them to decrease the size
of successive annual budget deficits each year and to achieve a balanced
Federal budget within a few years after its passage. In the face of these
legal requirements, the F.Y. 1992 budget deficit was approved to be
$66,300,000,000 greater than that of the 1991 F.Y.; an increase of almost
25 percent! This is an appalling, intolerable situation. Even idiots realize that

you cannot solve problems of excessive spending and huge budget deficits that threaten to bankrupt the country *by continuing to increase spending!* We have to believe that our elected officials and their bureaucrats know that also. If that is true, it poses serious questions to us. If they are competent to do the job they are elected to do? if they understand the gravity of the problem? and if they know the basic actions required to solve it? why do they disregard all of this and proceed with business-as-usual? or worse yet, with actions that are counter-productive, actions that only exacerbate the problem?

How did your Senators and Representatives vote on these issues? And why did they vote the way they did. You have the right to know! In fact, you have a duty to find out, and to react to that knowledge and any conflicts it may present to your beliefs on the matter, on future trips to the polls. If your elected officials are among that class of Socialist Democrats or the smattering of Socialist Republicans who vote for every spending bill; who seem to have a permanent grip on their hallowed seats of power in Washington, and *you* continue to vote them into office; then we can not unilaterally fault them. In that case, it is incumbent upon *you* to share the blame; and it would be helpful if you could explain to some of us; *your* thoughts as to how our government can be made to work if everyone follows your lead!

It is important that we understand clearly what we are talking about here. We can simplify our deliberations and facilitate our understanding by considering two scenarios:

Scenario No. 1
### Continue the Rush to Socialism

Continue the adoption and implementation of the form of socialism that is being imposed on the citizens of this country. In the classical form of Socialism, for example, that in Sweden; the people of the country made a conscious decision to commit to that form of government. It was agreed that the government would "take care of the people"; from the cradle to the grave! In return, it was understood that the government would levy and the people would pay the necessary taxes to cover the costs.

The socialism being imposed on our country differs from the classical form in several important respects. We'll refer to that being imposed on us as "*yellow*" socialism. Implementation of *yellow socialism* in the United States is not the result of an explicit mandate from the citizenry at the polls. As a matter of fact, most people in this country probably are not consciously aware of our drift (plunge?) toward socialism. Socialism is being gradually and quietly thrust upon us by the liberal factions of our government; Democrats aided by a few liberal Republicans—people that we, never-the-less continue to elect to office time after time after time . . . The continual acquiescence of government to demands and emotional pleas of small groups of people with special interests is a major factor in this drift. It is done without identification of, or regard for the possible adverse impacts upon us, individually and upon the viability of the country itself. Our government organizations are gradually taking on the responsibility for "*taking care*" of all the people in the country; the needy and the not-so-needy; cradle to the grave. Beyond that they are gradually accepting responsibility for "*taking care*" of large numbers of our institutions.

For example, by their actions, they have created an innovative classification of banks that are, "so large that the country cannot afford to allow them to fail"! Smaller banks that do not meet their criteria for such special treatment are allowed to fail. We should not be surprised then to witness a frenzy of action in the world of banking, that involves mergers of smaller banks, into larger ones; designed, of course, to ultimately get all of them under this special umbrella of protection. Is that a desirable situation? I suspect it is not! It is entirely possible that controlling bank growth so that none of them ever reach that size, might be a far better solution.

*Yellow socialism* is most clearly characterized by the obvious fact that those who are imposing the system on us, have no plan for, in fact, no intent to pay for most of it. Where "classical" socialism accepts the responsibility of paying for its programs on a real time basis; *yellow socialism*, doesn't worry about paying for the costs of its programs; ever. These cost are simply added to the national debt! and left for future generations to worry about. Our government officials fall prey to the emotional "tug" of doing everything for everyone; but they are not able to bring themselves to enact tax legislation to cover the costs. "Emotional Idiocy" in action; creating "An Era of Fiscal Idiocy". And the ultimate result, financial collapse of our government, and its subsequent inability to "*take care*" of anything or anybody! Picture our situation in this country with financial failure: *no* funds for Social Security payments every month; *no* Federal retirement checks; *no* government guarantee of accounts in banks, savings and loan institutions or credit unions; slashed government payrolls; *no* welfare or health protection for anyone, even for the most needy among us; *no* government subsidies, even for the most worthy causes; inoperative military forces; etc., etc. Universally, socialism has failed to do the job. Our government's failure to finance its social programs will only hasten the time of our demise!

Life under Socialism has been characterized as follows:[7]

## THE SIX BASIC CONTRADICTIONS OF SOCIALISM

1. Under Socialism, everyone works, but there is nothing in the stores.
2. There is nothing in the stores, but everyone has everything.
3. Everyone has everything, but everyone is dissatisfied.
4. Everyone is dissatisfied, but everyone is for the system.
5. Everyone is for the system, but no one works.
6. No one works, but there is no unemployment.

A maze of double-talk. Is there any reason to believe that our experience will be any more successful than that of the multitude of others that have tried it and failed? Not that I can think of! The long-term projection of our scenario points to certain failure. It is sheer folly for us and our nation to ignore the lessons of history in this regard!

Scenario No. 2.
*Revert to Free-market, Democratic Principles*
We can revert back to the democratic, free-market economy that brought us the wealth and good life we now enjoy. We can cut back on government spending on all programs; begin to bring our citizens, all of them, back into the real world: begin to wean the people from the big-government, sugar-daddy pacifier they have come to rely upon; prohibit new, costly, unfunded programs; balance the Federal budget; and then develop and implement a plan in which the balanced Federal budget contains an element that provides for ultimate repayment of our massive Federal debt.

To be sure, this option will require some downward adjustment in the standard of living of all of us. Some will be affected more than others. But, by taking control of our own destiny, *NOW*, we may be able to escape massive deprivation and human suffering such as was encountered in this country in the 1930's or such as existed in the final days of the Soviet Union, in parts of eastern Europe, and in third-world countries.

Implementation of some level of this option is necessary, if this nation is to survive, long-term, and if we are to be able to retain some important aspects of our elevated standard of living.

---

[7]   Readers Digest Magazine

Why is it that our system is not working? Why are our officials unable to make decisions responsive to the needs of the "nation"? Why is it they are unwilling to confront the tough issues? How long can we sit idly by and let them "run from" their responsibility? Do conditions have to get as bad as they are in the Soviet Union; in eastern Europe; or in third-world, developing nations before we are willing to do what has to be done? We'll try to shed some light on this whole subject as we proceed.

During the time of operations Desert Shield and Desert Storm, one of Abigail Van Buren's, columns captured my attention for the contribution it might make to this inquiry. Like many of you, I often read some of the advice columns in the hard media. A look beyond the gratuitous promotion of "mind control and adjustment" forms of counseling, found there, can provide interesting and important insights into "how America is thinking" about some of the issues we face as a nation.

As we have discussed earlier, many teachers seized upon the opportunity of the Desert Shield—Desert Storm operation, to divert students' attention and interest away from their normal basic educational (?) pursuits; to matters relating to the war and the warriors representing us in the Gulf area. One practice was to have the children write letters to service personnel in the war zone.

In one such instance a sailor on a ship in the Persian Gulf, received such a letter from a high-school student here in the states. He was so affected by the contents of the letter that he shared a portion of it with "Dear Abby". She, in turn, shared a small segment of the student's message with her readers, as follows: "I now you are doon your best to pertek our nation fum them and I want you to no we are prowd of you." In his transmittal the sailor reacted with the following comment: "God help America if our kids are graduated from high school spelling and writing the way they do."

Of course, we all react differently to revelations of this sort. The fact that our public education systems are failing, seems to be widely accepted. But, it would be instructive to ask ourselves, "just how bad is the situation?" Is this case unusual? or does it represent a normal or average condition in our society? I must admit to some level of apprehension about even asking those questions and reaching for the answers. But, of course, we must! Limitations in the intellectual capability of our people as a contributing factor in the evolution of our problems needs to be identified and quantified.

Of course, it is not unusual for the readers of Abby's column to "talk back"; and they did in this case. The three responses she shared with us in a subsequent column are interesting. They can help us understand how some of our people react to adversity; to charges of incompetence; to claims that our government organizations are not working; etc.—the kinds of assertions that are necessary in our discussions of the nation's problems.

One of the responses quoted in the follow-up column was from a parent of a child with a learning disability. The writer was critical of the sailor's response; suggesting that the letter may have been written by a student with a learning disability. It continued that we should not be so quick to criticize how a person expresses himself/herself. Instead we should be thankful that the child took the time, made the effort and exhibited the courage to write.

This brings into clear focus, two widely diverse views of citizenship and how we should live it. What the "parent" suggests may be true. But, again it may not be; odds are that it is not! If, in fact, this student represents an educational norm in our society, we need to know that. How else can we energize society to "fix" the problem? The passive, unquestioning attitude proposed by this "parent" is a classic example of what has gotten us into this mess. If we propose to allow that suggested model of citizenship to prevail in this country, an adequate education is of little importance. Training our minds and developing senses of inquiry, analytic abilities and problem solving capabilities are a waste of time, if we are not motivated or willing to use them.

The sailor was demonstrating a stellar class of citizenship that we should champion and encourage. First, he was serving his country, in a perilous arena, in a time of need. Secondly, he cared enough about his country, the one he was fighting for, to recognize the possible importance of his discovery—and then to do something about it. His is a model of citizenship that our forefathers, those people who drew up the ruling plan for this country, would understand and appreciate.

Of course, we all react emotionally to situations of impaired capabilities. It is important to understand that, even if this student did have a learning disability, there is absolutely nothing about what happened here that reflects adversely on him or her. It does reflect serious questions upon our public educational system, when someone—anyone—of such limited literacy, has been advanced into high school. Educational systems will work properly, only when advancement is based on the learning achievements of the individual. When that mode of operation existed in public education, years ago, it was not uncommon to find students of advanced age still in elementary or early high school grades. The undesirability of such a situation was recognized. The answer—the system was consciously and intentionally changed, to advance people on to the next grade whether or not they were prepared to achieve in face of the more difficult curricula of the higher grade. The logic of this change is difficult to grasp. It certainly was no favor to the student who was advanced beyond his/her capability. It should have been obvious that this practice would only delay or completely sidetrack those students' trail to the literate world. Beyond the adverse impact upon the slow learners, this procedure has denied other students the opportunity to proceed in an orderly manner with their learning experience.

That change made no sense then! It has demonstrated beyond question that it makes no sense now. In fact, our educational systems will not, cannot, work with it in place!

The second response to the high school student's statement came from a high school teacher. The absence of denial in this response, by someone so close to the situation, tells us that such grievous shortage of skills in students at that level of their development probably is not unusual. Such recognition, from inside the system is helpful. The teacher respondent goes on to give us some reasons, from his/her perspective, as to why the teaching and learning we expect in our schools is not happening. They included the following:

— A teacher has the student for only 50 minutes each day.
— The learning experience during this time is inhibited by other activities such as, roll call, discipline problems, correcting papers, intrusion by disturbances in the hall, etc.
— As an average student of today, Johnny hates school,—he seldom has a pen, paper or textbook with him.

The above list of problems areas is not complete. It is, as you might expect, slanted to the teacher's point of view. It stresses problems posed by the students and is essentially silent on problems resulting from people and processes within the school systems.

This response is consequential because of the "*all important*" nature of the interface between the teacher and the student. This interface is the "make or break" point that ultimately determines whether or not the educational system works. Effective relationships and interaction between the teacher and student does not guarantee success of the educational system in meeting society's needs. On the other hand, no educational system will ever succeed without an effective interface at this point. The teacher's knowledge of the subject, his or her desire and ability to teach, the enthusiasm and innovation he/she brings to the classroom; and the example he/she sets will play an important role in achieving success at this point. Recognition of this factor in our society is limited and shallow. Analysis of the problem is superficial and ineffectual.

But, of course, success of the system also requires a cooperative, dedicated student body that is dedicated to learning; one that shares some of the characteristics exhibited by young children entering our educational systems today, through kindergarten and first grade classes. Protection and stewardship of their boundless sense of excitement, expectation and eagerness to participate, to do new things and to learn should be a primary goal of all of us. Instead, our continuing experience demonstrates that, as these children progress up through the system, this beautiful bubble will burst and as early as the third or fourth grade some of them will begin to deviate to that hostile pattern of disillusionment and nonparticipation that is threatening to dominate student bodies in many of the upper middle school and high school grades.

As the children progress into the higher grades the "mix" of students in the system changes. Some kids still "come to learn"; others are there only because they are forced to attend. The learning efforts of those students who are still earnestly engaged in gaining an adequate education, and who are effectively interfacing with the system are radically impacted by the tactics and total confusion interjected into the system by those who are in school, only because they are forced to attend. We read of instances where black students who are achievers in school in many areas, are taunted by the non-achieving students and in some cases even by faculty; mocked "because they are acting like white people". Chicago educator and author Jawanza Kunjufu has written a book that discusses this general subject, entitled, "To be Popular or Smart: The Black Peer Group."

He tells us that these disruptive kids are disillusioned, they have rejected the system, many of them have developed a sense of wisdom? that convinces them that an education is not necessary for them. We should not be surprised to hear them proclaim that, "The government will take care of them." That is the intuitive message most of them receive at home, on the street, and in the schools! An education is not a necessity!

In an attempt to justify the forced attendance of the disruptive group in school, it is easy for the public to hypothesize that, "A miracle will occur in the lives of all of these misguided youngsters. They will "see the light"! turn around in their thinking, recognize the error of their ways and proceed to let the learning experience work its magical influence on their lives. Experience demonstrates clearly that such hope is sheer folly in most cases.

At the same time, the magnitude of the damage caused by their presence in the learning institutions is obvious to any astute observer. However, that side of the picture is essentially ignored; little or no effort is exerted in detection, analysis, and implementation of effective corrective action. Decision makers for these systems, elected and bureaucratic, proceed as though the problem does not exist! *And no one challenges them.*

The practical benefits of forcing these types to be present in schools are not well established. Of course, in an *era of emotional idiocy*, having all kids in school is soothing to those that do not look beyond the emotional realm in making their decisions! The logic of such forced attendance seems not to be questioned. This is a serious matter. It deserves attention, it begs for a sane explanation; or it deserves to be changed.

Such dubious actions are popular with those we elect to public office. After they enact such laws, it never seems to occur to them to revisit the situation, determine how well things are going, and where necessary make adjustments. Their present attitude seems to be that if they thought of it and they enacted it; it is the best of all possibilities—it cannot be improved upon!

Among us lesser mortals, of less ego and a lesser sense of self importance; there is an old saying—a truism—that applies here:

**"You can lead a horse to the water,
but you can't make him drink."**

This particular contributor to Abby's column signed himself/herself as "A Disillusioned Teacher". We can appreciate and understand that well-intentioned, capable teachers in our present systems are "disillusioned". The perspective and assistance of such people will be an important ingredient if or when serious corrective action is undertaken.

The third response to the Abby column was different from the other two in interesting ways. It was obviously submitted by a young person, either in or recently graduated from high school. It was very short, no excuses here. It was upbeat, aggressive and oriented to the future. It was signed, "Educated in Indiana". Its implications are, the most informative, the most telling and the most chilling of the three. We need to look at it carefully.

The primary points of this response were:

1.  The writer disagree with—condemned—the generalization in what had been written about the inadequate education status of the younger generation.

2. It assured us that America will not fall apart when his/her generation takes over, and
3. It expressed sincere appreciation, on behalf of all educated high school students of America, to those serving in the armed services in the Gulf and elsewhere.

The intimation of the "Educated in Indiana" sign off and the nature and tone of the contents make it clear that—in the eyes of the contributor—his/her education is a very good one.

Now, that may be true; his/her education may be everything that is desired and needed. But again! it may not be! How is the recipient to know? The arrogance of making such strong, all encompassing statements on such complex far reaching issues point to the strong possibility that egotism may be the master here. Who, of sound mind, would propose that anyone could speak for all of the educated high school students in America? To presume that they all agree on anything?

And who, of sound mind, would propose that they understand all of the ramifications of the huge, mysterious, complex, management problems of running this country effectively; and of knowing first hand the capabilities and motivation of all of our citizens to the point that they can accurately assure the rest of us that everything will be okay when their generation assumes command?

The intent here is not to be critical or abusive of the contributor. The position expressed is undoubtedly shared by legions of his/her peers and many others.

The idea that we Americans are proud (egotistical) in our approach to life is not new. For as long as most of us can remember, Americans have felt that ours is a superior culture, that we can and do, do things better than anyone else, and that the high standard of living we enjoy serves as evidence that such is the case. There was a time when we could point to evidence that helped to confirm that this was the case. As individuals, as organizations, and as a nation we excelled in most things that we did. However, evidence of our decline in ability and performance during the past few decades is unmistakable. The proficiency of our systems, the productivity of our workers, and the quality of many of our products and services simply do not "measure up" in the new world of developing global markets. As a society, we are not totally oblivious to this fact. The problem is given "lip service"; but little else.

What seems to be lacking is the intelligence and humility, on our part, to recognize and react to undeniable evidence that we are no longer at the head of the pack; that others are out producing us in quantity, quality and price. They are systematically developing a citizenry that is better educated, more focused, more ambitious and more effective than we are. And we are sitting on our laurels, seemingly unconcerned and uncaring!

This third contributor to Abby's column obviously believes that he/she has received an excellent education. This poses an intriguing question, "What can he/she (we) use, in our society today, as a trustworthy indicator or measuring device to make such a judgement?" The first thing that comes to mind is to rely on the grades received in school. Again, that was a reliable indicator at one time in our history. But! unfortunately, that is no longer true. Like so many other situations in our society, that device has been corrupted, by the practitioners in our political arena and in our public education systems.

This was effectively demonstrated in a recent "Letter to the Editor" of a local daily paper. A father wrote relating a good-news/bad-news experience he had encountered. The good news—one of his children brought home a thesis paper from school which had earned a grade of B+. The bad news—his deep disappointment when he looked over the paper and found large numbers of misspelled words, numerous punctuation errors, erasures and corrections done in a careless, sloppy manner. The father related his deep disappointment and wonderment at how our kids will ever be challenged to do good work if we continue to reward them in this manner for such mediocre effort.

In earlier times, a persons ability to gain employment and to advance up the career ladder was a reliable indicator. But, of course, other artificial factors have been legislated into the process by our politicians and bureaucrats; factors that are systematically given legal priority over *ability* and *merit* in hiring and advancement actions. As a result, this indicator is no longer reliable!

We are left with a situation that produces a dichotomy of beliefs in our people. One that has the potential for misleading and seriously impacting our effectiveness in all that we do.

Ill-conceived government action is denying the country of its ability to use its best qualified people throughout the work force; in both the public and private arenas. Less than honest judgements and actions relating to a person's performance, in school or on the job, is a disservice to all of us and to the country. It is also a disservice to that person. It denies him/her the ability to identify weaknesses; "what they don't know"; the areas that they need to work on to improve. Chaos, inefficiency, inadequate quality control and loss of competitive position results from people of limited ability being misled in this way.

***Simply put, members of our work force have been robbed of their ability to, "KNOW WHAT THEY DON'T KNOW".***

As a result people who believe that they are competent, that they know what they are doing; are in actuality working "over their heads" and creating utter chaos. Such deficiencies cannot be ignored forever. But, how are they to be identified and corrected? when they are hidden!

We don't know the extent to which forcing the use of less than the best talent available to us in positions in our work force contributes to our inability to compete; but we know it is a factor! Possibly a major one. There are, of course, other factors that must be considered. But, orderly, effective solutions to management problems such as ours, must start with step by step analysis to discover weaknesses and then developing and implementing corrective action for each identified problem area. That is, orderly, evolutionary resolution; as contrasted to massive, totally disruptive revolutionary changes where everything is changed all at once, whether it is part of the problem or not.

This situation calls to mind the following very thought provoking statement:

---

### THE TRULY WISE

The man who knows not that (i)
He knows not aught—
He is a fool; no light can ever reach him.
Who ever knows he knows not and (ii) would fain be taught—
He is but simple; take thou him and teach him.
And whoso, knowing, knows (iii) not that he knows—
He is asleep; go thou to him and wake him.
The truly wise, both knows (iv) and knows he knows—
Cleave thou to him and never—
more forsake him.[8]

An Arabian Proverb

---

[8]   The Public Speaker's Treasure Chest; Revised Edition; Harper and Row.

Please take the time to carefully study and understand the full meaning of that proverb. It cleverly describes four types of persons; workers; citizens. All four are surely present in our society. Some questions that rear their ugly heads are, What is the prevalence of the type (i) person in our midst? How many people are operating in a type (i) environment, but could (would) fit the mould of category (ii) if exposed to knowledge of their deficiencies? What is the true measure of the losses we are suffering because large numbers of our most competent, the truly able, are denied access to positions where their contributions would make significant improvements in the performance of our public and private enterprises?

A complacent society provides a comfortable environment for the continued hibernation of the type (iii) personality. How much might they contribute if they were awakened and given a fair chance to participate.

And, of course there are some persons among us who qualify as the "truly wise". Unfortunately, they are seldom able to rise above the din of the aggressive, noisy, special interest groups. Lack of access to positions of prominence and power limits their contribution. The "squeaking wheel gets the grease in our society"; usually by legal edict. Legislators who are elected and sworn to do their best to manage the affairs of the country, to represent the interest of the majority of the people; routinely succumb to the demands of small groups of demanding, noisy, protesting special interest groups for laws that assure them the special treatment they demand.

# CHAPTER 10

As this is being written, public opinion polls indicate that over 60 percent of the people in the country recognize and are concerned about the inexcusably inept performance of our present government institutions and the people in them. A plurality of that magnitude seldom occurs on any issue in this country. Given that high level of agreement on the subject; we will accept as factual, from this point forward, the notion that serious problems do exist. And, we will proceed with analysis and identification of corrective measures that will point us toward ultimate solutions. Always motivated by the fear of losing our ability to continue using this form of government and reaping the benefits that it provides us.

In that vein, let me present, for your consideration, one other finding of fact. It is this: "*They*" **are not going to solve these problems!** *They* being identified as the incumbents in our public institutions and, to a large extent, in the private sector also. The existence of these problems, is not a new revelation. The "movers and shakers" that we trust with managing our public and private affairs have known of their existence for many years. In some instances, they have given lip-service to them. By their actions and by their inaction, they have demonstrated, beyond any doubt, a total inability or unwillingness to understand, improve or resolve any of the multitude of problem issues. In those cases where they have been moved to do something; their actions have only made matters worse.

Foreboding as it may seem, if these problems are going to be solved, it is up to "*you*" and "*me*" to take the lead. Of course you and I cannot do everything that must be done to achieve success. We must find ways to enlist the aid and assistance of others. The "war" is being lost because large numbers of relatively small, misdirected, special interest groups, have learned effective, devious ways of "buying" or otherwise influencing decisions in the halls of power. As was so aptly demonstrated during the recent Senate Judiciary Committee hearings for Clarence Thomas; an organized telephone attack, by one or two thousand loud, crafty, scheming women; results in tremors within the government establishment, that are felt throughout the nation. Does that mean that the position taken by the protesters represented the will of the people? Hardly! In a nation of 250,000,000 people, 2000 women represents 0.0008 percent of the people; far short of 50.00 percent plus one (125,000,001) that makes up a majority.

For several days a large audience of U. S. citizens sat glued to the "tube" watching the theatrics. They were treated to yet one more "soap opera". That surely was not the most important business the nation had to deal with during that time.

This country, its form of government and the freedom and other benefits it provides for us, simply cannot continue to exist as long as the majority of its people are silent. When they do not participate; their ideas and wishes are totally subordinated to the demands of special interests!

Referring back to the Arabian Proverb in the last chapter, it should come as no surprise that a type (iii) electorate is totally inconsistent with the needs of a democracy. That is, an electorate that meets this criteria:

> And whoso, knowing, knows
> not that he knows—
> He is asleep; go thou to
> him and wake him.

That is our charter, yours and mine. To awaken the sleeping silent majority, to develop a realization within its ranks, that our democracy, any democracy, can continue to exist, only if the people participate; actively forcefully and intelligently. The real test of the democratic form of government that is playing itself out in our country is not necessarily one of whether or not democracy can work. It is instead a test of our people; whether or not they care enough to make it work.

It is interesting, to observe the interest, dedication and zeal with which people in eastern Europe forced democratic ideas and ideals into the new governments being formed there in the early 1990's. Having recently thrown off the shackles of Communism and Socialism, they had glowing visions of what their lives, and their countries, could be under a democratic form of government. And they were determined to give it a try!

To then turn and see the complacency and lack of interest by citizens of this country, who stand to lose all that those people hope to gain; is alarming and sad. Our fate should not surprise us. "Government of the people, by the people and for the people," will not work without the continuing, active, intelligent participation (demands) of, "*the people*".

There is a fundamental need for our silent majority to organize and to become proactive in the process of government. What a bizarre situation! The majority must organize, become active and demanding; to *force* its own public and private servants to do the work they are elected, hired and paid to do!

Most of our people are totally involved in trying to provide for themselves, and their loved ones. There are not enough hours in the day to do that and then to manage, supervise, and do the detailed work we pay those people to do! That is why we hire them! If we must get more involved; we may need to organize for that purpose. We could call the organization a *C*itizens *A*lliance for *R*eclaiming *D*emocracy, *E*thics, and *M*orality in our government and our country. The acronym CARDEM describes the relationship between the organization and our servants; the expectation that they do the job they are put there to do, or they will be replaced by someone who can and will! Effectively motivated and operated local, state and national chapters of such an organization could be of great benefit in resolving our problems.

How can we begin to identify the problem issues; the relative significance of each; the causal factors that contribute to their existence and evolutionary development; and finally actions that need to be taken to effectively improve conditions and resolve the issues?

Fortunately, we have some clues to help us in the identification and rating of importance of the "causes". If the problems were confined to isolated segments of our society, that would point us in the direction of identifying the process and personnel requirements that are peculiar to those activities where we are failing. How are they different from those of the activities where we seem to be getting the job done? Unfortunately, a cursory, overview of the situation, strongly suggests that such is not the case in our situation. Where can we find instances where our public institutions are doing a good job? Because I am retired and because I am interested and concerned about these issues, I write a lot of letters, do a lot of prodding and prying information from a wide variety of public organizations. What I find is appalling. There are hidden organizations of substantial size, operating around all of us, whose budgets for people and funds never reach the light of public scrutiny. Whose spending is regularly increasing at the rate of 25 percent per year or more. The level of ineptitude and total disregard for the public's best interests and it's ability to pay is chilling. The incompetence everywhere. It is either not recognized or ignored by those incumbents who work there; who we pay handsomely for supervising and managing those activities responsibly and efficiently!

Beyond the public sector, similar, critical observations and inquiries into the effectiveness of operation and management in the private sector provides us with little justification for comfort or confidence that the job is being well done there. The media is full of reports of gargantuan failures within the Savings and Loan industry; in banking organizations, large and small; and in the Insurance industry. There is a common thread that runs through these activities. A measure of success in all such financial institutions, will depend upon the understanding of and proper utilization of mathematical analyses and probabilities. When viewed critically, evolving events and crises in this arena provides little, if any, basis for confidence in quality of the work force there.

The mass media reports with great fanfare, the prosecution of a few of the more notorious top managers of such failed organizations; especially where their abusive use of resources, have been conspicuous and flaunting.

That such abuse may have contributed to the failure of such an organization is not to be denied. However, it is highly unlikely that such a failure, especially of large institutions, could be exclusively caused by the actions of one person. More likely than not, such a failure results from the individual and collective ineptitude of employees throughout the organization; employees at all levels whose lack of qualifications and abilities to effectively do the work are either not recognized, or they are recognized but not confronted and dealt with. And, what happens to these people when an establishment fails and its doors close? Many of them will find jobs in other similar organizations, and continue to contribute to the destruction of the industry and the country. A more frightening possibility, is that they will be hired to teach in our educational systems; where they can pass misinformation and faulty perspectives on to a new generation of the American work force.

Of course, the obvious deficiencies of management abilities and entrepreneurship in our world of private enterprize is not limited to these financial groups. Businesses, large and small, are failing in record numbers throughout the country. It has been common practice to blame this phenomenon on depressed economic conditions that sometimes grip our country. To be sure, that can contribute to the situation. But any realist will recognize that there are other important factors involved here. Decline of the financial viability and "health" of many of our important manufacturing (steel, auto, etc.) and service corporations began a long time ago and has continued through extended, "economic-boom" times.

Examples of businesses in this country that are clearly well managed and able to hold their own in a global marketplace are not easy to identify. The Boeing airplane company and the Microsoft, computer software company are two that come to mind, that are exceptions to that rule.

You probably would not be surprised, if it were suggested here that the inadequacies of our educational systems might be a pivotal, contributing factor in all of these situations. Weaknesses in the educational system are usually discussed as one of our many problems; separate and unrelated to all the others. That surely is not the case. Major educational deficiencies in all of the basic learning groups and in supervisory and management skills are, contributory to failures in all public and private-enterprize, business activity.

In the past, tracking the quality of education in our public school systems has been based, primarily on the results of standardized tests. Systems such as the Metropolitan Achievement Test (MAT), can be used to test children's abilities at certain points in their educational development. For example, the state of Washington used the MAT series for testing at the 4th, 8th and 10th grades levels for several years. The deterioration of the quality of education, as documented by the continuity of such testing, proves to be an embarrassment for a lot of people working in that activity.

Mass media reporting on this subject is usually moderate in its criticism. It also does not forcefully press for corrective action. The headline of a recent, local, media report read, "Most students above state average on MAT".[9] Even editorial comments are cached in language designed not to upset anyone. Is it too much to expect the media to be supportive of action to correct such critical problems? They certainly have been actively involved in creating them! Many states offer the Scholastic Aptitude Tests (SAT) to their graduating seniors in high school. The SAT tests are standard throughout the nation. The results of these tests are often one of the factors used by

---

[9]    Feb. 15, 1991; Vancouver, WA; Columbian

some colleges and universities in selecting the members of their incoming freshman class each year.

A headline in another local newspaper read, "Oregon students No. 1 in nation on SAT scores".[10] Then in much smaller print, a sub-heading, "However, both the state and national averages take a tumble". The article goes on to say that the national average SAT scores in the verbal portion of the exam fell to a new all-time low. Lamar Alexander, one time Secretary, U.S. Department of Education, is quoted as saying that, "The simple fact is that even our best students generally don't know enough and can't do enough to assure success in tomorrow's world." Given his access to information, the staff available to him for analysis of that data and his position in the system, it seems prudent to respect his opinion and comments on the subject as being objective and accurate.

If his statement is true now, and the young people entering the work force are seriously deficient in skills; how long has that been true? How far back, has such ineptitude been the norm? Or translated to reveal the true concern; since age and years of service usually translate into promotion into positions of greater responsibilities, how far up, into the supervisory and management chain, has this malignancy progressed?

Teachers' unions, and many others in the education field who feel threatened by the depressing results of these testing methods are anxious to make the case that the scores of these tests are not truly representative of the ability of graduating students to perform in our working environment. That argument is challenged by historical evidence demonstrating that as the scores have gone down, the abilities of our workers and the performance of our society have decreased in proportion to that decrease. In a true, world-market economy that has to be seen as a serious handicap.

It is incomprehensible that a nation that *professes* to be so concerned about the welfare of its children; is so passively unconcerned about this situation. Where are the parents? Why are they not sitting on the schoolhouse steps and demanding improvements? The parents seem not to grasp the fact that ***they*** and ***they alone* are responsible for the quality of their children's education. They are foolishly waiting for the Federal government, the state, the school board and/or the educational systems themselves to solve the problem. And the truth is that will never happen. *"As long as they, the parents, are willing to settle for less than the best, that is what they will get.***

---

[10]    August 27, 1991; Portland, OR; Oregonian.

Where are the "do gooders" who are so "Johnny on the spot", when it comes to forcing enactment of other legislation which is supposedly for the benefit of children. In contrast to the many other issues that they pursue so passionately, *there is nothing in this situation that will benefit them.* And we learn something of their true "colors".

We referred above to some interesting reactions to "standard" testing systems that are used throughout the country. School employees, especially the teachers and their unions, do not appreciate annual reminders of the inferior quality of the product they deliver. In many instances they oppose the use of the tests. By edict of the public education establishment, use of the MAT tests was discontinued in the early 1990's in Washington State. The announcement of the termination of those tests was not accompanied by a commitment as to which system would be used in its stead or when it would be put in place. Elimination of one system or replacement of a system by another one, serves the interests of the "educational establishment" by breaking the continuity of test results. It will be difficult, if not impossible, to relate the effectiveness of the educational systems performance before and after the change.

In another instance, history has shown that girls usually do not score as well with some of the SAT tests as do the boys. The difference is attributed, by some, to the fact that girls, as a rule, do not take as much math in high school as do the boys. You just have to know that such a situation will not escape notice and assault in our society today. It is ideally suited for attack by that relatively small group of fractious, noisy, and demanding women who have become so adept in beating the system; to their own benefit and to the disadvantage of the rest of us; men and women alike, and to the detriment of the nation.

Their assault is being focused on two fronts. They are campaigning to coerce more young ladies to enroll in the math courses. And they have effectively campaigned to change the contents of the tests within the systems; for the express purpose of including material that will allow the girls to score better!

In this society many have learned to be surprised by nothing. Anything and anyone is fair game for the special interests! It does not follow that we must sit idly by and not "fight back".

Whereas, the general public seems not to be vigilantly aware of the potential gravity of the "educational" problem and its dynamic affects on the "world around us"; we are beginning to see conclusive evidence that its presence and its importance are being recognized in the business arena.

Competent business leaders are being challenged by the situation in ways that cannot be ignored; they understand that something must be done and that the educational system is not responding in an effective way. They realize that if they and their businesses are to survive, they must do what is necessary to assure an adequate supply of qualified young people for infusion into their work force.

Businesses are addressing the problem in several ways. In some instances, they have had to "dumb-down" the work. That is, they spend time and money to provide machines and work processes that fit an undereducated work force. Companies that are forced to go this route, are handicapped by the fact that this mode of operation is usually more costly; and their competitive position in the near-future market place is jeopardized. The additional peril of such action, one that is even more worrisome to *competent* managers of organizations that make this move, is that the quality of its work force will not allow it to adopt more complex future technologies that may be required for them to remain competitive in the longer term.

Another way of addressing this problem, has been to identify the educational needs of the employees, and set up "on-site" courses at their facilities to improve skills in these areas.

In other cases, businesses are embracing the position taken by the educational systems; that the lack of money is the reason for their shoddy performance. What is needed to solve this problem is, **"more money"**. They then contribute money directly to those schools from which they draw most of their new employees. In a way, an organization that opts for this alternative is telegraphing to an astute observer; the presence of ominous weaknesses within its management team. Funding for the public educational systems increased between 80 and 100 percent during the 1980's. The adult employees in those systems benefited a great deal in higher salaries and perks. The children, their parents and the taxpaying public have been left holding the bag. In most instances, the quality of education during that period went down! It does not take a genius to know that the problem goes much deeper than just "more money". One would expect that a management team, one with the "American Spirit", that aspires to successfully contend in today's competitive market place, would be more penetrating and intelligent in dealing with such a situation.

There are other situations in which companies are making some of their talented employees available to teach selected subjects in the schools which supply most of their new young employees. This procedure appears to be more attractive to organizations that require employees of relatively high technical abilities.

One final indicator of the gravity of this problem from the perspective of some industrialists can be gleaned from the actions of Japanese companies that own and manage large industrial operations in this country. Key management and supervisory people and their families are usually brought from Japan for the purpose of directing activities at these facilities. The high priority that those people assign to giving their children a quality education is demonstrated by the fact that special, private schools are often provided for the children of these families. They assign a high priority to providing those children an education that is comparable to what they would have received in Japan!

That both the test scores and the quality of our work force have been declining in recent decades; are recognized, well-supported facts. However, the evidence available does not define in a quantitative way the relationship between the two. I have not seen information that will help us correlate the literacy level with the ability and performance of our work force.

One study that has recently been reported in the media in the Pacific Northwest part of the country deserves some attention. In the late 1980's and early 1990's, the Oregon State Legislature created, "The Progress Board" for that state. The charter of the Board was to set a variety of social and economic bench marks for Oregon and then to chart its progress in meeting them. Creation of the Board represents an innovative and possibly productive approach to identifying, quantifying and solving some of the problems faced by the state and its citizens. A cursory look at the Board membership and their approach to the work before them, would seem to suggest levels of understanding and objectivity appropriate for the job. We should be able to view the results of their work with some confidence.

The Board spent $234,000 on a study, designed to give the state a first peek at the literacy levels of its adult population, and to relate that information to their abilities in the work place. The polling was done in the first half of 1990. The pollsters claim a margin of error of plus or minus 3 percent for the results.

The testing was divided into three categories: Prose Skills (reading); Quantitative Skills (mathematics); and Document Skills. The testing within each category was then divided into three levels: basic, intermediate, and advanced. The results were also presented by age group, to show the trend in the literacy curve for the people of the state, over time.

In reading skills, about 77 percent of those tested achieved at the basic level. This level of reading skill was depicted to be the ability to read a short sports article and to find basic facts that are included in it. Scores in reading skills plummeted as the level of difficulty increased. The intermediate level of reading ability was portrayed as the ability to identify and list evidence in a newspaper column that supports the author's argument. Newspaper articles are, of course, meant to provide the general public with a form of coverage of the day to day, "history in the making"; presented in a way that can be easily read and understood by the masses. Unbelievably, only 39 percent of those polled could achieve at this intermediate level of reading.

Although achievement at the advanced level of reading skill, as it was defined in the testing, would not seem to be a very rigorous test of one's reading ability; it did significantly tax the abilities of those polled. The advanced level was depicted as having the ability to, identify from a list of tax forms the proper one to use, based on information referred to in a magazine article. In this instance, as in the previous one, most magazine articles are supposedly written for easy reading and comprehension.

Again the results of this section of the test are far below what most of us would have expected. A mere 8 percent of those polled achieved at the advanced level. That is, 92 percent of those polled were not able to accomplish this task.

Literacy in the reading skill is, of course, a fundamental requirement to achieving well in other areas of the polling process. One category included in the poll was related to the ability of those polled to read and understand documents. The basic level of this category was characterized as the ability to locate a meeting time on a memo. About 75 percent of those polled were able to achieve at this basic level. Determination of the correct medicine dosage using a dosage chart and a child's age and weight was representative of the requirements for achieving at the intermediate level of this category. Sixty five percent of those polled *could not* achieve at this level. About 95 percent of those polled failed to achieve at the advanced level of this category. Eighty-two percent were not able to use a bus schedule and select the proper buses for given arrivals and departures! Ninety-six percent were unable to effectively analyze and interpret information contained in four graphs that related information during periods of economic recovery.

It is interesting that much of the discussion of the mathematical part of the poll was referred to as "Quantitative Skills". The simple word "mathematics" seems to cause some level of paralysis in many of our people. What a shame! the subject can be so interesting and it is so important.

Mastery, limited to just its basic elements can be of such great value and bring so much satisfaction to those who "bite the bullet", and learn the basic principles and how to apply them.

The implications of the results of the mathematical portion of the poll are even more astounding than are the other portions. In the mathematical portion of the poll, 78 percent of those tested achieved at the basic level. The other 22 percent had great difficulty totalling two entries on a deposit slip.

Testing at the intermediate level in the quantitative skills category utilized information on a sample restaurant menu. You order a Lancaster Special sandwich (listed at $1.95) and Onion Soup (listed at $0.60). When ready to leave, you give the cashier $3.00, how much change would you receive from the transaction?

Needless to say, this is not a complex, nor difficult mathematical problem. And yet! the poll demonstrated that 73 percent, more than two thirds, of Oregon's adult population could not consistently develop correct answers to this and other similar, simple, practical mathematical problems. [11]

The implications of the results of this study are sobering for Oregon and its future. It represents *a crisis of major proportions!* We must proceed with caution in any attempt to correlate the problem nationally with that in Oregon. If other states have performed similar studies the results have not come to my attention.

A similar national study that was done in 1985 used many of the same questions used in the Oregon study. In the national study, only young adults, ages 21 to 25 were polled; on average, Oregonians in that age group scored slightly above their peers in the national study. A sobering situation!

We need to face the question of the believability of the recent study results. For example, the study tells us that only about 5 percent of the adult Oregon population can perform at what the study called the advanced level. The 95 percent who could not perform at that level were unable to accomplish some tasks of very modest difficulty: 1. To identify the proper tax form to file, based upon information in a magazine article; 2. To determine the gain from biweekly and monthly investment programs using a savings bond advertisement; or 3. To correctly select appropriate busses for given arrival and departure times on a bus schedule! If, in fact,

---

[11]   Sources-Portland, OR-Oregonian; Oregon Progress Board.

this study accurately portrays the literacy level and ability of the work force in Oregon and/or in the nation, one marvels that conditions in our society are not magnitudes-of-order worse than they are.

We are faced with yet another puzzling circumstance. Statistics tell us that 20 to 25 percent of our adult population are college graduates. How are we to rationalize the inference gleaned from that statistic and the study results, that all college graduates cannot perform the relatively simple tasks required to achieve at the advanced level in the poll? But, apparently they cannot! if the results of the poll are accurate. Viewed in yet another perspective, how is it possible for 20 to 25 percent of the population to graduate from college when only 5 percent of the population can achieve at the advanced reading level in the poll. Experience tells us that reading, understanding and application of information in most, if not all, college text books presents challenges far more difficult than those required to achieve at the advanced level in the poll.

On the other hand, it seems improbable that members of the Board and/or the contractor that did the study orchestrated the study to magnify or to simplify the severity of the problem. The potential advantages of such manipulation to any of the participants are not readily apparent. It is also possible that the design and logic of the study are flawed. Even if such flaws exist, the message of the study would not necessarily be invalid. It seems reasonable to assume that objectivity prevailed in the design, performance and conclusions reached with the study.

We can only conclude, at this point, that credible evidence exists to indicate the probability that the literacy level in our country is substantially lower than we have imagined; and that that factor is a major contributor to the inability of our public and private enterprises to operate in an effective, competitive manner.

# CHAPTER 11

Freedom is nowhere to be found
When people are over taxed, and
Over regulated.

Douglas Wilder
Governor of Virginia

The situation that we encounter here is a very subtle one. Awareness of the fact that there are some among us who would deceptively and fraudulently present themselves as having abilities far beyond the talents, knowledge and abilities that they actually possess, is not a new phenomenon in our society. On the other hand, recognition of the possible presence of legions of such persons in our midst, who are *unknowingly* passing themselves off in such a manner; is another thing.

The nature and scope of the problem that results from masses among us, of limited literacy, knowledge, and abilities; *WHO DON'T KNOW WHAT THEY DON'T KNOW*, has not received the attention it demands. This brings us face to face with an insidious, perilous dilemma. This is a problem that will not resolve itself; and it will be very difficult for others to solve. We can expect that those in the work force who possess the problem attributes, will vehemently resist the concept that such a problem exists, let alone, accept that they are a part of it. In a nation of proud people, who are often egotistical far beyond what is merited; we can expect that those who contribute the most to the problem will be the most egotistical, the most vociferous and the least responsive to any attempts to correct the situation.

Review of the historical, evolutionary development of our government processes and institutions, reveals that this country's leadership in earlier times recognized this as a potential problem. We can assume that they regarded it as a serious threat; because they didn't just sit around and look at it, or talk it to death. They did something about it! Their actions pointed to the truth and applicability of the old adage, "an ounce of prevention is worth a pound of cure". In designing a system to prevent such problems from developing they exhibited levels of intelligence and restraint, that are, unfortunately,foreign to those in control in our halls of government today.

They implemented procedures which required that persons who set themselves up in business as medical doctors or dentists prove that they had the knowledge and skills to do that work correctly. Only qualified people were allowed to work in these fields.

Licensing programs were established for architects; engineers; surveyors; etc. The goal was to provide the general public with a level of assurance, that the design and construction of buildings, bridges, energy systems, water and sewer systems; in fact, the whole cross-section of public buildings and of the public-service infrastructure facilities be safe, functional and have a useful life that would justify their costs. To assure that only qualified people made the critical decisions required in those exacting, complex projects.

With the passage of time, the creeping intrusion of "big brother" government into our lives, and the slithering of socialism into our government institutions, the licensing procedure has been imposed on more and more activities. The situation has progressed to the point that, in many communities today, if you need to hire someone to do a $100, more or less, concrete sidewalk job; you must get a permit from your city or county government to do the work (on your property, not theirs) and the person you hire must be licensed and bonded to do that kind of work. And, of course, there are always fees to be paid for all of the permits and licenses. The extra income and personnel requirements of such permit and licensing activities, fit well into the "empire building" dreams and visions of the modern politician and bureaucrat.

Carried to its present status in many principalities today, your efforts to hire a gardener-handyman to cut your lawn, will require that this person be licensed and bonded to do this $10 to $20 job! Decades ago these licensing systems were policed to assure compliance. More recently, the interest of the establishment seems more devoted to collecting the fees than it is to enforcement.

The licensing process has always had some curious irregularities. For example, the licensing requirement does not extend to many architects, engineers, etc. who are on the payroll of government agencies. But! consulting architects, engineers, etc. who do design and other kinds of technical work for those same agencies must be licensed! Large federal utilities that have for decades pushed the frontiers of what is possible in design, construction and operation of huge electric transmission systems have done that work with unlicensed technical employees on their own staff. The genesis of the idea that government employees need not be licensed, probably dates back several decades to the time when applicant qualifications for government jobs were rigorously and effectively screened, using extensive and intensive batteries of examinations in general and specialized, technical disciplines. And when, only the best qualified were hired, based on those test results and other pertinent factors.

Of course, that system is no longer operative. As a reaction to pressures generated within this, "age of emotional idiocy", legislators embraced and forced upon all of us, "*their better idea*"? New laws that they enacted, mandated that qualifications related to a person's ability to do the job, be totally eclipsed by a candidate's sex, color, nationality, physical impairment, etc. For a brief moment in time, it was inferred that meeting "quotas" for each of these categories was required. Then it became obvious that, even filling quotas would not appease their demands! Look around in our society, today, and you will see entire organizations, in fact industries, that are totally dominated by members of these "so-called" minority or special interest groups! And, chances are good that you will find that they are still hiring 90 to 100 percent from "special" rosters of applicants! No where is this abuse of the civil rights of members of the silent majority greater than in hiring for government positions. The concept of hiring the best qualified applicant has been totally discarded. As a matter of fact, media disclosures have shown situations where vacancy announcements for government jobs have stated that, "*only unqualified persons should apply*". "*Qualified applicants will not be considered*"! **CAN YOU BELIEVE THAT? ITS TRUE!**

A work force can, of course, be assembled on the basis of ability, or on the basis of these other factors. Proponents of the new system, especially those who benefit from it's special privileges, would have us believe that the two systems are compatible; that nothing is sacrificed in quality of worker; or quality or quantity of work, when hiring is handled in such convoluted, insane ways. The present, pathetic operating record of most of our public and many of our private institutions, must be viewed as undeniable evidence that this new system is contributing in a major way to our impending demise!

There are other examples that clearly demonstrate the fallacy of the abstraction that proclaims that government intervention can be effective and of benefit to the citizens and the country. What better example than our banking and money management industries which flooded the American economy with a bath of financial debt in the early 1990's. That part of our society that we must all depend upon for effective management of the finances of the country appears to have no procedure or processes in place by which it can assure us of the competence of their employees; workers or managers. A dilemma of crisis proportions appears when we stand back and comprehend the pivotal relationship between effective management of this financial industry and our own monetary viability as individuals and as a nation. Even those of us who have no relationship or connection with the failing financial institutions, find ourselves saddled with the obligation for repayment of the losses. Citizen responsibility for a costly bailout of the owners, the Board of directors, the officers and the employees of the institution! The result of the government's assumption of responsibility for guaranteeing the accounts of the enterprise; followed by its total neglect to do the necessary, effective review and oversight; and to take timely corrective, intervention action when it is clearly indicated that is necessary.

THERE IS AN IMPORTANT POINT THAT NEEDS TO BE EMPHASIZED HERE. UNDERSTAND AND CAREFULLY CONSIDER WHAT THIS MEANS. YOUR REQUIREMENT TO PAY "YOUR SHARE" OF ALL OF THIS KIND OF DEBT HAS NOTHING TO DO WITH YOUR "ABILITY TO PAY"! *YOU ARE REQUIRED TO PAY YOUR PORTION OF THESE LOSSES—PERIOD.* THESE ARE TAX OBLIGATIONS; THEY WILL BE COLLECTED! BODY AND SOUL—YOU ARE RESPONSIBLE FOR THEM. YOU WILL PAY WHAT THEY DETERMINE TO BE YOUR SHARE OF THE LOSSES; *AND THEN*, IF THERE IS ANYTHING LEFT, YOU CAN PAY YOUR RENT, BUY FOOD, CLOTHE YOUR KIDS, PAY FOR YOUR TRANSPORTATION TO WORK, ETC. IF YOU ARE UNABLE TO PAY YOUR SHARE OF THE LOSSES; *THEY WILL CONFISCATE* YOUR HOUSE, CAR (S),ETC.; *EVERYTHING YOU OWN IF NECESSARY*; TURN THESE ITEMS INTO LIQUID CASH; PAY YOUR SHARE; AND PUT YOU AND YOUR FAMILY OUT ON THE STREET. *YOU HAVE NO RIGHTS TO YOUR ASSETS UNTIL THEY HAVE FINISHED WITH YOU.*

And then, of course, they will lead the parade of do-gooders pleading the case of the homeless and the needy; preying on the conscience of the rest of the people; seeking to develop feelings of guilt in those who for some reason, at that point, still have a place to live in, who are still able to survive.

We should define the term "they" in the preceding statement. Of course, "they" refers to all of the elected and bureaucratic government officials, all of them! each and every one! who participate in the design, development and implementation of these ridiculous schemes. But we should not stop there! "They" also encompasses, our friends, neighbors, associates, and ourselves; when they and we sit idly by and allow them to do it! Even worse, we reward them for doing it to us by re-electing them to office; time, after time, after time.

Prior to the implementation of synthetic government hiring practices, young people, men and women, went into the financial industry with the idea that it would be a lifetime career. Advancements up the career ladder were; at least, from an outsiders perspective, based upon knowledge and performance of the individual. The system provided motivated, knowledgeable, and competent employees on a continuing basis. But then things changed. More government intervention! The industry has not shared with the public the new criteria that they use in hiring and promotion decisions. That it has been very significantly changed is obvious to any astute observer.

Quotas, as touted by Federal mandates are obviously being met, and then some! Walk into any savings and loan institution or bank, large or small, and odds are that 90 to 95 percent of the staff that you encounter will be female.

These lamentable situations result from the requirements of two, less than brilliant, government edicts now operating in the work place. First, a passive attempt to comply with equal employment opportunity laws, executive orders, etc. Secondly, the same genius that saddled us with those constraints, extended the problem one step further. They created additional innovative, insane and counter-productive laws which were related to motherhood and apple pie by their stated requirements for, "equal pay for equal work"! Were the motives really that honorable? or was this yet another slick trick, another lie, foisted off on the passive, silent majority by their servants? As ultimately implemented, equal work was generally translated to mean that everyone in the same room of the work place should get equal pay. As implemented, there is little or no evidence to demonstrate that the level of pay was in any way related to the knowledge, ability, or productivity of the individual. It appears that all who were impacted by the implementation, received increases in pay. Of all of the hundreds of thousands of personnel actions cut on this issue, I suspect that few, if any, were found to be overpaid. Forces operational within our present bureaucratic steamrollers, play only to the theme of **MORE! MORE! MORE! More programs; more facilities;**

**more employees; more pay; more perks; more autonomy in the work place with more freedom from supervision, regulation and productivity measurement and requirements! And, of course, the need for more and more of our dwindling resources!**

Finally, the most striking circumstance of all, in which the public is not provided with any reassurance as to the knowledge, ability or competence of people who serve in very responsible roles, involves those we elect to public office. These are people who often have little or no experience in business or in any of the fields of endeavor they will encounter on the new job; people who have never managed anything, possibly not even a household budget; and we put them in charge of managing our impossibly complex affairs of state! Here are people whose level of literacy, ability and *real* intent are unknown to us. They are routinely elected to office on the basis of campaign promises that are seldom fulfilled. Once in office, they routinely pass legislation that creates new programs or that expand existing programs that require enormous new expenditures of the limited funds still available to the tax payer, the general public. They dive into these new ventures knowing only that they will be *very expensive.* The fact that they don't require reliable estimates of the program costs, is probably part of their management plan. Availability of firm cost figures might put them in the uncomfortable position of having to justify the staggering expenditures to their constituents using priority tables, cost/benefit analyses, etc. It is so much easier for them when such information is not available. They may rationalize in their own minds that cost is not important, since paying for most of the actions during their tenure is not part of their plan. From their perspective, enacting new legislation that will increase taxes is so messy. It's easier, and safer politically, for them to just add these new costs to the national debt! And let our kids, and our kids, kids, worry about it!

There are always proud, dedicated people in our society; in any society; who are existing on, "the margin". Individuals and families who live on the, "razor's edge", financially, between the ability to be self sufficient and falling into the chasm of dependence upon others for the necessities of life. Here are people, those we elect and their bureaucrats, who routinely commit other people's resources; yours, mine, our friend's and neighbor's, with no concern for the hardship that their action may be causing those who must pay. Each time that they impose new financial requirements onto the taxpaying public, some people and some families who have been existing at this margin, financially, are forced into insolvency; they lose their homes, they have no place to live, they can no longer feed or cloth their children, and they join that part of society that must look to the rest of us for everything.

Our public servants are not concerned that they have taken the very "bread of life" off the table of one group who was, "making it on their own", to provide more parks, swimming pools, a multitude of new public buildings and campuses which they will then fill with more public employees, substantial salary increases for themselves and others at the public trough, annual cost-of-living increases for all of the millions who receive salary, retirement payments or other kinds of reimbursements from any government organization, more money for school employees on the pretense that the quality of education will improve, and so on, and on, and on, . . . !

As the members of the general public skimp on their spending, trying to get by, often having to do without even necessities of life; these public servants? (pirates) routinely continue to pass measures, spending massive additional amounts of public funds for various and sundry nonessential items. Items that will contribute nothing of real benefit to society; items that do not address our need to resolve the problems we face. Items that may, in fact, aggravate conditions and make things worse.

Do you understand the irony and the importance of all of this? As a society, we have recognized, at least in a superficial way, the advantage of trying to assure some level of competence in a part of the work place. We have implemented licensing systems in some of the professions, in some blue collar activities, and for gardeners. We have done nothing to protect our interests in areas of major financial activities. And, most important of all, we have done nothing to identify problems and protect our interests in any of the political arenas.

A person or organization that mows our lawn for a $15 fee, must be licensed and bonded. But! people who commit us to millions, billions, and trillions of dollars of expense and debt, have no licenses, are not bonded, and they have no basic personal financial responsibility to us or to society, for actions they take; even when misinformation and possible fraud are involved!

**We have established guards for our piggy banks, but our gold mines are open and unattended; the big money is there for the taking! And they take it, from all of us!**

Having acknowledged that our nation has life threatening problems, and having committed ourselves to try to do something about it, we need to identify the causal actions that are at the root of the problems. The discussion in this chapter points us in directions of interrogation, some of which, are new and not previously developed.

What are the levels of literacy, experience, judgment, interpretive skills, and business acumen of those that we elect to public office? Are we wise to trust and delegate to them the stewardship of this nation's survival? In our detached approach to citizenship we have watched, passively, as legions of special interest groups attack the system and take what they want; leaving the residue for others.

If we have thought about it at all, most of us have probably labored under the impression that the average level of literacy of the citizens of this country is quite high. High enough, for example, to believe that, if we apply ourselves, we can successfully compete in the new international, world economy; against other developed and developing nations. And we have seemingly assumed that the abilities and performance of our present public and private leaders measure up to those of their predecessors whose stewardship of the American dream left us with this legacy with its many advantages we enjoy as a society.

The fact that we have accepted such assumptions, in spite of conditions in our society, is, in itself, a reflection of our ineptitude at managing our affairs. An alert citizenry might well recognize the problem without the confirmation provided by the Oregon Progress Board study and others like it. But! with the results of that study and some others in front of us, it is incomprehensible that we would still not recognize the magnitude and importance of illiteracy as a problem and its impact on our society.

If a predominate percentage of our work force is at such a low level of educational development and ability, impacts on performance and our economic welfare have to be enormous. A matter deserving our highest priority of concern!

How do we characterize the 95 percent of the people who, according to the Oregon Progress Test, cannot perform elementary tasks, such as:

1. Identify the proper tax form to file from among several referred to in a magazine article, or
2. Determine gain from biweekly vs monthly investments using a savings bond advertisement, or
3. Use a bus schedule to select the appropriate bus for given departures and arrivals.

Are people literate, simply because they can read? Or does the true test of literacy require that people understand what they read and be able to apply it to daily life?

Two interesting definitions appear in the **1989 Edition** of Webster's Encyclopedic Unabridged Dictionary of the English Language.

There we find:

> "literacy—1. the quality or state of being literate, esp. the ability to read and write. 2. possession of an education: *to question someone's literacy.*"

and immediately below that:

> "literacy test", an examination to determine whether a person meets the literacy requirements for voting, serving in the armed forces, etc.; a test of one's ability to read and write."

I must confess that the definition of a "literacy test" intended for use in determining competency to vote and to serve in the armed services catches me a bit by surprise. In my 60 plus years of life, I have never seen a voter challenged and obliged to demonstrate a minimum level of education and knowledge of how our society works, before participating in this very important activity. In my time, the emphasis that has always been to get *everyone* registered so they can vote. If the person is breathing, they can vote. And a corollary policy, if a person is breathing they can run for any office in the land; if they meet the age and citizenship requirements!

A legitimate argument can be made for the concept that a certain level of literacy should be required of people who vote or serve in the armed services. The argument is even more persuasive that such a requirement should be levied on those who would serve us in elected or bureaucratic positions.

But, once again, such an idea would surely be challenged by the reformers among us. Given the warped, presently accepted definition of the words, "civil rights" and "equal opportunity" it is not possible for our society to seek out dedicated, intelligent, competent people for our important work in the public and private arenas. The most depressing aspect of this entire subject is that the titans of public service and private enterprise, quietly acquiesce to the strangulation resulting from such senseless public policy; even to the point where their enterprises fail.

This can lead us to disturbing disclosures as to the competence and trustworthiness of our justice system; especially the Supreme Court. The Justices acceptance and, in fact, sanction of all of this would lead us to believe that in their wisdom:

1.  All of this complies with all aspects of the constitution! It reflects the intent of the folks who wrote our Constitution? That is their job! Creating new rules; new legislation is specifically and intentionally not a part of their position descriptions.
2.  Each justice has carefully considered the requirements for voting and concluded that literacy—the ability to read; knowledge of how our system of government is supposed to work; and continuing knowledge of how well it is working are not necessary for a person to cast an informed, effective ballot. That our system will work even with an illiterate electorate.

If, in fact, they believe the above to be true, they owe it to us more simple souls to state their case, to prove to us that their position has been carefully thought through and that it is correct. If the case they make is not convincing; to us or to themselves, then their subsequent actions, alone or in concert with other government entities, need to respond to "truths" that are supportable.

The idea of questioning the integrity of the Supreme Court might trouble some readers. In an ideal situation that would not be necessary. But! keep in mind that in the Constitution and in the establishment of our government the Judicial Branch and all of its components are "simply" the third of three branches that makes up its total. Equal to the other two! not weaker! not more powerful! but equal. The Supreme Court and the rest of the justice system are staffed with mortals; not Gods. Each of them is guaranteed the same personal rights as you and I! No more! No less! I know most of us forget that! I suspect that most of them do also!

And finally and most importantly, they; all of them work for us. If they don't do the job that must be done; they can and should be replaced! If this system of government is to work—at all—everyone, especially those in highly responsible positions, have to be held accountable for doing the work they are paid to do.

How effective and productive are these elected officials in the work they do for us? In their selection, supervision, and control of the mammoth, ever expanding public work force. Are they spending our money wisely? Are they doing what is necessary to make our governments function? Or are these people a primary reason why these systems are not working?

We need to seek answers to those questions; and follow up with actions that will put us on the path to recovery!

# CHAPTER 12

I am the kind of fellow who is always
willing to give people the benefit of my
inexperience in various lines.

I saw a team of two donkeys stuck
with a heavy load.
I asked the farmer if he had tried
twisting the tails of the donkeys.
He said he knew all about that, and that
he was saving it for the next hill.

**Tom Collins**

The analogy between our situation and that portrayed by Mr. Collins might be quite accurate. Donkeys are characterized in our society as having a *mind of their own*, of not being very intelligent (that may or may not be true), of being stubborn and of generally being more trouble than they are worth. It is said that, "If you want to get a donkey's attention, you have to hit him over the head with a 2" by 4" board. Such action probably would best precede Mr. Collin's, twisting of their tails. In the final analysis, however, the character of these animals is such that we can never be certain of victory in any encounter with them.

Such is the nature of our predicament as we try to resolve some of the issues that plague us. We must not underestimate the difficulty of the job that faces us. The attitudes that must be dealt with, are deeply entrenched. The people we must impact are accustomed to making the rules for *others* to follow; it has been understood for years (decades) that those rules do not apply to them. They are used to having their own way, in all things; not because they are always correct in the positions they take on issues, but simply because they are who they are—king pins? on the wheel of fortune of life in this country. They are accustomed to a high level of respect; given simply in honor of the positions they occupy, not because that respect has been earned by the quality of service they render to the country.

The above statements are generalities, of course. Each characteristic mentioned there and additional points that we will present in what follows, will apply in varying degrees to each individual in the class of actors that is under scrutiny. In the public sector it is appropriate, for us to make such generalities. With few exceptions, it is the *herd instinct*, the actions of the groups that are killing us. It is not a requirement that all social democrats or republican party members of Congress, or in the state legislatures vote alike on all issues; but the exceptions to such solidarity of voting patterns are rare. Such actions do not accurately represent the preferences and best interests of all of the people in the country. They do protect the reputation of each elected member within the party hierarchy. To do otherwise, to vote a personal position, when it is at variance with the party line, would pose serious problems later in their political careers, when their own seniority might qualify them for a committee chairmanship or other position of power in the organization.

Who are these people, these public servants who are systematically **"trashing America"**? What are their real motives? short term? long-term? Do they really understand the myriad of implications, impacts and repercussions that reverberate throughout society, as a result of their actions? do they *just think* they understand; or do they just not care? What is their intelligence quotient, their level of literacy on the basis of the testing and measurement system discussed in the last chapter. Are they able to read and understand the voluminous and complex legislative bills that they are called upon to pass or reject? If they cannot, and it is certain that many (most?) of them cannot, upon what do we base our confidence in their actions? If they have those talents, do they take the time to use them? And do they then vote in accordance with their personal feelings and convictions on the subject or do they throw that aside and submit to the "herd instinct" with their vote.

We know some things about them. So some of what follows will not surprise you. If it does sound new, it is probably because we have not taken the time to put it all together in a way that allows us to see the entire picture; one that gives us a clear perspective of the total situation.

They are obviously people of great egos and substantial ambition. But! what traits, abilities, and experience do they bring to the job? Are they qualified for the jobs? Are they the best qualified people available to us for these important positions? Having accepted the fact that the system is not working, what evidence do we have that will allow us to identify the reason for their failure?—intelligence limitations?—incompetence?—flawed character?—shortage of integrity? honesty? candor? or ? ? ?

We might attack this problem and the above questions using highly technical, management analysis techniques. However, limiting ourselves to such an approach, one that would be beyond the ability of most of our citizens to understand, would carry with it an implied final judgment that the people cannot understand our system of government. That, in turn, leads to a logical conclusion that our concept of, "*government of the people, by the people and for the people*, will not work. That undesirable conclusion is lurking out there. It is one that should be allowed to stand only if we cannot find ways to overcome it.

Our needs will be best served if we utilize a reasoned, logical approach in our discussion. One that will allow everyone to understand and participate; one that will allow everyone to factor in and react to their own perspectives; to arrive at their own decisions. This method is consistent with the idea that a government, of the people, by the people, and for the people can, in fact, work!

Who are these people who are trashing America? Our analysis will focus primarily on the Federal government; it's elected, appointed and bureaucratic elements. Such analysis, comments, and criticism of the federal situation is readily adaptable to the problems at other levels of government. People who look forward to advancing from state and local levels of public jobs to the federal scene, will look to those presently in the federal positions as role models and mentors; and we can expect that they will pattern their efforts, actions, and methodologies after what they see succeeds at the federal level. "Succeeds", as used here relates especially to the all-important consideration in the minds of all of them; the ability to get reelected, reappointed, etc.;—to keep their jobs.

Although we could begin by considering any one of the three branches of the Federal Government, we will start by concentrating our attention on problems associated with the Legislative Branch. It will become apparent that the source of many of the problems throughout the government service can be traced to ill-advised actions there. The Legislative Branch consists of two houses; the House of Representatives and the Senate. It is generally assumed that the founders stipulated in our Constitution that the members of the House of Representatives be reelected every two years; to provide the "*people*" with a means of controlling the actions and direction of their government as the needs and conditions changed year to year; to assure accountability of government to short-term needs. We can understand that from their perspective, they had no doubts but that the "*people*" would actively and energetically avail themselves of the opportunity and responsibility to exercise control over their government.

On the surface, at least, it would appear, that two-year terms achieved the goal of making the House responsive to the "people"; However, a more in-depth examination reveals a flaw in the concept that appears to have been overlooked by the founders. What is really happening, is that the House regularly responds to aggressive demands by small groups of people with special interests. They seem to be unable to separate the special-interest noise (static), from the authentic signals from society that presents the more comprehensive picture of the problems facing the nation. It is not surprising then, that their actions often (usually) are counter productive, creating more problems than they solve. One might conclude that they have never taken the time to sit down together and quietly and thoughtfully decide and agree upon what their real mission should be.

Do you remember the story related in a previous chapter, of the experience David and I shared in our canoe? House of Representative actions are comparable in many ways to those of David. They close their eyes to the big picture and respond to minuscule problems many of which are submitted in highly-charged, emotional presentations. Situations that have a sense of immediacy about them in the minds of a few of their constituents. Their reaction is to one of emotions. One which is blind to the overall, short term impact of their actions and to the long-term future consequences.

A couple of examples that will help us develop a common understanding of what is meant here:

1.  Several months ago one of the committees, of the Congress, took testimony from two mothers who were grieving the deaths of teenage sons.

    One of the boys had been killed in a car accident while delivering pizzas for a pizza parlor. For reasons that were not clear from our media coverage of the hearings, the grieving mother blamed the government and the rest of us for not protecting her son from the circumstances that led to his death; that it was someone else's fault that he had that job and that he lost his life doing it. There was no indication that the boy's employer had broken any specific laws.

    The second boy had been killed while working in the proximity of what was referred to as dangerous machinery. That statement, by itself, raises questions as to the level of understanding of those involved in the process! Anyone who works around machinery of any kind, must understand that all machines can be hazardous and must be used with a great deal of care and respect. Again, for reasons that were not clear, the mother felt that the government and we were responsible for the boy's death. She was pleading for action on the part of the committee, "to prevent similar occurrences in the future."

Of course, we all have feelings of sympathy and concern for families who have suffered such losses. But impulsive action of the federal government that will affect the daily lives and viability of the total population, 250,000,000 million American citizens, in response to such singular instances hardly seems prudent or wise.

But, as a result of the hearings, the committee apparently brought pressure to bear on the people in the Executive Branch, at the Department of Labor. They, in turn, instituted a nationwide, "witch hunt"; an investigative program and crackdown on the broad category of business enterprises that were hiring young people. Many fines of significant size were levied. The government likes fines, it is a convenient, covert way for them to feed additional funds into government coffers. It is logical to assume that large numbers of teenagers lost their jobs. Employers can be expected to do the smart thing in such a case. If hiring teenagers carries that kind of exposure, to punitive damages, resulting from ambiguous laws, they will shift to hiring other unemployed members of the labor force. And our kids take another blow below the belt; one that further impedes their ability to become integrated into society.

2.　The second example gained more publicity. You may have followed it on television and in the hard media. Sara Brady is the wife of Jim Brady, President Reagan's Press Secretary who was gunned down in the same incident in which the president was injured, several years ago. As a result of that incident, she became an activist, determined to get gun-control legislation passed by the U.S. Government.

We all feel concern for the discomfort, pain and suffering that Jim has had to face on his long, difficult road through therapy to whatever level of recovery he will ultimately achieve. And, I suspect many would support a measure that would assure us that such a situation would never again occur. But even the supporters of her proposal did not claim that benefit, if the bill was passed.

On the other hand, government intervention with any kind of gun control laws, faces confrontation with provisions of the Second Amendment to the Constitution. It states: "A well-regulated militia being necessary to the security of the free state, the right of the people to keep and bear arms shall not be infringed." Those words state the case for citizen's rights to own and bear arms; all kinds of firearms, very clearly. Legislative groups at all levels of government are beginning to chip away at those rights by singling out certain types of firearms and making it illegal for citizens to own them. Such regulations are not likely to survive a challenge to the U. S. Supreme Court. If, in fact, the majority of our citizens, support some other position with respect to the ownership of firearms, an amendment of the Constitution is the appropriate way to deal with the issue.

There is nothing about Jim's specific case that would indicate that he, the President, and others would have escaped injury on that fateful day, had her proposed legislation been in place.

Never-the-less, Sara, one person in over 250,000,000 was able to capture the attention of members of Congress, testify before subcommittees and committees; and to ultimately get them to act to place restrictions on firearm ownership and use! This despite the conflict of their action with provisions of the Constitution and the polling information showing it to be in conflict with the desires of the majority of the country's citizens.

I am not a member of the National Rifle Association, but for reasons of my own, I support some of their positions on issues. Are you surprised by the statement that, "our police and justice systems are ineffective; that they simply are not working"? I suspect you are not. In many locations in this country, no one is safe; at home or away. Totally innocent, tiny children, teenagers and adults are randomly killed on a daily basis; in all sorts of scenarios; by drug impresarios, marauding gang members, and others who routinely live outside of the law. No gun-control legislation will take or keep guns away from those people! Gun control is not the answer; its passage will only increase the vulnerability of the law-abiding citizen to the terrorist.

If you are not yet faced with such gruesome, frightful conditions in your community, it would be a mistake to credit your good fortune to the effectiveness of your police and justice system. Instead, recognize that you are just lucky. Be thankful that the criminal element has not moved in and challenged them in your community. When that ultimately happens, the lawless will prevail in your situation, just as they have in other instances.

An example will help to illustrate how all of this relates to you and me. For months during the fall and winter of 1991-1992 people living in a neighborhood on the near-east side of Portland, Oregon suffered persistent, unrelenting vandalism to their property. Vehicles that they had to park outside on their driveways or at the curb were especially vulnerable. Most residents of the area were victimized several times during that period. It was not unusual that individuals would have accumulated hundreds of dollars of damage and loss.

Early one morning, at about 2:00 AM, a man who lived in that neighborhood heard a noise outside his bedroom window. When he looked out the window he saw two young men systematically vandalizing his vehicles and those of his neighbors. For reasons that will become more clear as we proceed with the story, his first thought was not to dial 911 and get the police out on the case. Instead he picked up his shot gun and went out to confront the perpetrators. In the process of trying to escape, one of the boys found himself trapped in the neighbor's, fenced back yard. His only avenue of escape was to run toward and past, in very close proximity to, the property owner with his gun. In such a situation, it is not possible for the person protecting his property to know whether or not the criminals are armed. More likely than not, they are. Not knowing for sure, what he faced, the property owner fired his gun as the intruder ran toward him—and the young boy was killed.

Of course, the situation captured the attention of the community, the media followed developments closely. Officials of the local police and justice systems immediately lunged into the discourse, telling the people of the entire area that they should not take such situations into their own hands. They stressed that in such situations, victims should call and report the situation to the authorities at 911. Such advice was always accompanied by assurance that the police would respond immediately to calls. The whole event was ultimately reviewed by a Grand Jury and the property owner was not charged.

Now lets move a few weeks later to February 24, 1992, when the details of another case in that same general area were described in a column by Phil Sanford, a columnist for the Portland Oregonian daily newspaper. He introduced this situation as a satirical example of the outstanding effectiveness of the "Community Policing" procedures practiced by the Portland police and many other departments throughout the country.

A lady and her husband owned a small business known as the Dragonfly Gardens. They specialized in selling high quality perennial, bamboos, bonsai, herbs, etc.

Shortly after they opened in February 1987 the place was burglarized; they lost about $400 worth of material. Two fellows, one of them a state employee, were caught and convicted of the theft. Soon after the first instance, the business was hit again. Regular attacks continued, occurring about every six weeks. In each case, the average loss of merchandise was about $600. In each instance owners also faced bills of about $800 to repair the chain-link fence; where the intruders went through it to gain entrance to the property. Early on in this episode, when a break-in was discovered, the owners notified the police and they actually sent an officer out to the property. A bit later, when the owners reported new attacks, the only police response was to send out forms for the owners to fill out and return to the police. And then! a short time later even that was discontinued; the police seemingly ignored the reports; from the owners' perspective there was no response by the police.

In September 1990, the establishment was hit three times; in October 1990 twice, and then on both December 9th and 10th, 1990. The December 10th hit was calculated to be the 40th time the property had been burglarized. We can all relate to this situation. What is a citizen to do in such a case? Why do we have laws, expensive police forces and massive, expensive mazes of justice facilities and personnel; if not to protect law-abiding citizens who are trying to do the right thing and get along? What is a victim to think? to do? What is the message being sent out to the public by their expensive protective services organization? There would appear to be only two alternatives: simply give in to the perpetrators and suffer the losses; or take the matter into your own hands and do what you have to!

I could have forgiven these people, if they had picked up their shot gun and taken care of the problem, themselves. But! they were more patient and far more inventive! After a few telephone calls, the lady owner was able to contact an acquaintance of hers who was a member of a local motorcycle gang. She asked if that group would be willing to patrol their property every night, along with several others in the area for which the gang was already providing such service. It was agreed that the Dragonfly would be included in their patrols. The end-result was interesting and telling. Phil reported that on a few occasions the patrol caught pairs of would-be burglars and they gave them a choice. They could go back where they came from and tell their friends not to come around this property anymore; or, something was going to happen to their knees and teeth. ABRA KA DABRA, a miracle happened, the December 10th break-in was the last of the costly string of burglaries suffered by the business.

It would be a shame not to learn all that we can from such a situation. It is interesting to learn that there is a language that even the criminals understand and respond to! It would seem that problems such as this can be handled without violence. But, that is not likely to happen until the people demand the protection they are paying for and that they deserve. It also seems obvious that it will not happen as a result of the efforts of our present police and justice systems; stymied as they are by rapidly expanding reams of nebulous laws; legions of attorneys lapping at the public trough; and unlimited dollars to fund all of the costs of undirected, senseless, unending prosecution and defense procedures. Continuing public criticism of and attacks on the police, who may get a bit rough as they deal with dangerous, habitual perpetrators of crimes against the public is not helpful.

I am not able to comprehend why some of our friends and fellow citizens are willing to work for us in such perilous, thankless activities as they encounter in police work. But, I am thankful and appreciative that they are. And I will support them as long as they continue to serve the needs of the people.

On the other hand, if it gets to the point where police positions can no longer be filled, or where the justice system becomes totally ineffective (it doesn't have far to go!) we all need to look at the alternatives available to us. Hiring your local motorcycle gang may be one good answer! Assuming the responsibility of protecting your own family and property may be another. One thing is perfectly clear; the founders of this country, the writers of the Constitution, and those hardy patriots who have preceded us in the two hundred-year history of this country never wavered in their determination that the rights of the people should not, will not, be sacrificed to a lawless element of society.

If dogs or wild animals severely injure or kill people or damage their property, the animals are hunted down and destroyed. Animals act from instinct; they don't know right from wrong. A good case could be made for less severe reprisal against them. On the other hand, humans who engage in such destructive, lawless activity, knowingly and continually; understand what they are doing. There is a limit beyond which society should be expected to mollycoddle and tolerate such people who routinely and intentionally live outside the law in such violent ways. Our present practice is to put them away "in storage" *for the rest of their lives*. And then they are released back into society at some future date, only to repeat their offensive activity over and over again. In addition to the heavy burden of pain and suffering that our present practice places on the innocent of society, it also results in a staggering financial burden for all of us to bear. It costs millions of dollars for trials, the taxpayer usually is stuck with the attorney's fees for both the prosecution and the defense. Those incarcerated often receive medical care that is superior to that available to many law-abiding citizens on the outside. I remember reading, not long ago, about a person serving a life sentence for a series of murders, who was provided with bypass heart surgery. And all the while law-abiding citizens of limited means cannot afford that and a multitude of other medical procedures. And, they expire for lack of treatment of frailties that are routinely treated successfully in our health-care system today. Statistics show that the normal yearly costs of confining each individual in our prisons systems is $30,000 to $50,000. The heavy financial burden of maintaining the present tens or hundreds of thousands of such persons in our prisons buys nothing of lasting benefit to society. And still, legislators everywhere are passing new laws, ad infinitum, intent upon capturing more and more persons in their webs, for committing what they consider to be undesirable actions. At a time when our prisons are overflowing, when those in charge of such facilities find it necessary to release convicted felons just to make room for new, incoming captives; it is foolish to be enacting new laws and regulations that will compound the overcrowding situation with people whose violations are of little adverse consequence to society. Such action certainly poses valid questions as to the level of intelligence we employ in the public sector.

At some point in time we must come to realize that this country cannot afford to do anything and everything it wants to do. We will then be forced to establish priorities on spending. And we will come to realize that all of that money going to support criminals could be used much more wisely by providing medical and a variety of other services to needy, law-abiding citizens.

Of course, the "Era of Emotional Idiocy" fuels perpetuation of President Lyndon Johnson's "Great Society" myth, that a country as rich as ours can afford to do anything and everything it wants to do. Four and one half trillion dollars of Federal debt later, it seems logical that any "thinking American" would question his position!

The point of all of this is this; there are things that can be done to substantially decrease the intensity and cost of criminal activity in this country. Gun control is not one of them. The country may not yet be ready to adopt the severe practices that are required to do the job. In the meantime, innocent, law-abiding citizens will continue to pay the price with their lives and with pain and suffering of injuries until the general population gets fed up; until we all reach the point that we are no longer willing to accept a class of citizenship inferior to that accorded the criminal element in our midst. In the event that does not happen, and society continues to abdicate its responsibility to protect the innocent; the ability of the individual to possess arms for the protection of himself and his family becomes an all-important "right"!

Cases such as this demonstrate one very important flaw in the operation of the Legislative Branch. It is their proclivity to micro manage. The above ladies who gained access to the seat of power for whatever reason, are but three of the 250,000,000 of us. That their cases might be presented in letters to their senator or representative is understandable. That their positions warrant full blown exposure to legislative committees, and that the committees would act upon their requests is not. The success of such efforts has resulted in massive numbers of "crusaders" for all kinds of very narrow minded causes.

At a time when our economy is falling down around us, thousands of people are losing their jobs weekly, our major industries are being displaced by foreign suppliers, the balance of trade is a serious problem, the national debt is skyrocketing, etc. etc.; our legislators have more important work to do. It did not come as a total surprise to learn recently that one of those auspicious committees was busy holding hearings on PMS, Post Menstrual Syndrome! Is there no limit to the knowledge and abilities of the people we put in these important positions?

The Constitution called for Senators to be reelected every six years. This provision along with the requirement that most legislative actions be approved by both houses of the legislature was obviously designed to provide some continuity and stability in the direction taken by the government.

It seems useful to take a minute and portray character attributes that are important to us in those that represent us in these important elected, legislative offices. To set the stage for doing that in a meaningful way, let me suggest a test each of us should take just prior to going to the polls to vote people into political office. Take each name that you have decided to vote for, and ask yourself this question:

> "Do I trust this person enough, have enough faith in his/her knowledge, ability, judgment, and integrity that I "feel easy" about handing him or her a book of my blank personal checks, signed at the bottom, with instructions that they are free to use the checks on anything that meets their "needs" test?"

Would you feel comfortable doing that with everyone you vote for? Does that sound like a reasonable arrangement? Or is it a scary suggestion?

Whether or not you hand them the checks, this is exactly the power that we delegate to our public servants. They go off to Washington, your state capitol, the court house or the city hall and they spend your money. Their actions result in tax liabilities that are taken off the top of your income; you get what is left after *all* of the demands they create are satisfied. There was a time when public servants understood and respected the intimacy and importance of their relationship with their constituents.

How many of your public servants meet that test today? My answer? None! Of course this line of reasoning exposes a major problem that we all face when we go to the polls. We find ourselves in a position of necessarily voting for many candidates whose abilities and integrity do not meet our standards. It is not an unusual situation when none of those on the ballot meet our criteria. And, we are forced to vote for the unqualified candidates that most nearly meets our criteria.

This is a major handicap in our system. There is a simple solution. If I, as an individual voter, feel that none of the candidates for a position are qualified, I should have the option of voting for, "None of the Above". "None of the Above" would be an option on the ballot with every position listed. A candidate, to be elected, would have to receive 50 percent plus one of the votes cast for that position. If no one received that majority of the vote, that position would be left open until the next election cycle; or a special election would be held. Given the authority we delegate to the people we put into these positions, leaving a position open is preferable to putting unqualified, ineffective or dishonest persons in them.

We are all aware of the big push presently enjoying great popularity with the social-democrats, at all levels of government, for "*health care for everyone*". The **emotional tug** of such a proposal in an **era of emotional idiocy** is immediately obvious to all of us. The type of medical program being championed resembles many others around the world that are known by the name, "socialized medicine". Why is it not called that here? A strong probability is that the self-interests of elected and bureaucratic public servants dictates their prolonging the deception of our people as long as possible, perpetuating their belief that ours is a democratic, free-market society. The longer they can delay the awareness and acknowledgement of socialism here; the more social programs they can pass and put into operation; the more people they can get *under the spell*—that the government can and must do everything for them; the more people that come to believe that *the government* owes it to them; the better are their chances of bringing a system of total socialism to the country!

It is unfortunate, but true, that the longer people live under the umbrella of government care, the more doubtful they become about their own abilities. For most persons involved, the ultimate impact of long-term dependency on government support, is loss of self-confidence and self-esteem to the point that the concept of being able to support themselves dims! And they give up on the effort to do so.

Of course, socialized medicine is not a new idea; it has been around for a long time. It has been (is being) tried in a number of countries; and it has essentially failed in all of them. Will such a program work for us? If it is intimated that it will work here, in the United States, how are conditions here different from those in places like Sweden, Canada, etc. where it is not working? Where its enormous costs are inundating the economy and the ability of the people to pay for it; and where the demand for medical services severely out strips availability. Where patient's needs are queued onto waiting lists and they must often wait months or even years for many kinds of surgery and/or treatment for life threatening conditions; or the kinds of ailments that respond best to immediate attention. That dream of "health care for everyone", that spurs our emotions, becomes a myth. It loses much of its allure if it cannot provide us with the, "when needed—as needed" health care presently available to most of us. People who die waiting for health care that will eventually be available are just as dead as are people who die because the service is not available due to its cost! A major difference is that the delay inherent in the socialized medicine scenario affects everyone. In so many people's minds that seems to be so much more fair; those who can pay for the service die, "waiting" just like and in the same proportion as those who cannot pay. Never mind that the total number of deaths in the country for any given period of time will probably be greater than it is under our present system. When everyone has to wait, many will die who could have been saved by immediate treatment.

How much will this program cost the nation? Each one of us? How will it be paid for? (Will it be paid for?) Why is it that the costs and a method of paying for it are not a part of the discussions and debate of the issue? The program "sells" so much better when "costs are ignored!

What evidence is there that under such a program, medical treatment for the nation will be better than it is now? Worse than it is now?

The irony of this situation is that we can observe, even at these early phases of implementation of such a plan that trying to provide health service to everyone; will probably jeopardize our ability to provide acceptable health service to anyone. This is especially true if "yellow socialism" continues to dominate the nation's program planning and implementation. The logic of this is so obvious. One has to wonder, does all of this go over the heads of our leaders? can they read these signals? do they understand their significance? or are they so wrapped up in the emotional aspects of the situation that all of this eludes them?

It is no secret that most elected officials have little or no knowledge or experience in any of the many and diverse fields of endeavor for which they now become "top management"; the board of directors, so to speak, for a city, a county, a state, or the United States. By their own admission, most of them, on the occasion of their first election to office would confess that they do not consider themselves to be experts on any of what they will encounter on the new job. The attainment of expertise in the work, comes with time; it takes some longer than others to gain this expertise. The length of time that it takes is often more a function of the egotism and arrogance of the individual than it is a function of the true intelligence and ability of the individual.

Many of them are relatively young, this may be the first job they have ever had. Some are college graduates, some are not. Saying that is not intended to imply that the college graduate is better qualified than the non graduate. The true meaning of having a college education in today's society is a bit blurred. In earlier times, institutions of higher learning worked toward legitimate, defensible goals of teaching young people, "how to think"; to be objective, to identify and prioritize alternatives. They exposed them to the concepts and application of logic, analysis and problem solving. And they, then sent them out into the world; a new light, a new mind, a new perspective and new insights into what they encountered there. And the country prospered!

But, in so many instances, that system has been replaced by one that sits idly by, while the minds of the students in *our* colleges and universities are impregnated with the biases and warped perspectives of the faculty and the staff they encounter there during this very vulnerable time of their lives. They are taught what to think; not how to think. And instead of bright lights and new beginnings the graduates bring forth characteristics and concepts of kamikaze pilots, blind to the multitude of alternatives available, and determined to blindly pursue and to further the cause(s) of their mentors!

The credit for failure of our system should not be unduly assigned to young persons in the political arena. There is plenty of credit to go around. Advanced age of participants may equate to better qualifications; but that is not always the case.

A notable example of this phenomenon, is a grandmotherly type person, who is presently about half way through her first, two-year term in the House of Representatives of one of the states in the pacific northwest. During her campaign, she claimed, as pertinent management experience, having had at one time a position of some responsibility with the Campfire Girls or the Girl Scouts. She now has two or three actual months on the job, this is a part-time legislature. With this experience has come great wisdom and confidence. Her letters to constituents, letters to the editors, and point-of-view articles in the media, leave little doubt that, at least in her mind, she has attained a high level of expertise in the affairs-of-state in her state; a state with an annual budget that exceeds $10 billion. In the articles she speaks out boldly and expertly? on complex matters; she presents her authoritative position on all issues; she freely criticizes other experienced legislators, especially those whose position differs from her's; and *she votes solidly and consistently with the social-democrats of the institution who were so instrumental in getting her elected.*

It goes without saying that any system, including systems of government, will fail if it's management complexity and demands exceed the knowledge, experience, ability and competence of people available to do that job. What is not so obvious, as it applies to public service, is that massive, complex systems also require a total work force with higher than normal capabilities in many professional, white collar and blue collar specialties. It is also not so obvious, that a democratic, market-oriented, free-enterprise system of government, requires a "match" of sorts, between the complexity of the operation and the educational achievement level of the general population. Proper operation of a governmental system that depends upon the knowledgeable, active and effective participation of the general population, requires that the people be able to discern on a continuing basis how well their governmental systems are working. What is so easily attributed to submissive, uncaring neglect by our citizens in meeting their responsibilities of citizenship, may very well be the result of their inability to understand the world around them and to make rational decisions when or "if" they go to the voting booth. Whether their inability to perform is due to the complexity of the system or a deficiency of the education provided them, is of little consequence. In our case, ineffectiveness of public participation is probably due to both factors. This is one area where the malfunction of our public school systems may be having massive and serious adverse impacts on the nation far beyond what has previously been understood.

Some understanding of this relationship between the educational level of the people and the complexity of the system of government, calls into question the intelligence, logic and the sense of our leader's efforts to prejudice those nations whose previous form of government did not work; toward the democratic, free-enterprise form that we *profess to have*. If we have such a high level of confidence in our *alleged* system, why are we so aggressively moving to cast it aside; to be replaced with one comparable to those that failed them? And, why are we trying to convince them to use the system we are rejecting?

Although the democratic, free-market system of government worked well for us for a long time, our government today is being methodically violated by incompatible actions. If our system is not good enough for us, why do we recommend it to others? And why are other important considerations, such as the ability of the people to understand and participate effectively; hidden from the people of the U. S. A., as the system is covertly changed?

The governmental systems developing in the transitional nations have one important advantage over the U. S. They are not constrained by a 200-year accumulation of legislative intervention and strangulation. As newly evolving systems, they will be more simple and unimposing. As a result, the people will be more able to understand and participate effectively. That may also be part of the reason why our early experience in governing ourselves was more successful than it has been more recently. The complexity of our system has grown to the point that it defies understanding by anyone! A point that, once recognized; can and should be a part of any plan of corrective action.

On the one hand, these servants of ours operate as individuals. But the true measure of their genuine contribution to the best interests of the country is directly related to their performance as institutions. Knowledge of the subject; identification and objective deliberation of the alternatives; give and take debate; reaching majority decisions that do not compromise the best interests of the country; and finally supporting that decision even though it is not everything an individual had hoped for are all required of the participants if the system is to succeed.

So! how have they performed, are they performing, as a group? Please carefully consider that question on the basis of the success or failure of the programs that control your lives.

Take some time to think about this; make a list of the actions they have taken or programs they have implemented that from, your perspective are achieving the best possible results; a list of those that are not achieving everything that they might; and finally a list of those that are, in your mind, actually working to our detriment, as individuals and as a nation.

This deliberation can begin to point up some interesting observations. The defeat of Judge Robert Bork, and the later close vote of approval for Judge Clarence Thomas in their quests to become members of the Supreme Court would seem to imply that a large number of our Senators believe that our legal system, as it has evolved from the service of Chief Justice Earl Warren and his liberal associates and disciples, is doing a good job! Many of them have been willing to have the court act in a legislative manner; deciding cases on the basis of what they, the judges, believe is best for the country—as long as the biases presented by such decisions were compatible with their own. They strongly resist return of the court to its original intended mode of operation—to interpret the application of the Constitution to today's problems and to interpret the intent of the Legislative Branch, as the cases before them relate to the laws enacted there.

It is difficult to comprehend how anyone could view the present nature of our society, with its wide spread violence, the vanishing values of morality and ethics, the inability of society to deal effectively with trouble makers and criminals, the drift of our society from one representing the wishes and desires of the majority of the citizens to one dedicated to surrender to the loud, largely emotional, generally uninformed, undisciplined, and uncompromising demands of small, special-interest groups.

# CHAPTER 13

We live in puzzling, illogical and irrational times. As we individually and collectively go about our business day after day, week after week, year after year, it is impossible for anyone with any sensitivity and intellect, to be unaware that all is not well in our little corner of the world! Of course, there will always be a segment of the population who will go along in their world of little dreams, blind to situations that threaten their affluent, comfortable "way of life". But! it should be reasonable for the rest of us to assume that at some point; the symptoms of trouble that emerge from the system will become so obvious that a majority of the voting public would recognize them. And, that most of them would make the extension of logical thought to the point of realizing that "life in Camelot" may be available, only to those who are smart enough, ambitious enough, and dedicated enough; those who cherish it enough to voluntarily and aggressively do what is necessary to preserve it.

In looking at our situation closely, we can begin to understand the importance of interpersonal relationships in a free society such as ours. When we get to the point that we finally recognize that we are in trouble; important additional questions immediately arise. One important one being, "how our present conditions compare with those ten years ago? twenty years ago? thirty years ago? etc. What is the trend? short-term? long-term? Are things getting better? or are they getting worse?

In a society where the teaching of national history in the public schools is not considered to be especially important, members of the younger

---

[12]    Dan Valentine's, "Spirit of America" American Essays No. 9 Copyright 1972

generations will be unable to effectively deal with such questions. That places all the more burden on those of us who are old enough to remember. It also places a premium on the ability of all of our citizens to span generation gaps; the willingness of young and old to relate to each other, to communicate clearly and accurately, information that paints a true, unbiased picture for the younger persons.

We are not alluding here to the trite, hackneyed expressions that often flow from the elders to the youth; about "the good old days". Persons who are not at least approaching their 30th birthdays; will find it difficult, if not impossible, to join us in making a comparison of the world we lived in twenty years ago, say 1970 and our world today. Most of them were not there, in 1970. Many that were there, were of an age that precluded their ability to comprehend in an analytical way the world around them.

But beyond that it is important to realize that, if by some magical way, we could allow them to experience those days; they still would probably reach different conclusions than would most of their elders.

As I sit writing this on March 5, 1992, on an IBM compatible personal computer with word processing, I and millions like me who own such equipment are facing tomorrow with some trepidation. The threat is that thousands, or possibly millions of IBM compatible machines have been infected by the Michelangelo virus. It is, supposedly, keyed to strike havoc into the lives of owners of the machines tomorrow; Michelangelo's 600th birthday. The threat is that the virus will systematically destroy the contents of the magnetic disks in those machines infected by it. For most of us, the presence or absence of the virus; where or when it might have gotten into our machines and the possible total amount of damage are not known. Most of us will not take advantage of the availability of software that will identify its presence and eliminate it, if it is there.

So, too, it is with our people. Each of them is a product of the environment in which they reside, their experiences and what they are taught by parents, friends, associates, teachers, and all others with whom they come into contact. If the full truth and impact of this concept were known; we, as parents, grandparents, or just people who care, would surely not be so complacent and passive about what happens in our public school systems, on our streets, on our television sets, in theaters, etc. And, parents of young children would not be nearly so willing to thrust their infant, preschool and elementary age youngsters into institutionalized settings where their primary source of learning will be their peers. What they hear there and whatever seeps into their minds, as a result of all of these relationships and experiences will lie there as part of their being; and will, when the opportunities present themselves, influence their thoughts and actions, in positive and negative ways, on matters great and small!

Unlike the situation with the Michelangelo virus, it is very difficult to identify, with any degree of certainty, the presence of such frailties and influences, good and bad; abilities and inabilities, that make up the psyche of a human being. In the important matters of literacy and quality of education, where reliable testing is available, it is customary for public educational systems to resist using available test systems. The results of such tests threaten the job security of the administrative and staff employees of the systems involved. They hold enough power to force their will onto the communities. And, passive parents and the general public fail to intervene and force corrective action!

In this light, the problems we are presently encountering should not be a total surprise. The following information is quoted from an article in the Vaughn Street Journal in June 1980.

\* = \* = \* = \* = \* = \* = \* = \* = \* = \* = \* = \* = \* = \* = \* = \* = \*= \*= \*

## ADOLESCENT VIEWS MIGHT OPEN YOUR EYES—WIDE!

Results of a recent study by the Opinion Research Institute of Princeton University reveal some interesting, perhaps frightening, attitudes among high school students.

— So much for the free market, 82 percent polled think there is not need for competition in business. Added to that, 53 percent feel government should do more business regulating.
— Fully 40 percent were at a loss to name any advantage capitalism holds over communism. A rousing 67 percent don't believe there is a need for profit in business.
— Some of the other results:

    — 63 percent favor government ownership and operation of banks, railroads, and steel companies.
    — 62 percent believe the government is responsible to provide jobs.
    — 61 percent think employees should not produce all they are capable of.

— 56 percent of the females interviewed had "no opinion" as to whether government should take over industry.
— 55 percent think the best way to improve standards of living is to increase wages without increasing production or prices.
— 50 percent thought government contributes most to national prosperity.
— 30 percent of the males interviewed had "no opinion" as to whether government should take over industry.

\* = \* = \* = \* = \* = \* = \* = \* = \* = \* = \* = \* = \* = \* = \* = \*= \*= \*

Where do you suppose those young people are today. We can imagine that many of them have gone on through the public school system, obtained teaching certificates; and are now teaching today's generation of learners. And, in the process, viruses of another kind find their way into the minds of our people. They perpetuate themselves there, and become a part of the thinking process—the psyche—of future generations of Americans, lying in wait to impact, in their own ways, the future destiny of this nation!

In 1945 Dr. Spock published his book, "A Common Sense Book Of Baby and Child Care". Anyone who has faced the challenges of becoming parents of young children knows something of the apprehension, possibly bordering on panic, that many new parents feel. The awesome responsibility, the lack of experience and specific knowledge, and the intense desire to do the job right—to assure that "your" child will have every possible opportunity to succeed in life!

His book was one of the first efforts of ordinary people to "sell" themselves as "experts" in rearing children. The value of his book, to new parents and to our society, would have been greatly enhanced if he had limited his advice to matters in which he had some expertise; such as diet, physical development of the child, and possible medical problems that might be encountered along the way as the child grows and matures. But, of course, that was not what happened. Throughout the book, we encounter the presentation of fatherly (godly?), authoritative, statements and advice relative to the control and direction of the mental development of children. The author acknowledges that prior to the implementation of the reforms suggested in his book new parents looked to their own experiences as children, and the methods used by their parents as a major resource in developing their own parenting skills. But, references in the book that press new parents toward acceptance and use of his "new" concepts are abundant. There are clear implications that his newly recommended methods are proven and that they will achieve superior results in the quality of new persons and citizens emanating from the system. If it had been taken and implemented in moderation, his proposed program might have resulted in substantially different results over the long-term. That did not happen. Many of the young parents of that time, and in the intervening years, accepted the new theories totally. His book and ideas enjoyed a level of sacred respect in many homes that exceeded that reserved for the Holy Bible. And, of course, legions of other "self proclaimed" **experts** have added their "straw-house" pronouncements to the liturgy of the parenting field.

Having been an active participant in the rearing of two children, the old way; and having been a critical, involved observer in the rearing of several generations of other American youth; I confess that I do not consider myself an "expert" in the field! That has led me, on occasion, to the question, "What does it take to become an expert in this field?" The answer that seems to come back to me is that, "They learn it from books, *written by other experts.*

Most of us can relate to this issue. Those who have succeeded in raising their children to be self-sufficient, motivated, loving, caring, responsible citizens, using the "old methods" would not profess to be experts! They are more inclined to recognize their own frailties and to thank the good lord for the encouragement and support he gave them along the way. Parents who have raised their children, especially those who have worked closely with more than one child; will understand and testify to the vast differences in personality; and in physical and mental needs of any two children—even those of the same parentage, and in the same family environment.

Of course, not all young parents fell for the emotional lure of expert, "fool proof", parenting methodologies; but many did. And still do! Existence of the Era of Emotional Idiocy; the trend to react to emotional tug and ignore conclusions reached as a result of your own personal logical, intellectual considerations; greatly increased the amount of acceptance of the "expert" advice.

Anyone who has been around young children to observe and ponder the wide diversity of their interests, demands and behavior; would rise to question the ability of any human being, even one that calls herself/himself an "expert", to provide advice that would accommodate all of those differences, and still be able to generate positive results in the development of every one of the millions of children in this country and around the world; including your own?

This country faced its first major, organized, undisciplined, unprincipled problem with its young people in the early and middle 1960's. It probably is not an accident that those young people represent the first generation to grow up with many of their numbers having been raised under the tutelage of these experts and their theories. It does not require any stretch of the imagination to suppose that there is a direct relationship between the training they received and the problems they have caused; are causing.

The evidence of the 1960's and the behavior of some members of subsequent generations of our youth who have matured under the direction of these people and their programs raises substantial questions: Are their theories helpful? does their program bring about positive results? or is it indicated that it is a sham—that better results can be achieved by instinctive, conscientious, family-oriented direction and management of the child rearing activity? Experience dictates that those questions need to be pursued more aggressively; suggesting the need for a comprehensive, intellectual examination of that whole field.

The force of the powerful promotion activities, used in "selling" you on the idea of using their advice, methods and programs in rearing your children, relies heavily on emotional coercion; exploiting the relationship between you and your children. Their approach being something like this, "If you really care for your children, you will surely do what is best for them! You need to come to us for advice and assistance in rearing them! We have the answers to your many weighty questions." Never lose sight of the fact that it has not yet been proven that their methods do not cause more problems than they solve. And, further that you, as parents and a family, can probably do the job much more successfully without external intervention.

If study of this field led to nothing more than "truth in labeling" requirements, that would be a big improvement. Lacking serious study of the effectiveness of such "expert" involvement, we find government officials assuming that their involvement is constructive. And, through legislation, they force elements of the program on all parents, even those who have wisely rejected their use.

Yet another example of a foolish, arrogant, adventure of government use of power and loss of control!

Our governments have demonstrated clearly, their inability to effectively do most of the things that they have attempted. It should not be necessary for us to suffer through yet one more of their experiments to prove that they have nothing constructive to contribute to the process of rearing our children. The best results occur when that job is left to the family; mothers and fathers relying on their instincts, and reacting to their mutual love for all members of the family. Any government intrusions on this scene is only detrimental; it detracts from the overall success of the effort!

Assured absence of outside intrusion into the rearing of their children will help parents to understand the totality of their responsibility in this important function. That realization may have an impact on their decisions for establishing priorities for themselves and their families.

The future holds no promise or hope for a population that places service in the work place, with its fleeting position and prestige; above personal relationships, especially those in the family. That a government of supposedly educated people would become so proactive as to lure its citizens into the work place, away from dedication to family and interpersonal relationships, and responsibilities is beyond my comprehension;—it is unforgivable! But it is a common event in our society today!

I will never forget the shock I felt a few months ago when I encountered the message emblazoned in large letters across the front page of the magazine section of a local Sunday newspaper. There, for all to see was a statement that so eloquently displayed the sorry state of affairs that now exists in some activities in this country.

## WHO WILL CARE FOR OUR CHILDREN?

And a major part of the magazine was devoted to a lot of diatribe about the terrible problem we face with the shortage of child-care facilities, etc., etc., that dominates the attention of so many during these crazy times! **This is the discourse of a literate society? ? ? ?**

Can you imagine how much hell would be raised if our government forced young parents to put their children into state-funded day-care centers so they could be nurtured and reared to government specifications?

And yet, as long as it is their idea; to do so in the pursuit of ownership of big, expensive cars; to live in big houses; to belong to country clubs; to be a member of the "in" crowd; to live the great life; it's OKAY! ! !

During the latter years of my career, I occupied demanding, executive positions with responsibility for managing several hundred people and programs involving hundreds of millions of dollars per year. The load was burdensome, but I still made time to work with the Boy Scouts of America, my son's troop, and I devoted time to our family activities.

There are unstructured ways that word of those kinds of activities is communicated to your many associates in the work place and in the community. The people around you know of your interests, your activities, your work ethic, and your dedication. That is one of the ways you are judged in leadership roles!

Many of the people that worked for me were older than I was. I'll always remember several of the things that happened to me in such circumstances. Two are pertinent to this discussion.

I always operated with an "open-door" policy. Employees were encouraged to discuss with me problems or opportunities for improvement in our operation. On two different occasions, older gentlemen, who reported to me, came into the office, closed the door and, with tears in their eyes, each essentially said, "Harry, you will never be sorry that you took the time to work with, and get to know your son during these busy years of your life; years which are also important, formative years in his development. I did not do that when my boy was that age. Now he has grown up and is out on his own. I am trying to make up for that lapse now, but there just is no way to make it happen! We seem to have lost that opportunity forever. Realization of that fact devastates to me!"

With the passing of the years, my relationship with my son, Eric; my daughter, Deborah; Rosalee, my wife; and our extended family are enriched. The truth of the words of those two associates become more and more evident.

My fear, and the reason I have discussed this here, is that those of you who are progressing through that stage of life, may not have the good fortune of having friends or associates who will call this critical situation to your attention. And, like my two associates you will miss the opportunity to develop and share these glorious relationships! Once lost, the chance to recover seldom presents itself. Please don't let that happen to you!

# CHAPTER 14

It was just three years ago that I first sat down to begin writing this treatise. In the beginning I was spurred on by a perception that the government(s) of this nation were not working. The functional paralysis suffered there seemed to me to pose a serious problem. Few of our citizens were concerned about it to the point that it was being discussed publicly; there was little, if any, concentrated, aggressive effort within the establishment to identify and implement corrective action. Indications were that "the people" who, in our system (a government *of the people, by the people, and for the people*), must be held accountable for such negligence and failure, were asleep; they lacked the intellect to comprehend the gravity of the situation, or they did understand it and they just plain did not care!

Emphasis in the early chapters was focused on trying to awaken the people of the country; to challenge them to look at the "world around them" more critically; and if this focus of their attention resulted in their increased concern; to stimulate them to constructive action that would benefit us as individuals and as a nation.

The disparity between writing about this type of evolving, real-time subject, as contrasted to writing fiction or about historical theses was not considered to be a major problem at the time the work was begun. Writers of fiction and historical works do not face the kind of evolution and changing scenarios that have been encountered here. The subject matter; in the case of fiction, emanates from the mind of the author: in the case of historical themes, it is fixed in time and place by the events that occurred during the era being covered. This consideration, combined with the "mine field" of irrational liability laws praying upon the people of this nation helps explain why prospective writers here, today, usually choose to present their subjects in thinly veiled, theoretically fictional ways.

Much of the information presented here, has been available in some form in mass media offerings. However, collection from those sources requires more time than the average working person in our society can devote to such an effort. It also requires that time and effort be exerted to identify and to eliminate the self-serving, personal and organizational biases that have become an unfortunate, inherent part of the offerings of the mass media as it reports the "news" to us. It is, the intent here, that we attack the situation, "head on". That we analyze, translate, and present the results of such an effort in a reasoned, logical, easy-to-read form; for your perusal, in establishing your own contribution to solving our problems.

The nature of this work, results in it containing perceptions, ideas, interpretations and tentative conclusions of the author. With that in mind it is appropriate, to remind the reader, once again, that this approach is used because it is thought that it will best stimulate the, "target population"—out there—to become involved in thinking through the many issues discussed. It will do this where the reader tends to agree with the information and conclusions presented; it will do so even more effectively where the tendency is for the reader to disagree, in part or in total.

That we all agree, at this stage of consideration on all of this, is not to be expected. What is important, is that a large segment of the voting public give careful, honest, in-depth attention to our problems; that we find a practical way to communicate with each other; that such communication and debate can be achieved in an objective, intelligent, respectful, forgiving, and constructive format. That in this activity we will be able to rationalize that each of us will need to sacrifice some of the benefits that we have been receiving; in the interest of achieving a more secure, acceptable future for all of us! We must all work to maintain more thoughtful, caring relationships with each other; to identify and pursue issues that are truly important at the national level; and to intelligently push aside and ignore highly-charged, emotional, destructive debate on issues of lesser moment. One can only imagine what other people of the world think of us as they view this ongoing spectacle. Everyone talking at the same time, no one listening to the other's thoughts, and absolutely no tolerance for opposing points of view.

Is this how civilized people solve problems? Is this an accurate representation of the personal ability and the character of the citizens of this country? Is it an accurate indication of the limits imposed upon us by the growing threat of illiteracy in this country? Isn't it perfectly clear in this heated debate, as in any serious disagreement, that everyone cannot possibly gain everything they want from the confrontation? Isn't it clear that such divisiveness is poison to the country; and that we must move on to more important things? Not that long ago, the country was buffeted by arguments related to the Equal Rights Amendment; another issue that involved the question of expanding the special rights for the women of this country; even beyond what they already enjoyed. There is a lesson that needs to be learned here. These distractions of the national attention away from items of genuine significance to our national interest; to issues that are inconsequential, nationally; has coincided with our inane surrender to increased involvement of feminists in policy-level, decision making in our society. Where women are put into important positions, not because they are qualified for the job; but, just because they are women; quotas are sacred, they must be met!

Such instances of national stress are not an accident; they occur as the result of a divisive program being pressed by a part of our female population, who are willing, in fact, anxious to do anything and everything they can to improve their own circumstances at the expense of the rest of us.

My original assumption, as I began this work, was that the subject being discussed, the relationship between the people of this country and their governments would be stable enough that we could discuss issues and press for citizen involvement on a "real time" basis. In normal times that may have been possible; but these last three years (1989-1992) have not been "normal". Change has been massive and of great significance in the lives of nations and of individuals. The events of these times helped to ignite an awakening of a segment of the American people and to kindle their interest and involvement in their government.

We experienced military operations Desert Shield and Desert Storm. The thoughtful, aggressive and effective, leadership that exhibited itself there, by

President George Bush; the Chief of the Joint Chiefs of Staff, Colin Powell; the Secretary of the Department of Defense, Dick Cheney; and the Secretary of State, James Baker, surely played some causal role in arousing the people. The gridlock we had become accustomed to seeing and detesting was cast aside. The people, all at once, saw what the Executive Branch could achieve, if freed of paralyzing intervention of the Legislative Branch. The leadership displayed in this action was especially noticeable when compared to the faint-hearted inaction and reaction of the social-democratic leaders of the Congress; some of whom we had come to believe were well informed and competent in analysis and judgements related to our military readiness and ability.

It became obvious that huge segments of our population were "hungry" for some demonstration of leadership ability within that circle of people they had chosen to lead this country. President Bush's popularity vaulted to unheard levels of acceptance; ninety plus percent of the people were favorably impressed by the job he was doing.

The contrast between the performance of the Executive and the Legislative; along with a number of serious problems of administration in the Legislature served to arouse the voters and stimulate them to greater involvement. Somewhat later, the announced intention of billionaire, Ross Perot to enter the 1992 presidential race, provided some additional impetus.

The stability originally assumed by the author no longer existed. Historical events, of great consequence were occurring right here in our own nation. That being the case, the plan for this presentation was modified to include discussion of some of that evolving historical activity that will surely be viewed, years hence, as significant in the maturation of our country. As a country, we had traveled a short distance down the road to public awareness and involvement that I had set out as the goal of this work.

Relating this discussion to certain historical events will help us to identify and deal with the struggle encountered by some of our citizens as they try to understand and judge the organizational and operational effectiveness of their government institutions. It may also give us some clues as to what it will take to alert the electorate to the problems and to stimulate them to action.

I have previously confessed to being reared by honest, hard working, and patriotic parents. Parents that taught me to respect my elders and others in places of responsibility in our government. I have recognized and told you of the misgivings I feel, when deviating from those teachings. But, massive amounts of information documenting the failings of our system and the people who are charged with making it work have been written and printed, where the authors have respected all of those niceties; and they have been ineffective! They have "struck out"! Given that fact, and the deep concern that I personally feel about our situation; I am compelled to proceed with a more solemn and unusual approach.

As this is being written, both of our major political parties have held their 1992 conventions. President George Bush and Vice President Dan Quayle will be on the Republican ticket; and Governor Bill Clinton, of Arkansas and Vice Presidential candidate Senator Albert Gore from Tennessee will be on the Democratic ticket. They have begun what will probably be a "ho-hum", uninspiring, conventional campaign. It is unlikely that any of the serious, but controversial—real issues will be addressed in the months that this marathon goes on.

In the real world, Federal spending levels to this point in the fiscal year are validating the National budget for this fiscal year. It appears that the projected $400,000,000,000 deficit, will be achieved or exceeded. And yet, there has been no suggestions or discussion; no action being taken by either the Executive or the Legislative Branches that could and should be taken to control and decrease spending. The kind of thing that any of us would demand of the management of a business organization in which we owned stock or otherwise shared in its ownership and destiny.

And most noticeably and regretfully the two houses of the Congress continue to legislate in the same old, reckless manner. Spend! Spend! Spend! with no restraint; no restrictions.

An inconceivable situation. I simply cannot rationalize to myself that we have achieved this level of national debt and are experiencing this continuing rush to perdition, through the efforts of literate, dedicated, patriotic public servants. AND SO! I find myself going one step further in doing what seems to be necessary in our effort to effectively extricate us and the country from these problems.

It comes in a statement that is not new to my thinking process; but one that I have never before seriously considered putting in writing:

These massive, unmanageable problems and the jeopardy to our country's continued viability can only be attributed to—

## *"THE FOOLS WE ELECT TO PUBLIC OFFICE"*

A statement that, on the surface, would seem to clearly state an opinion and to reflect an appraisal of scope. However, we can increase the focus of our attention and substantially elevate the level of our mutual understanding of that statement with some additional discussion.

Although the word "fool" is widely used by all of society, its meaning as we use it here can be focused by looking at the meaning[s] of the word. The Webster's Encyclopedic Unabridged Dictionary of the English Language provides eleven different meanings for the word. The ones that seem most applicable to the way we use it here are:

When used as a noun—

1. a silly or stupid person; one who lacks sense.
2. —N/A
3. a person who has been imposed on by others and made to appear silly or stupid
4. a weak minded or idiotic person
5. an ardent enthusiast who cannot resist an opportunity to indulge his enthusiasm

When used as a verb—

10. to fool around, to putter aimlessly; waste time
11. fool away, to spend foolishly, as time or money; to squander

To be sure, persons who may feel that we are referring to them, may resent that implication. I guess that is the way it has to be. We have to find some way to penetrate the psyche of those offenders who are "doing this to us". That is the first step in achieving any positive action. Those who work with the problems associated with chronic alcoholism, tell us that the first and by far the most difficult part of any successful treatment program for that malady is to get the "user" to admit that he/she has the problem. So it is with what we are trying to accomplish. Experience clearly demonstrates that more socially acceptable critique just wont do the job. We must accede to "stronger medicine".

To go one step further, those elected officials who feel impacted by the statement, will do so because of conscience; because we will not name them here. We should recognize that this reference does not apply to "all elected officials"; there are some who are intelligent enough to know right from wrong; who press for constructive actions; only to be consistently out-voted by the majority. Their clear thinking and courage in publicly supporting what they believe is proper, is essentially lost to posterity. The fools prevail.

The reference does apply to the majority, who continue to exacerbate our situation and are blindly, carelessly or foolishly taking the country down the road to ruin. It doesn't just apply to the *leaders* of government institutions, whose foggy visions determine the misguided direction of our governments; and who "pull their rank" to intimidate the lesser mortals there into blindly supporting their favorite programs.

The representation of being fools does apply to those lesser mortals as well, those who have not yet gained the seniority to command leadership positions, but who allow themselves to be forced into bondage by the powerful few. The philosophy of representative government such as ours, is that each citizen receives equal representation. We go through a time consuming and very expensive audit of the country every ten years. It is called a census. One of its main purposes is to redefine political boundaries and to reassign elective positions to conform to the changing demographics of the country. All of this to assure a modicum of equality of representation in the system. Spineless participation by office holders and their subservience to the allocation of power on the sole basis of seniority makes all of the census effort a sham.

As introduced here the concept of the "fools we elect to public office", applies to all elected officials at all levels of government and other activity where our system reverts to the use of elected persons to transact the peoples' business. State, county, city governments, and public utility groups; as well as the federal officials that are the subject of our concern.

We have acknowledged that the thoughts we are embracing here are very uncomplimentary to those to whom our characterization applies. It is important that we not lose sight of the next step in an analysis such as this. One that questions the character of those of us who consistently vote to return "fool" incumbents to office—year after year; decade after decade. One that raises the question as to whether or not, we as citizens and contributors to the problem are simply perpetuating the condition that—"fools beget fools".

Presentation here of my list of those that I believe fit into the "elected fool" category would probably be non-productive. What will be productive is for all of us to consider the idea. Is it credible? And if it is, for each of us to make our own lists, and to especially consider the character of those that your vote will help put into the system for future service. If elected, will they help us get back on track or have they demonstrated clearly that they are part of the problem. Patriots' use of this concept, upon entering the polls, presents an accurate and revealing manifestation of the intellect and the character of the electorate. It goes beyond voting solely on the basis of narrow, highly-charged, emotional issues of the day. It is a measure of whether or not we are smart enough, honest enough, dedicated enough, and patriotic enough to deserve the multitude of benefits that this government can provide for us if it is properly managed.

The probability of success would be greatly enhanced, if those in public office would honestly assess their own contribution to the system and react to the conclusions they reach. Since all of us will be making, but not publishing for public consumption, our lists of "fools in public office", those in office will be able to understand and benefit from this exercise, only if they personally participate in it. If they are a member of the "fool brigade" it is up to them to make that judgement and react accordingly. To repeat a concept stated earlier—there are many among us, including (especially) those in public office, that simply "DON'T KNOW WHAT THEY DON'T KNOW". However, if they can bring themselves to honestly address this question, many of them will recognize where they fit in this spectrum of causal and curative aspects of our problems.

The incumbent's self inquisition and appropriate reaction will be extremely useful in helping us achieve some level of improvement. But, real success surely will happen, only if you and I—all of us—honestly and effectively do what we must. There are individual assignments that citizens must identify and perform if we are to make the system work. Doing so is made more difficult by our heavy dependence on the "hard" and "electronic" media for the input information we use in the process.

Those early patriots who wrote and put into place the foundation documents of this nation, demonstrated high levels of vision and trust with the guarantee of free speech to individuals and groups. Through their vision they recognized the advantages flowing from the people's freedom to critique the performance of their servants and the government that they provided. They demonstrated faith, that future generations would not abuse the power that flows from such a "right". Their foresight and intent is somewhat veiled by the seeming unwillingness of today's media organizations, reporters, editors and anchor persons to present information objectively, without shading what they present and the way they present it to fit their own biases. Citizens, would surely be able to do their job better, if those organizations performed more honestly and effectively. That probably will not happen. Doing so would decrease their ability to "shape" society to fit their vision of what it should be, it would raise their costs, and it might adversely impact the "bottom line", profit figure on the balance sheet. The same dedication to "seniority control" that contributes to the paralysis in Congress; seems to exist in most media organizations. However, we cannot cite defects in the media as a singular excuse for not doing what *we* must. Much of the information we need is there, if we are willing to take the time to seek it out, to peel away the scum that tends to conceal its real meaning and importance, to analyze it, and then to react to it.

During the summer of 1992, the city of Los Angeles once again experienced an extended period of fiery, deadly riots following, and supposedly in response to, a jury verdict that essentially found four *white* Los Angeles police officers innocent of charges brought against them in the beating of Rodney King, a colored man they had stopped for a traffic violation. A sequence of the beating had been captured on video tape by a citizen in the area with a home video recorder.

For reasons that they should be forced to justify, the electronic media made a crusade out of the incident. In the months between the time of the incident, (in March of 1991) and the time that the trial was held and its verdict announced (in April of 1992) that very brief video tape was shown nationally and locally thousands of times; day after day, week after week, month after month; by the three major television networks, by the Public Broadcasting System and by the many cable news outlets. It should be obvious to any rational, lucid person that that small section of tape did not constitute all of the evidence that would be developed over the several months of investigation that preceded the trial. Organizations licensed by the Federal government to serve the public in media services, should be required to provide that service in an honest, conscientious, responsible manner.

The massive, over reporting of this incident is a classic example of the media's dedication to fanning the flames of any and all race—or class-distinction situations that arise; especially if the actions of middle-class, white males are involved. Their gross over reporting of this case can only be characterized as thoughtless, reckless, and irresponsible. In the minds of many citizens the case was tried on the tube; results of the trial were a foregone conclusion. Those policemen were "**guilty of a crime**"! That is especially interesting; when, in any other situation, most citizens would realize and admit that they were not lawyers; that they did not understand enough about the intricacies of the laws, and their application to this case, to make an honest judgement of guilt—with or without access to *all* evidence available. Given a chance to react objectively to the situation, most people would admit that for justice to prevail, the case would have to be crunched through the court system and a decision made on the basis of the honest interaction of the evidence and the definition of what constitutes a crime under the law. Had this been a case of white policemen beating another white man or of black policemen beating another black man; the tapes *might* have been shown once or twice and the incident would have been forgotten. If our laws and their enforcement were truly "color blind" there would have been no lawsuits lasting years. Policemen involved would not have been fired. Tens of millions of dollars of public funds, tax money collected from you and me, would have been saved in attorney fees and in million dollar settlements with the victim spawned by the case!

Little wonder then, that the emotions, especially those of some African-Americans who continue to imagine themselves to be victims of the system, were highly sensitized; and when the court found the officers innocent, and the verdict was announced; the colored people in a segment of the city of Los Angeles found it to be a convenient excuse to "raise hell". And they did! burning, looting, and gaining a modicum of revenge on the non-black persons who were unfortunately in the area at the time. And, of course, other non-black nationalities and the "establishment" black people; those who try to live within the law were not spared in the attacks. They were attacked and victimized along with all the others. Before it was over, something over 50 persons had been killed. Property damage was estimated to be in the billions of dollars.

This Los Angeles riot deserves more attention than we will be able to give it here. We refer to it here to demonstrate the gross mismanagement that we have come to accept from the elected and bureaucratic incumbents to which we entrust our system. A possible sign of hopelessness of our ability to make our system work, especially with the existing organizational, procedural, and staffing arrangements. It may even signify that the system, itself cannot be made to work.

This year, 1992, is a presidential election year. As an aside, it has also been a bad weather year. A devastating hurricane swept across Florida and on into Louisiana. A short time later a major hurricane hit one of the Hawaiian Islands. Did this create a hand ringing question in Washington, D.C.? What to do? Of course not! they did what they always do when they face any problem? They threw money at it. A race of the political factions ensued; each striving to out-do the other and win the favor of the "people"? Federal action ultimately promised to pour billions of taxpayer funds into "rebuilding" the affected areas. Dollar amounts are simply pulled out of the air. The effort is unstructured, there is no plan that presents a rationale for determining which facilities are to receive federal funds and which are not. Detailed cost estimates are not available to support justification for individual project amounts or the total need.

Of course, the mass media is right there in the middle of these situations as always; with editors, anchors and pundits pressing for more help; and criticizing the lack of immediate and total response; now! Their pressing and ever-present question being, why is it taking so long for the funds to become available? A typical headline being, "CONGRESS FIDDLES AFTER L.A. BURNS", in the May 25, 1992 issue of U.S. News and World Reports. Such questions and pressure generated by persons who have never managed anything, who have no idea of what it takes to organize such a logistical problem, and people whose one and only responsibility is to report to the rest of the nation "*what*" is happening on a day to day basis in the affected area; do not serve us well. When the media does more; when they editorialize their impatience, and when they force acceleration of the process; effectiveness, efficiency, and cost control are sacrificed.

I suspect that most of us would support a plan to provide some relief and assistance to the victims of such natural disasters. However, especially in times of financial crisis, does it make any sense to carelessly allocate and spend our limited national resources? Strangely, the public either passively accepts or passes out kudos for a job well done! What a shame! The funding decision was made in about 11 days. Can anyone develop a plan to spend that much money wisely in 11 days? Of course not!

This brings us back to the L.A. situation. Can you guess what our government's solution to that problem was? OF COURSE! more billions of dollars for aid and for *rebuilding the area*. This solution has been applied in several situations in the past. It never solved anything. Most such areas, after the rebuild, will slide back into the same miserable condition that had previously caused the problem to erupt.

And, where will the money come from to pay the costs of such commitments? Will plan expenditures for lower priority budgeted items be deferred, and the funds diverted to this higher priority need? Such thoughts never enter the minds of these movers and shakers. That is a concept that is completely foreign to them. This is, after all, taxpayer's money! There's more where this came from!

For decades, it has been the practice of the federal government to step in and assist people and areas impacted by major natural disasters during a transitional period. The trend to do more, to increase response, revealed itself in the reaction to another hurricane that hit the Atlantic coastline and after the debilitating earth quake that hit the San Francisco bay area a few years ago. History tells us that without some intervention such as creation of a policy to serve as a guideline in these instances, the costs of federal participation for funding transitional periods and for rehabilitation will continue to sky rocket.

Discerning citizens are left with some lingering and troubling questions. If the government is going to respond in this manner, what is the incentive for property owners who live in these areas of high exposure to "Act of God" disasters, to buy their own catastrophic insurance? The answer would seem to be, not much! What is the ultimate result of uncontrolled extension of this practice? It's cost to the taxpayer and its affect on the insurance industry in the country?

The "ERA OF EMOTIONAL IDIOCY" is alive and well!

Given our present leadership, there is only one sure-fire answer. Congress must enact a law that prohibits the occurrence of such major natural disasters, especially *during an election year.*

A fundamental issue being examined here, is whether or not our government system is working. We have previously, concluded that it is not.

The election process, however, is a critical part of our total system of government. It's appeal to the multitudes, worldwide, is obvious. It is the first thing nations retreat to when they are throwing off the bonds of totalitarian regimes. The campaign of our 1992 presidential election year is nearing it's final stages. It is appropriate that we divert our attention briefly to assess, in some detail, the performance of our election process; how well is it working this year?

An election procedure that works well would:

1.  Be successful in identifying from all of our people, a small number of the best qualified candidates to compete at the polls for the elective offices to be filled in an election. This process has to weed out those candidates who are not willing to put the needs of the country at the very top of their priority list in all actions taken on our behalf as stewards of the national interest. That is the ideal! We probably can survive with something a bit below the very best.—*But! it seems clear, that our system fails this test, miserably.* Qualified people seldom run for office. They are not likely to succeed if they do.

2.  The voters must have access to accurate, unbiased information on the candidates and on the operational needs of the government system.—*The media **must** clean up its act if we are to ever succeed here!*

3.  The voters are able and willing to do their part; **in a *discriminating and intelligent way*.**—*Much improvement is necessary here.*
4.  The candidates elected must be trustworthy and honest. They must **keep the faith** with those who elect them. They must conduct themselves, in office, in accordance with the promises made during the campaign.—*Indications are that this will not happen until the electorate integrates this character element into the criteria they use in judging candidates' qualifications.*

So what about this year?—1992? How well is it working?

### * * Campaign Interlude * *
### September 28, 1992

With the federal Government's 1992 Fiscal Year coming to an end, reports indicate that the predicted $400,000,000,000 deficit for the year will become a reality. To help us understand the magnitude of that, it translates into spending just over $45,000,000 more than we took in, every hour, 24 hours per day, 365 days per year!

The U.S. trade deficit soared in the month of July 1992 to the highest level in two years. For the month our exports exceeded our imports by about $8,000,000,000. And, as a result, there is now 8 billion more American dollars in the hands of other nations and nationals; an important lever with which they can and will interject themselves into the affairs of our nation.

The U. S. economy continues in deep recession; tens of thousands of American workers find themselves joining the ranks of the unemployed each month. The prospects of most of them finding any new job, let alone one that pays what they had been receiving are very grim.

On the campaign trail—we are moving into the final days of the struggle; 35 days to go.

Candidates of the two major parties usually register an increase in the polling data immediately after their party's convention. True to form, Arkansas Governor Bill Clinton, democratic candidate for the presidency found himself with a commanding lead in the polls after the Democratic convention and prior to the Republican convention. The assumption by most pundits and expert observers seemed to be that President Bush would at least regain the lost ground in the polls after his party's convention.

The "bump" in the president's rating after the Republican convention, was disappointing. He did not regain what he had lost. And Clinton has enjoyed a 10 to 20 percent lead over the president throughout the intervening time.

The two candidates have traveled the country, ocean to ocean; and from Canada to Mexico; on grueling schedules, often seven days a week. It is apparent that both of them want the job! Each is obviously convinced that he has the skills and ability to do the job. And yet, after several weeks of this rigorous effort, hundreds of whistle stops and speeches by both men, and the expenditure of millions of dollars; the voter's knowledge of either party's programs remains essentially the same as it was immediately after the conventions.

Clinton has seemed to put the problem of possible infidelity behind him. It is interesting to speculate whether this is the result of his convincing the people that, "it never happened" or if the level of morality and ethics in our country has plunged to the point that the voters no longer perceive such activities to be important considerations in our critical societal decisions. He has, however, continued to face the original and some new revelations relative to his apparent evasion of military service during the Vietnam war.

The general design of this Democratic convention deviated from past practice in some important ways. The Democratic party has begun to recognize that the "tax and spend" imprint of their on-going practices; may work to their disadvantage in the presidential race. Governor Clinton has perceived that label as damaging to his chances for success in his presidential race. His plan has clearly been to isolate himself from the liberal, socialist faction of the party during the campaign. He has worked to convince the voter that he is not one of that group; but that he is instead a moderate in his party. The implication being that things will change toward more fiscal restraint and increased sanity in operation of the government in his administration. The *"establishment"*, social-democratic leaders of the Congress and of the democratic party were conspicuously absent from his convention. Where were they? Why weren't they there? as they always had been in the past? Was this campaign really offering something new? or is this simply a ruse, designed to fool the people?

Given his lead over the president, Clinton's campaign strategy has been to maintain a "holding pattern" and sit on the lead. The strategy has also involved an intense and unrelenting offense, charging the president with unilateral responsibility for the economic problems of the country. Clinton assurances that his program will turn things around are abundant. He has been unwilling to venture into any new areas of discussion and commitment unless he is forced to do so by polls showing that the president is gaining.

Clinton's claim to be a moderate is threatened by his choice of Senator Albert Gore of Tennessee as his vice presidential, running mate. In his years in the Senate, Gore never saw a spending bill he didn't like and support; unless it was for national defense. The Senator has seemed restrained in his freedom of action and participation in the campaign. He has spent a lot of time following Clinton around on the campaign trail.

As election day approaches, information is becoming available on who Clinton is considering for appointment to some of the key cabinet jobs in his administration. This is further jeopardizing his supposed disenchantment with the ultra liberal wing of his party and its democratic members in the Congress. The list of possible appointees is dominated by liberal members of Congress. All of this probably goes over the heads of most voters at this time.

President Bush has been working very hard in an earnest effort to convince the people that his continued service in the White House is the best option for the country. His Republican convention was of the more traditional design. Participants represented a wide cross section of republican party members; with their convictions ranging from moderate to ultra conservative.

His strategies have included a number of different approaches. He has talked about the "tax and spend" nature of Clinton's proposals, and during his term as governor. He has talked about a number of other weaknesses and failures in Arkansas during Clinton's tenure as governor. He has talked about the absence of any Clinton experience in foreign policy. He has talked about the hypocrisy of a person who evaded military service of his country, ordering today's young people into military action.

The polls have responded slightly in the president's favor. But, do what he may, he has not been able to break the apparent hold that Clinton has on a plurality of the people. He has been unable to make a major impact on the polling advantage held by the democratic challenger.

The frustration flowing from the president's lack of success is escalated by the fact that polls show a large "undecided" segment of the electorate that does not "feel easy" with the prospect of voting for either candidate. Existence of that indecision; the fact that people are still open to accept logical reasons for voting one way or the other, stimulates the president to try to find the words that will win them over.

If any of the campaign oratory of this campaign survives to go into the history books; it probably will be that of Dan Quayle, Republican, Vice Presidential candidate. In his challenge to the entertainment industry, he criticized inclusion in the story-line of the television program, Murphy Brown, the "out-of-wedlock birth of a baby to the leading character, Candice Bergen. His point was (is) that stars such as Ms. Bergen are idols to vast numbers of teenage girls. Exploitation of this theme can only have denigrating affects in the minds of teen age girls, an area where the nation already faces a massive problem of teen-age pregnancy and illegitimacy; children becoming parents of children. It is conceivable that his position, and actions may have a lasting impact.

His criticism was not, however, limited to this one instance. For years, elevated levels of profanity, immorality, obscenity, violence, and evil have gradually become more accepted and championed in the hard and electronic media. The limits to what is allowed have been incessantly under attack. And barriers have continued to fall to the point that there are no longer any absolute limits. Almost anything goes. In its head-long charge for profits, the industry has demonstrated no conscience or willingness to discipline itself.

The people's concerns about escalating indecency, perversion, and depravity are increasing. They are questioning and their concern is growing about this trend; it's obvious impacts on the character of our people; and the quality of life we enjoy. Dan Quayle originally made these remarks early in the campaign; but the subject is still receiving more than a little attention. The entertainment industry has helped to keep the subject alive by taking up the challenge and reacting in very public and obnoxious ways. As a result it is entirely possible (probable) that this issue may develop a life of its own, and stay in the public eye. People who sense and are deeply concerned by the deterioration of our sense of "values" in this nation, may get involved and ultimately demand correction by the "establishment". Such a movement is not without powerful "tools" of its own, should it decide to act. Continued existence of the individual shows, and the industry itself, are dependent upon advertising money paid by sponsors. Organizations that expect that their expenditures here will improve their position in the market; increase their "sales". Regional or national boycotts on the products or services advertised on offending programs are appropriate and they will be effective.

The apparent character of the industry and its attitude toward the problem was effectively displayed on the September 20, 1992 program, "This Week with David Brinkley".

Charlton Heston and Richard Dreyfus offered some interesting comments about the contrast between the product being produced by "Hollywood" and what the people of the country seemed to want. The decline of the financial performance of the major electronic media networks was offered as evidence of this condition.

Mary Steenburgen, star of *Parenthood* and *Time After Time*, and a close friend of the Clintons was also a guest on the program. The discussion brought out that Ms. Steenburgen, was a single mother who looks to the entertainment industry for her livelihood. She lives in a small town, in the mountains, about two hours out of Hollywood. She has two small children; one 11 and the other 9 years old. In concert with the theme of the program; George Will asked her if she would want her 11-year old to watch "*Married with Children*". Her response was especially telling. She said that her children do their homework every night and that they are not allowed to watch TV during the school year. That is an interesting commentary on the industry; one that, if heeded and followed by the rest of us, would serve the country well! It also lends some credibility to Mr. Quayle's criticism and supports the idea that the issue may continue to be debated.

And then, just when it appears that we can begin to focus on the possible outcome of a two-way presidential race; we learn that Arizona volunteers for Ross Perot have collected and submitted the necessary number of signatures to put him on that state's November ballot. We also learn that with success there, he has achieved the goal originally established for his campaign. His name had been qualified for inclusion on the ballots of all fifty states. His continuation of the effort, since his public withdrawal in July, had either escaped the attention of the media or it was thought that the effort was not news-worthy.

During the intervening time, he had also published a book, "United We Stand", which rose to be included on the best-seller list. It articulates specific details of his program for managing the nation's business during the next four years, if he is elected president. His plan is characterized as being realistic; it is, therefore, also austere. The plan attempts to spread the pain of gaining control of our fiscal hemorrhaging, fairly among all citizens. His economic plan would result in major decreases in the nation's budget deficits each year.

Mr. Perot cites as one reason for his return to the political arena, the absence of any realistic, responsible strategy by either of the major-party candidates to decrease the annual deficits; and ultimately to "work off" the national debt. As a matter of fact, there is some agreement among a large number of "experts" that the programs proposed by the major-party candidates will increase the annual deficits above their present level!

Mr. Perot's public reemergence has resulted in much speculation as to whether or not he will become a candidate. He had pulled out in July 1992, when the democratic convention was winding down. The reason he gave for that action was his belief that the major-party candidates were going to respond with discussion and commitments directed toward the real issues. His reemergence as a visible participant, symbolizes his disappointment in what has transpired in the campaign in the intervening time; the absence of candor and substance in the actions of the major-party candidates since July. He feels strongly that his reinvolvement, will serve the best interests of this country that has done so much for him. His campaign expenses have been paid almost entirely with his own personal resources.

As part of the process leading to his decision of whether or not to re-enter the campaign, he called the 50 state directors of his coalition, "UNITED WE STAND" to Dallas today (September 28, 1992). During the day the group will listen to presentations by top managers of the Democratic and Republican campaign staffs, who have made the trip to Texas to speak to the group. Their mission is to try to convince the Perot group that their candidate's program *is* responsive to the needs of the country. This is a totally new and unheard of wrinkle in our election process!

The 50 state directors will return to their home bases; poll their groups; and report their findings back to Mr. Perot. Ross indicated that he would make his announcement on October 1, 1992. Some new excitement has entered what was getting to be a very boring campaign; with the same blather being repeated over and over again by the active candidates.

And what has been happening in the Legislative Branch during the past few months? The answer; Not much of consequence.

Many initiatives that the President had sent up for their consideration and action continued to languish in the inactive files of the democratic *leadership* (?) of the House and the Senate. These are bills which were designed by the Executive Branch to respond to our societal needs; to relieve the massive unemployment problem in the country; and provide some stimulus to move the country out of the recession that is causing so many of our people so much pain.

Can you understand and explain why these "real time problems of the people", have no priority for action in the minds of our legislative agents? Instead of dealing with these real, existing problems, they have opted to spend their time creating new ones. They have carefully selected bills pending action, that they knew the President would veto. Bills that promised more goodies to the people, more expense and governmental interference in the lives of businesses and the people. The Family Leave bill is an example. This is a bill that would force businesses to give employees extended periods of leave, without pay, away from the job in the event of illness or other problems at home. As expected Congress passed the bill and the President vetoed it. Just as he has over thirty others in recent months. Congress has been unable to override any of his vetoes.

And they continued to spend money for *critically?* needed facilities: For example, in the Portland, Oregon area it was announced that:

1. $3,750,000 in Federal money has been set aside for a planned Oregon Trail interpretive center in Oregon City, Oregon which is at the end of the Oregon Trail. (This, shortly after a new multimillion dollar, Oregon Trail, interpretive center opened near Baker, Oregon—courtesy of Senator Mark Hatfield and the generosity of taxpayers from throughout the nation.) Here is what is important about this item; the story goes on to say that Representative Mike Kopetski, *Democrat*-Oregon, was instrumental in getting the money for the project. Of course, Mr. Kopetski is running for reelection. This windfall, to be spent in the midst of his constituents, is surely designed to help him get the votes he needs, or

2. The House committee approves wildlife refuge center! The bill was proposed by U.S. Rep. Jolene Unsoeld, *Democrat*-Washington; who is, of course, running for reelection against a Republican opponent.

You should expect that, regardless of where you live in this great land, if your incumbent representative or senator is a democrat and is seeking return to his/her position; you too, should expect to read or be told of similar pork barrel projects. Projects which will bring federal funds into your area, to benefit that incumbent in the race against any opponents.

Sadly, we see nothing in this interlude discussion of the performance of our government during the current political campaign that gives the slightest hope or leads to any expectation that the system; the government or the election process is working—at all!

What is most distressing about this situation, is that, in a time of desperate national need, a time when the economy is in deep recession, millions of people (who want to work) are unemployed, tens/hundreds of thousands of new people are joining them in the unemployment lines each month; the Congress turned their backs on the situation—on the people! Although bills that had originated in the Executive Branch and that would have begun to alleviate some of the problems, were awaiting action on the desks of key Legislative Branch leaders, they chose to stonewall the situation. Nothing of consequence was accomplished during this election year to address the perilous conditions we face! Or to help the millions of citizens who are out of work and need real help! the kind that will allow them to get back to work and earn their own way!

## * * End Of Interlude * *

The Los Angeles (LA) riot and inferno should also be remembered because of an incident that happened during its aftermath. In early May when smoke was still wafting from some of the burned out buildings in that area, it was reported that Marlin Fitzwater, White House Spokesman for President Bush had announced that:

> "We believe that many of the root problems that have resulted in inner-city difficulties were started in the '60s and '70s" programs of President Johnson's "Great Society."
> He went on to say that the poverty programs that were implemented there, ignored the relationship between "people's pride in their community and having a job . . . having the hope of income and improving their lives, and being able to own their own homes to give them a stake in the community."[13]

Now, let's assume that you and I are two discerning, caring, and patriotic Americans; blue collar, white collar or management associates in a business or some other setting where we share the responsibility for success of the operation, and where teamwork is necessary for the success of the enterprise. Or we may simply be friends or neighbors. Had we met on the street, at about that time; "where we live", chances are good that the L.A. problem would have been one subject that we discussed. We may have similar views and opinions on the subject or we may be totally and fervently at odds. Under such conditions, most *normal* Americans could, would, calmly discuss the issue, hear each other out, respect the points of view of each other; and in the end, each would go away wiser, understanding the arguments that support the other side(s) point of view. And, we would have gained a better understanding of the parts and totality of the problem.

---

[13]   Portland, Oregon-The Oregonian May 5, 1992.

Is it unreasonable for us to expect as much of those with whom we trust the nation's "affairs of state"? To expect them to be normal, caring, objective, people—"searching earnestly and honestly" for the solution that will best serve the nation and its people?? Such expectations are reasonable, but, of course, experience tells us such sanity in the political arena is not likely, especially in an election year! Nothing is apolitical in a presidential election year!

Instead of a logical, reasoned reaction to Marlin's statement, social democrats everywhere came unglued. The knee-jerk, spontaneous and instantaneous reaction from individual democrats and from all social-democratic bastions was one of intense disbelief that anyone would even think such a thing; let alone say it out loud, where others could hear it. The suggestion was met with their fierce denial; there could be no possible connection between the two! "LBJ's actions contributed nothing to our problems today!"?

And so! after brief, random tremors of charges and counter charges on the issue, the subject dropped from the menu of important public issues.

Can the social democrats provide evidence that will support their spontaneous denial? Probably not! They should be challenged to do so!

Can we or should we, forget about what may be such important relationships that may help us identify sources of our problems and ultimately help extricate us from the fiscal insanity that plagues us? The kind of problems we are facing haven't "just happened"! As a matter of fact, fiscal problems of excessive spending; spiraling, increasing deficits; pending bankruptcy and lurking financial ruin are almost always the result of human error. Humans cause such problems; and only humans can do what is necessary to overcome them!

If our problems haven't "just happened", there must be "causes" lurking out there, buried in our history; causal actions which must be sought out, identified and used as a basis for any successful corrective effort. We need to look for political actions taken which established new directions for our ship-of-state; actions which have not resulted in the beneficial results expected.

In what was a rare exception to our usual blind, irrational, unquestioning government performance; an astute, legitimate, and possibly important question had been asked. A reasonable, possible cause of some of our problems was advanced! and then dismissed without any intellectual consideration.

Had Mr. Fitzwater's statement been made by a member of the democratic party about action taken during a republican administration; would the result have been any different? Probably not! What a sad commentary, on our system and those we choose to manage it. Apparently any expectation of cooperation and patriotism across party lines is too much to expect; especially in an election year!

The events of the middle decades of this century, 1940's through the 1970's deserve our critical attention. Identification and analysis of issues need not pit the democrat against the republican, the liberal against the conservative, or the pseudo learned-elite versus the rest of us. It does not take a brain surgeon to comprehend meaningful interrogation of some of the events of that era; their short-and long-term, cost versus benefit effectiveness.

In the early 1960's, John F. Kennedy's (JFK) election, and his time as president were exciting times for those who lived through that period. That was especially true for those of us who were of his same generation of American.

Whereas, they had come to view our Federal government as some detached, far off organization that dictated terms that the people could neither understand or control; he was saying and offering something new! something exciting! He seemed to be recognizing each of us, as notable, responsible parts of the big operation that is our government. We could play a part, we could help!

I realize that most who read this will react by saying that politicians always exercise such ploys. That reaction is understandable. In the intervening 30 years, the early 60's to the early 90's, politicians have picked up on the use of this as a ploy. As a result it does have a hollow ring today. However, to those who were there and heard JFK outline his plans and programs, the idea was new; he was believable; he expressed confidence in our collective ability to achieve difficult (impossible?) goals; he commanded the support and respect of the masses, members of both political parties. A perception was electrically alive in the country that we could do whatever we set out to do!

One of the most commonly expressed aspirations of today's American citizen is the desire to pass on to future generations, the American dream. Each of us will have a different vision as to the contents of that "ideal American dream" that we want to pass on. Some, of our younger citizens may conceive of today's conditions as being that ideal. Many who have a wider selection of environments from which to select may well choose some other ideal. Many of those who experienced the John F. Kennedy years, will certainly see conditions at that time as their ideal.

America was truly the melting pot of the world. Family life was cherished; children were accepted as treasured gifts; their care, training and development were top priority in the minds of the parents and often of the grandparents. Jobs were available; qualifications, experience and ability to do the job, were still major considerations in the selection of employees for positions in the private and public arenas. Security of continued employment, was common for those who performed well. As a rule the level of pay bore some semblance of comparability to the value of the work to society. The mulish pursuit of material, financial and prestigious, ego-enhancing goals was tempered by the knowledge and acceptance of the fact that there were more rewarding goals to be sought and achieved in life. People cherished and guarded relationships with other people; within the family, the extended family and the community. There was time for recreation; time for hobbies; time to relax; time to think; time for reflection, meditation, and contemplation. And! we were somewhat relaxed about the ability, purpose, scruples, dedication and patriotism of the elected, appointed and bureaucratic servants in our government institutions. Those people still worked for us, the taxpayer.

President Kennedy's aura of leadership and his call for citizen participation were especially exciting. Some of his public statements in speeches, etc. have become prominent in the nations collection of notable quotations. That is certainly the case with the ones we will use here.

On the occasion of his acceptance of his nomination at the Democratic convention in Los Angeles on July 15, 1960, he said:

> "We stand today on the edge of a new frontier—the frontier of the 1960's—a frontier of unknown opportunities and perils—a frontier of unfulfilled hopes and threats. Woodrow Wilson's New Freedom promised our nation a new political and economic framework. Franklin Roosevelt's New Deal promised security and succor to those in need. But the new Frontier of which I speak is not a set of promises—it is a set of challenges. It sums up not what I intend to offer to the American people, but what I intend to ask of them."

And, on the occasion of his inaugural address in Washington, D. C., on January 20, 1961, he said:

> "And so my fellow Americans; ask not what your country can do for you—ask what you can do for your country."

"My fellow citizens of the world; ask not what America will do for you, but what together we can do for the freedom of man."

It is fair to say that many were flattered and excited by the confidence he expressed in the ability of the nation and it's people to achieve the "near impossible" when, in a supplementary State of the Union message to Congress on May 25, 1961, he said:

> "I believe that this Nation should commit itself to achieving the goal, before this decade is out, of landing a man on the Moon and returning him safely to earth."

That was giddy, incredible, inconceivable and yet inspiring stuff! The generations of Americans who heard that challenge had grown up, reading the Buck Rogers comic strip; convinced that such ventures were far beyond the state of the art that existed at that time; and yet they were in awe of the possibilities that it projected for human travel. But that had only been a dream! *Is this thing possible*?!

Any number of additional less celebrated JFK quotations could be added to further support the premise that his vision for the country was one that would assign high priority to non-governmental activities. It seemed clear that his vision for the nation did not rely on or include an aggressive, force-fed, costly, "welfare—state".

\* # \* # \*

And then suddenly, on November 22, 1963, we, individually and collectively as a nation; along with people around the world were stunned beyond comprehension! The President had been assassinated during his visit to Dallas, Texas.

\* # \* # \*

AND THE COURSE OF EVENTS IN THE EVOLUTION OF THE UNITED STATES, THE EFFECTIVENESS OF ITS GOVERNMENT AS IT RELATES TO ITS CITIZENS AND TO THE GOVERNMENTS AND CITIZENS OF NATIONS THROUGHOUT THE WORLD; WERE CHANGED IN SIGNIFICANT, RADICAL WAYS! CHANGES WERE MADE AND THE AMERICAN PEOPLE WERE PERSUADED WITH

*PROMISES OF "A GREAT NEW SOCIETY". ONE THAT WOULD SOLVE ALL OF OUR PROBLEMS; AT REASONABLY SMALL COSTS TO SOCIETY; THE SACRIFICE REQUIRED OF THOSE WHO HAD TO PAY FOR THEM WOULD BE MINIMAL!*

*THOSE PROGRAMS HAVE BEEN CONTINUED, AUGMENTED, INCREASED, ENLARGED, AND EXPANDED; YEAR AFTER YEAR, DECADE AFTER DECADE. RATHER THAN BEING INSIGNIFICANT, AS PROMISED, THEIR COSTS HAVE BECOME ENORMOUS. TRILLIONS OF DOLLARS HAVE BEEN SPENT ON THEM OVER THE YEARS. TODAY EXPENDITURES FOR THOSE PROGRAMS ALONE REPRESENT ALMOST HALF OF THE NATION'S TOTAL ANNUAL EXPENDITURES. THEIR PAYMENTS ARE DRAGGING THE COUNTRY INTO FINANCIAL INSTABILITY. ALL IN THE MANNER OF ROBOTS; OUR ELECTED AND APPOINTED LEADERS HAVE NEVER LOOKED BACK TO EXAMINE AND TRY TO HONESTLY DISCERN WHETHER OR NOT THE PROGRAMS ARE EFFECTIVE, WHETHER THOSE HUGE SUMS ARE ACHIEVING WHAT WE EXPECT, WHETHER THEY ARE ACHIEVING ANYTHING OF VALUE, OR POSSIBLY MAKING THINGS WORSE. WHETHER OF NOT OUR PROBLEMS MIGHT BE ADDRESSED IN ALTERNATIVE, MORE EFFECTIVE WAYS.*

*INSTEAD "THE FOOLS WE ELECT TO PUBLIC OFFICE", TAKE TURNS MOUNTING THE ROSTRUM IN THEIR RESPECTIVE SANCTUMS PRAISING ALL OF THE GREAT THINGS THEY HAVE DONE; CONDEMNING ANYTHING THAT THE EXECUTIVE BRANCH MIGHT TRY TO DO TO CUT COSTS; AND REACTING WITH GREAT DEMONSTRATIONS OF PAIN WHEN THE JUDICIAL BRANCH MOVES TO SHAPE THE PROGRAMS TO COMPLY WITH THE CONSTITUTION. THEY SIMPLY AND ERRONEOUSLY ASSUME THAT CONTINUATION OF THIS IDIOCY IS THE ONLY WAY TO PROCEED!*

# CHAPTER 15

Vice President Lynden B. Johnson had accompanied President Kennedy on his fateful trip to the southwest. He was with him in Dallas on the day of the assassination. The reins of government were rapidly, transferred over to him. He was sworn into office shortly after the public announcement that President Kennedy was dead; before Air Force 1 left Dallas to return President Kennedy's body, the new president, and the rest of his travel contingent back to Washington, D.C.

It is difficult, probably impossible, to relate the traumatic shock and sense of loss that prevailed throughout the country following the assassination. In a very real sense the fear that we all felt was similar to what we had experienced in the aftermath of the Japanese attack on Pearl Harbor, on December 7, 1941. Each tragedy had exploded on us as a total surprise! Stunned, we speculated in fear and apprehension what the new days might bring. Any confidence we had felt about the future was shattered.

As time passed; days, weeks and months; we gradually worked our way through the fear and depression that had so engulfed us.

President Johnson, had been a prominent figure in our Federal government, prior to his selection as JFK's, vice presidential running mate. It was no secret that he had long coveted the idea that he might someday occupy the presidential office of our country. When the assassination presented him with this opportunity, he was ready; he knew what he wanted to do. It would have been instructive and useful if he, or someone, would have encapsulated his program intent in words similar to those that President Kennedy had used. It would have went like this:

**And so my fellow Americans, *ask not what you can do for your country—ask what your country can do for you.***

But, of course, that never happened. Nobody rang a bell, set the alarm or did anything to wake up the country to the real meaning of the changes that were taking place. And we slept through the whole thing; **for thirty years and still counting!**

John Kenneth Galbraith was a noted economist, educator and author of the time. He had served as the administrator of the Federal Office of Price Administration from 1941 to 1943, and as our ambassador to India from 1961 to 1963. He served as a professor of economics at Harvard University from 1949 to 1967, and beginning in 1967 served as the chairman of the Americans for Democratic Action. He summarized his perception of the change from J.F. Kennedy's vision of what the country should be to that of L. B. Johnson, by saying:

> "There should be no doubt about it—Johnson was very much more a part of the liberal instinct of the times than John F. Kennedy was. Also, in comparison with John Kennedy he had a greater sense of what he could get away with and what he could do on the Hill. Johnson used his leverage with Congress to the hilt and more."[14]

Over the years LBJ had become skillful at manipulating the government "machinery"; to get things done "his way". He had also accumulated large numbers of chits from other powerful members of the Congress and loyal, powerful, appointed leaders of the Executive Branch.

He landed in the presidential office—running. Things began to happen, he presented his programs, pulled the strings, cajoled and threatened as appropriate to get the action he wanted. His programs were enacted and

---

[14]   Lynden; An Oral Biography, by Merle Miller; G. P. Putnam's Sons, 1980 (p342)

gradually the country settled into a new routine; one in concert with his vision for America—The Great Society.

Lest we lose the attention of some of our readers at this point, for reasons of political bias and intolerance; please note that the conservatives and/or republicans were essentially on the sidelines while all of this was happening. They did not play any role of consequence in the events. What we are looking at here is a very significant and probably fateful change in direction of the democratic party. The character, reputation, and direction of the Franklin D. Roosevelt, Harry S. Truman and John F. Kennedy years were simply abandoned. Their reasoned, logical, responsible and effective management styles and policies were rejected; and replaced with what has proven to be a hollow "pipe dream"; one that panders to and advances the "era of Emotional Idiocy" scourge that corrupts our society. And the country embarked on the long, tragic, catastrophic course that has brought us to our present level of socialistic dependence on government "handouts", financial disarray, and impending fiscal disintegration.

With one exception, the new president and the country took off and never looked back. It was necessary that the details of the assassination be investigated, analyzed and reported to the people. The president moved expeditiously to appoint the members of a Special Commission to do this job. Selection of someone to serve as the chairman of the Special Commission, posed a unique problem to him. He recognized the potential for controversy that might arise from any conclusions of the Commission. One complicating factor, in his mind, was the knowledge that some people suspected that Lynden, himself, had possibly been involved in planning and execution of the assassination. After extended discussions with a number of people about the selection of the chairman, he asked Earl Warren, the sitting Chief Justice of the U. S. Supreme Court at that time, to serve in that position. When first asked, Warren had misgivings about serving in both positions at the same time, and he declined the invitation. Only to be "leaned on" by the president a short time later, and convinced that he should accept.

The Special Commission delivered its report to the president at the White House on September 28, 1964. In it, the Commission accepted and adopted conclusions that appeared to be supported by what the American people had seen as they sat transfixed to their television tubes on the fateful day of the assassination and the days that followed. The theory accepted by the Special Commission and advanced in the report, was that a lone marksman, Lee Harvey Oswald, alone, unaided, and slightly crazed had killed the president from a sniper's vantage point in one of the tall buildings along the route of the presidential motorcade.

There are some interesting aspects to what has transpired since the report was issued. President Johnson had deep reservations about the accuracy of the report when he first read it. It is speculated that never, during his lifetime, did he believe the conclusions of the Warren Commission Report to be accurate! He is not alone in that position! In the years since it was issued, widespread public doubt as to its accuracy, has resulted in a clamor for new investigative work that would develop conclusions that are more faithfully supported by the facts and evidence in the case. Such new inquiries have been hampered by the lack of access to most of the important information, facts, clues, statements, autopsy reports, etc. that were collected and used by the Special Commission. Information has been sealed away in secret, protected files, all of these years! This, in spite of strong justification that has existed; based on the "public's right to know". The government has successfully resisted all attempts to open the files. This situation continued, unchanged thirty years later in September 1992.

Notwithstanding the unavailability of the "official" evidence used by the Special Commission; much information that has accumulated from other sources, makes educated judgments possible. Evidence available for the case, does little to support the findings of the Warren Commission. The one factor that most threatens the credibility of its report, relates to the seemingly impossible trajectory the shots fired by the assassin, would have to follow to support their conclusions.

I am technically trained, as an electrical engineer. I am also an outdoors man, having grown up with access to all kinds of firearms which my brother and I used to put meat on the family table for many years. My education and experience makes it impossible for me, and hordes of other persons, to accept the Warren Commission's theory and report. Bullets simply don't bend and weave around in a way that makes their theory possible.

A number of other hypotheses have been presented as to who was responsible. Oliver Stone presented one such theory in what proved to be a controversial movie earlier this year (in 1992). There is a book, "Appointment in Dallas: The Final Solution to the Assassination of JFK"; by Hugh C. McDonald, as told to Geoffrey Bocca; The Hugh McDonald Publishing Corp.; 1975. The book does not name the killer. Neither does it speculate on who paid for the hit. It does present the hypothesis that money was paid to a professional hit man (men) to do the job. It is not possible to vouch for the accuracy of either account with the limited information available to the average citizen today.

From other research, we can speculate that there were several possible sources of any payoff money:

1. It is no secret that Lynden Johnson hated the Kennedys with a passion. He detested them! And he would gain something he had always wanted if JFK was gone.
2. At the time of his assassination, JFK was seeking the help of some big-city mobsters; in a plot to get rid of Castro. At the same time, his brother, Attorney General Robert Kennedy, was working to bring those same mobster groups to justice. It is easy to surmise that all of this did not set well with the leaders of those gangs. Their methods of settling this kind of problem was consistent with what occurred in Dallas.
3. It is suspected, in some circles, that American encouragement and assurances under JFK played a role in the murder of Ngo Dinh Diem, President of South Vietnam on November 1, 1963. Some believe that President Kennedy's assassination was an act of retribution for United States complicity in that event.
4. It is no secret, that then, as now, there were great numbers of powerful persons, and organizations, who had much invested in and/or who had much to gain from the continuation of our government's progress toward liberal, socialistic constructs.

In retrospect, we know now that Earl Warren, at the time of his service on the Special Commission, was using the massive power of his position as Chief Justice of the Supreme court, to significantly bend and warp the meaning of the U. S. Constitution and, therefore, the laws of the land to conform to a number of personal, emotional perspectives of his own. The ease with which he was accomplishing this seemingly impossible task may have had some influence in the conclusions set forth by the Special Commission. However, physical scientists will hold firm in the belief that the laws of physics and the other sciences determine a "fixed" trajectory for the fatal bullet that is inconsistent with the assumptions that must be accepted to prove the authenticity of the Commission theory.

Successful identification of the real killer, would be of value in answering a second, possibly more important, question involved in the Dallas killing: "Why was he murdered?"

Is it just an accident that President Carter, himself a member of the liberal, socialist democratic movement did not face any assassination attempts during his tenure? And that Presidents John Kennedy, Gerald Ford and Ronald Reagan, all of whom represented some threat to the liberal's programs, experienced such attacks? by half crazed people? That may have just happened! and then again; maybe it didn't! Maybe there is some connection.

For reasons that are not clear, history is becoming a forgotten art in our society. The small amount of activity that we do see in that arena is seldom motivated toward constructive, useful incentives. Instead, they are inclined to take the form of studies and analyses of the past, designed to decimate what is already "in the books". Transparent studies, designed to prove a preconceived result are not unusual. Devotion to trashing long-held beliefs, can usually be associated with the "era of emotional idiocy" that precludes intellectual reason from prevailing. In these situations, the "establishment view" often conflicts with some minority desire to illustrate and prove their persecution at the hands of the "male white American". Examples are the crusades that are presently assaulting the previously accepted story of Christopher Columbus, and the historical story of "how the west was won". It is no surprise, that small "nationality oriented" minorities among us are pressing such campaigns to trash these parts of our history. Because such action is extremely beneficial in their efforts to solicit sympathy; to appeal to the guilt complex (the result of the emotional plague—excessive emotional sensitivity) so easily aroused in the rest of us, and to serve as justification for some retribution (usually monetary).

The ease with which such minorities are able to recruit support of their cause in the mass media and from the politicians and the pseudo intelligentsia of the nation is incredible. How better to assure success in the magnification of such nontraditional, contrived perspectives; than to incorporate them into the curriculum of our school systems? Feed the gibberish into the minds of our elementary school children. Expose and infect them early in life with "the emotional plague"; before they are able to think and decide for themselves what is truth and what is fiction! And what is most distressing, is the fact that announcements of such curriculum changes in the media (see the Portland, Oregon, October 9, 1992, daily Oregonian) do not provoke any response from the parents of the children who will be exposed and suffer from it the rest of their lives!

The loss of conjecture, speculation, questioning, and honesty of presentation that, at one time, led to study and analysis of our past is unfortunate. To totally eliminate consideration of honest, objective historical theses in the on-going, national, decision-making process is suicidal. The middle decades of the twentieth century, 1940's to the 1970's, were times of conspicuous and significant changes in the direction and philosophy of our governmental systems. Individually and collectively the passage and implementation of the program elements of President Lynden Johnson's Great Society played an important role in accelerating this country's rush to Socialism.

Unbelievably and unfortunately the elements and totality of his revolutionary dream have continued to be championed, supported and bulldozed through by social-democratic majorities in the Congresses in the intervening years. This, in spite of the fact, that there has been abundant, undeniable evidence that all of those programs are *not* achieving positive results or meeting the expectations that attended their creation. Transfer payment funding to finance the programs is *taken from* those who work, who try to support themselves and their families; people who pay taxes and are trying desperately to escape poverty and becoming part of the welfare scene, themselves. It is then *given generously and freely* to those who don't relate to any of that; who have the strange idea that the government (we the people) owes them the necessities of life *and more!* The costs of this nonsense have reached staggering proportions. These programs have not satisfied any vital need. Having committed to those massive transfers, and having spent trillions of dollars; the sacrifice of the payers, over several decades, has not produced any visible, lasting, tangible results. None-the-less, the government demands that we continue pouring enormous sums of our limited resources into this sump; annual funding of these failing programs increase at rates far greater than the increase of any of the accepted indexes that measure cost-of-living changes. What is more important, the rate of escalation for these costs far exceeds the rate of increase in income of those persons (families) who are living on the margin between self-sufficiency and welfare. The result has been to increase over the years the number of people living in poverty; from about 24,500,000 or 11.4 percent of the population in 1978 to about 31,750,000 or 13.0 percent of the population in 1988.[15]

Walter Heller, head of President Johnson's Council of Economic Advisers from the University of Michigan, advised him in the development of his War on Poverty program. Mr. Heller's expectation, and that of the President

---

[15]    The World Almanac And Book of Facts-1991

was that, "Lynden would be the president who eliminated poverty."[16] A lesson learned about the dependability of advice given by economists? The erroneous data President Bush received from his Council of Economic Advisors in 1992 concerning the expected recovery from recession was not that unusual!

In his January 8, 1964, "State of the Union", message President Johnson said, "This administration today, here and now, declares unconditional war on poverty in America." In his March 16th, 1964 message to the Congress, he said that the cost of his programs would only be $970 *million*—about one per cent of the national budget. Good intentions gone drastically wrong! By 1992, these entitlement costs had increased from $970 *million* to $730 *billion*; an increase of about 750 percent in 28 years! an average increase of 27 percent per year! In 1992 the costs of entitlements were almost 50 percent of the national budget; as compared to the 1964 estimate of 1 percent! Individual income taxes, the taxes that you and I and all other individual tax payers will pay in 1992, will total about $476 *billion*.[17] Take all of the taxes that we pay each year, and it will only pay for 65 percent of those entitlement costs! Can there be any doubt as to the success or failure of the program? And yet it continues to be championed by the social democrats in Congress and they insist that the taxpayer continue to fund it!

There is one more important piece of information that will help us understand what follows. During JFK's administration, his brother Robert F. Kennedy served as his Attorney General. In a speech on May 6, 1964 at the University of Pennsylvania, Robert said:

> "About one-fifth of the people are against everything all the time."[18]

This statement was printed in the May 7, 1964, Philadelphia Inquirer. These are not the kind of words that jump off the page at you; the kind that will obviously live and contribute something important to the future of the nation. It seems unusual that they have been preserved for us. But they have; and they will provide useful insight for our analysis and discussion.

---

[16]    Lynden; An Oral Biography, by Merle Miller; G.P Putnam's Sons, 1980 (p 362)

[17]    United We Stand; Ross Perot; Hyperion; 1992

[18]    The Oxford Dictionary of Modern Quotations; Tony Augarde; Oxford University Press; 1991

We can now proceed with interrogation of these problems and development of what may be some surprising discoveries about the roots and possible solutions for many of them!

Contrary to Kennedy's statement, the groups of people that oppose and "stop action on" everything our society tries to do is almost, always much smaller than the 20 percent that he quotes. Twenty percent of 250 million people in the country would mean that 50 million oppose the actions! We can begin to comprehend the gravity of our problem when we realize that in a usual situation, today, an insignificant, infinitesimally small fraction of one percent (for example 50 to 500 people—{0.0000004 to 0.000004 percent}) can successfully stop any and all things that we try to do. They do so, by simply pursuing their "rights" in our inept, costly beyond reason, ineffective legal system. A system constrained partially to the use of ludicrous laws passed by local, state and federal legislators. A system that seems to feel compelled to hear all cases, regardless of how minuscule the issue. A system in which the performers feel free to ignore literal, constitutional ramifications of the issues raised and to legislate their own biases into the results of the cases!

For example, identification of a site location; and design and construction of a safe, permanent storage facility for high-level, radio-active, nuclear waste is one of *the most important* things his country needs to do. A site has been located and its construction is nearly complete. However, a few people in the general area of that site; empowered by the ineptitude of our governments' actions are able to totally deny all of us the use of the facility! To be sure, it is not possible to develop storage facilities and operational practices for such material, and guarantee 100 percent, accident-free operation over the millennia of years that they will be used. That is exactly the reason that the need is so great for the facility. If such an accident is to occur, our planning and actions now should be directed to minimize the death, human suffering, destruction of assets and total cost that results! But, the detractors simply use this factor in another way; and they say, "Not in my backyard."

It is perfectly obvious that if the facility is to be built, *it will have to be in someone's backyard!* But, with every one in charge, with no one in charge, and with a vacuum of intellect and backbone in our governments; there is no way for the national interest to prevail. And in the meantime the hundreds of thousands of tons of this treacherous material that already exists, and the additional that is being generated in active reactors, must be stored in facilities which were built to provide only temporary storage—until the material could be moved to more adequate, permanent locations. The tragedy of this, is that these temporary storage facilities are located close to population centers and in the proximity to immense amounts of very productive real estate and large waterways. A nuclear accident in one of these locations could (will?) result in unnecessary heavy loss of life and in the loss of use of massive areas of the country.

What ever happened to the concept in our democracy, "that the wishes of the majority governs?" Not today! Not here, in the good ole U.S.A.!

These kinds of pivotal problems are exacerbated by the appointment of unqualified persons to important cabinet posts. Providing adequate storage facilities for nuclear waste is a responsibility of the Federal Department of Energy. President Reagan had a dentist serving as the Secretary of Energy during much of his administration. President Bush named an ex-commander of a submarine to that post. Looking into people's mouths all day, or viewing the world through a periscope does little to provide the necessary management or scientific skills for that position. As might be expected, "energy" problems continued to fester; little of consequence was accomplished during their terms. Clinton has appointed a female, corporate attorney whose qualifications are even more deficient!

Most of us expect our government to be as described by Abraham Lincoln; "of the people, by the people, for the people". The implication of that statement and of the way we elect our leaders is that in our "democracy" the opinions, the aspirations, and the objectives of the majority of the people will prevail; will determine the programs, the environment, and the morality for the nation. It also implies that the government will maintain a societal environment, a system of laws, in which individuals, and public and private organizations can do what needs to be done to serve the needs of the masses of people and the nation. Why else would we go to the trouble of electing our president and the other agents that we charge with the stewardship of the public's business? The people understand that; and it would certainly seem reasonable for us to expect that those we elect would understand it, also! But! do they?

There seems to be two possible answers to that question:

1. They do not comprehend it! Or worse yet
2. Our reference to, "the fools we elect to public office" in fact, proves to be an overstatement of their true ability!

We do not make such demeaning statements without some trepidation. But! Others have tried in innumerable ways to break the impasse, and create some action to resolve our problems. All efforts, to date, have failed to penetrate the cocoon that isolates our government leaders and the establishment from reality! We are positively and unequivocally determined, here, to do what we must to get through to the perpetrators!

*THE FACT IS THAT MOST ACTIONS BY OUR CONGRESSIONAL AND EXECUTIVE BRANCHES OF OUR GOVERNMENT IN THE PAST TWO TO THREE DECADES HAVE SYSTEMATICALLY AND EFFECTIVELY SHIFTED THE RESPONSE TO AND CONTROL OF OUR GOVERNMENTS AWAY FROM THE "MAJORITY" OF OUR CITIZENS. THEIR ACTIONS HAVE METHODICALLY SHIFTED THE POWER AND CONTROL OF EVERY ASPECT OF THE COUNTRY OVER TO THESE SMALL GROUPS OF ANTI-ESTABLISHMENT ACTIVISTS; PEOPLE WHO ARE SELF-APPOINTED AND SELF-ANOINTED. PEOPLE WHO SUFFER FROM THE EMOTIONAL PLAGUE; WHO ARE OFTEN INTELLECTUALLY ILLITERATE ABOUT THE SITUATION THEY ARE OPPOSING; WHO ARE RESPONSIBLE TO NO ONE; AND WHO HAVE NO KNOWLEDGE OR INTEREST IN THE ADVERSE IMPACTS THEIR ACTIONS ARE CAUSING FOR OTHERS!*

*DURING THE 1992 CAMPAIGN SEASON THERE HAS BEEN A GREAT DEAL OF TALK ABOUT THE "GRIDLOCK" THAT EXISTS IN OUR GOVERNMENT INSTITUTIONS IN WASHINGTON, D. C. OF COURSE THAT GRIDLOCK IS VERY VISIBLE AND IT IS A SOURCE OF GREAT DISGUST AND DISTRESS TO ALL OF US! HOWEVER, VIEWED MORE REALISTICALLY, GIVEN THE CONGRESS THAT WE PRESENTLY HAVE, THEIR INABILITY TO ACT CAN BE VIEWED AS A BLESSING. IN THE PAST FEW MONTHS, THE COUNTRY HAS BEEN WELL SERVED BY PRESIDENT BUSH'S VETO OF SOMETHING OVER THIRTY "HOKEY" BILLS PASSED BY THE CONGRESS.*

*THAT "GRIDLOCK", THE INABILITY OF THE WASHINGTON, D. C. ESTABLISHMENT TO ACCOMPLISH ANYTHING, IS JUST ONE PART OF THE PROBLEM. IN FACT, IT IS PROBABLY THE LEAST IMPORTANT PART!*

*WHAT IS MORE IMPORTANT, IS THAT IN SYSTEMATICALLY EMPOWERING THESE INFINITESIMALLY SMALL GROUPS OF ACTIVISTS, REBELS WITH A CAUSE, ANY CAUSE, THEY HAVE CREATED GRIDLOCK OUTSIDE OF GOVERNMENT, AS WELL! LAWS THAT OUR ELECTED OFFICIALS HAVE ENACTED WHICH NOW CONTROL THE, "WORLD WE LIVE IN"; ALLOW SMALL GROUPS, OFTEN EVEN INDIVIDUALS, TO DELAY AND/OR DEFEAT ANY AND EVERY ACTION THAT SOCIETY TRIES TO TAKE.*

*IT IS NO SECRET THAT THE CITIZENS OF THIS COUNTRY NEVER REACH A CONSENSUS AGREEMENT ON ANYTHING THAT TAKES PLACE HERE. THERE IS ALWAYS A FACTION THAT DISAGREES WITH THE MAJORITY OPINION. THAT PHENOMENON IS NOT NEW TO THESE TIMES! IT HAS ALWAYS BEEN THAT WAY. WHAT IS DIFFERENT, IS THE FACT THAT OUR GOVERNMENT(S), IN THEIR INFINITE WISDOM, AND BY THEIR RECKLESS, MISDIRECTED ACTIONS; HAVE TAKEN CONTROL OF THE COUNTRY AWAY FROM RULE BY THE MAJORITY OF THE PEOPLE; AND GIVEN IT TO SMALL GROUPS OF DISSENTING ACTIVISTS. THE FURTHER CONSEQUENCE OF THIS TRANSFER OF POWER IS THAT CONTROL OF THE COUNTRY IS SHIFTED FROM THE INTELLECTUAL, ORGANIZED INSTITUTIONS DESIGNED TO IDENTIFY AND IMPLEMENT THOSE POLICIES AND ACTIONS THAT BEST SERVE THE NEEDS OF THE COUNTRY; TO SMALL GROUPS OF LIMITED INTELLECT, WHO HAVE NO RESPECT FOR THE OPINIONS OR RIGHTS OF OTHERS, WHO HAVE A HUGE PROPENSITY TO TALK CONSTANTLY, AND WHO ARE RESPONSIBLE TO NO ONE.*

*WE HAVE ADMITTED TO EACH OTHER THAT WE ARE NOT BRAIN SURGEONS OR GENIUSES. I HAVE PROMISED YOU THAT WOULD NOT BE NECESSARY TO UNDERSTAND WHAT WE ARE DOING. IT WILL NOT STRETCH OUR INTELLECT TOO FAR, TO UNDERSTAND THAT THERE IS ABSOLUTELY NO WAY THAT THIS COUNTRY, OR ANY ORGANIZATION, CAN OPERATE—AND SATISFY THE WISHES OF EVERY ONE. WHEN EVERYONE IS IN CONTROL; NO ONE IS IN CONTROL. WHEN SUCH CONDITIONS EXIST, GRIDLOCK RESULTS! AND THERE IS ONLY ONE WAY TO CORRECT THE PROBLEM. DO WE NEED TO SPELL THAT OUT TO THEM?*

*THERE IS ABSOLUTELY NOTHING THAT SOCIETY AT-LARGE TRIES TO DO, MUST DO; THAT IS EXEMPT FROM INTERVENTION OF THE ACTIVIST SPOILERS. A DOZEN OR LESS REBELS CAN EFFECTIVELY DELAY AD INFINITUM, FOR MONTHS, YEARS, OR DECADES ANY PROJECT, REGARDLESS OF HOW BADLY IT IS NEEDED BY SOCIETY.*

*GRIDLOCK IN GOVERNMENT; GRIDLOCK IN THE PRIVATE SECTOR; GRIDLOCK EVERYWHERE—AND THE CONGRESS BLAMES THE PRESIDENT FOR THE PRESENT RECESSION. WHERE DO PEOPLE LIKE THAT COME FROM? AND HOW DO THEY END UP IN THESE POSITIONS OF SUCH GREAT RESPONSIBILITY??*

Having made such charges it is appropriate that we explain some of the rationale that supports that position.

Throughout our history, our social environment has been referred to, respectfully and with some pride, as the "melting pot" of the world. It is true that in the past, people of many ethnic, political, and religious backgrounds, from other places around the world, were assimilated into the population of this country. It is also true that the diversity of characteristics, abilities, interests, ambitions, and goals of all of those people contributed in a positive way to the kind of nation that we became.

As is so often the custom in our society, our leaders and many of our people blindly accept and act on the basis of untested assumptions. Among them are the following:

1.  That our country today, continues to be a "melting pot", where the people of different backgrounds, religions and ethnicities come together in a way that is in the best interests of our country. That the differences in their background, knowledge, perspective, etc. fit in and that the new mixture, with them included, makes this a better place than what existed before they arrived.

2.  That continued acceptance of massive numbers of foreign immigrants into this country, each year, and mingling them into the "melting pot" has the same positive impact as did the mixing of nationalities in the early days of the country. This nation's immigration policy seems to accept this theory. It also seems to be the basis for the soft, indifferent, non-enforcement approach taken in passively accepting the hundreds of thousands of illegal aliens that cross into this country's southern states each year.

3.  That all of these people come to "join us"; that their intent is to help make this a better place for all of us! The "real world" creation of their own "Little Havana" or "Little Mexico" civilizations within our borders somehow gets overlooked. And of course, if the existence of these mini-cultures is not recognized, judgments as to the positive or negative impact of their immigration are not made.

A convincing argument can be made that, in fact, this country is no longer the "Melting Pot" that it once was. It is instead, Colloidal". It is important to understand the difference between the two; the melting pot, and colloidal conditions. If these terms are new to you, we need to do some "lab work"; some experimentation to clarify their differences.

Find two one-quart fruit jars with lids. Take one, put 2 cups of water in it; add one-half cup of vinegar; put on the lid and shake. What do you have? In mixing they have created something that is new and different from either of the original ingredients; each of which contributed something to the new substance created. They seem to be compatible. The two liquids have mixed in a way that is analogous to our expectations under the "melting pot" theory.

However, to fully satisfy the criteria of the melting pot concept, one additional requirement must be met. The new substance must be an improvement over either of the original ingredients. Take a sip of the water you started with; then taste a sip of the vinegar. Now taste a sip of the substance that resulted from mixing them. Which is best?

Try this using other liquids in place of the vinegar; milk, catsup, syrup, etc. If the simple assumption used in justifying the continued, massive influx of immigrants applies here; the new mixture will always have characteristics that make it superior to *either* of the ingredients used to make it. Is that the case? Are your results here applicable to our "melting pot" assumptions? how might they impact our continuing immigration policies?

Now take the other fruit jar; add two cups of water; add one-half cup of motor oil; put on the lid and shake. Now what do you have? What do you know about that? Something has gone wrong here. The substances did not mix. Immediately after shaking the jar, the oil will be suspended in small globules floating around in the water. The water and oil have not mixed. If that jar is left to sit for a while the oil will separate and rise, to float on top of the water. The water solution with the oil globules floating around in it is not a "melting pot"; it is instead a colloidal solution. The two original ingredients are not compatible with each other; they will not mix; it is fruitless to try to get them to do so. Does that idea have application in considering our "melting pot" assumptions?

This nation was a melting pot at one time, and that was good! But that is no longer the case! I know that! And so do you, if you stop and think about it for a while! Where in our society do you find a "melting pot" of persons; black and white, red and yellow; men and women; young and old; workers, union members and management; rich and poor; working in harmony to advance the best interests of the nation?

What has happened to interrupt the progression of relationships that once made this nation great? We have stated the probability that "Great Society" programs begun during President Johnson's administration have contributed greatly to the problems we face. Programs that have continued to be supported and expanded; unchallenged and uncontrolled, by social-democratic majorities in the two houses of the Congress since that time.

What are some of the programs of his time, that may be at the root of our problems?

The Tax Reduction Act was enacted into law. It reflected the economic concept that under some conditions the federal government must spend more than it collects in order to stimulate economic growth.

A very broad civil rights law was enacted that attacked segregation, banned discrimination in public accommodations, and eliminated restrictions in job opportunities.

The Medicare system of health care to cover elderly people was established in conjunction with the Social Security program.

The Voting Rights Act of 1965 was enacted. It essentially removed literacy tests which were said to be unfairly preventing many blacks from exercising their right to vote.

Federal government involvement in financing primary and secondary schools was increased substantially; "to solve the problems in our schools for once, and for all time!!?"

Unemployment compensation was liberalized, the food stamp program was greatly expanded, opportunities for youth employment were increased very substantially.

Two new federal departments were created: Housing and Urban Development and Transportation.

All of these actions have several things in common:

— They all represented requirements for spending vast sums of money; such large amounts that the persons instituting the actions had absolutely no idea of the short- or long-term costs!
— They were not enacted because of any great need that existed in our society at the time.
— They represented extensive increases in the size of government and ill-advised intervention into the lives of the people, businesses and commerce of the nation.
— There were no program plans defining the year to year development, for measuring benefits against expectations, for following cost/benefit ratios, or for controlling costs.
— Magnitude of future costs, control mechanisms and financing methods were ignored.

— In retrospect, we can perceive that each of these actions have set into motion, forces and government action that are impeding the effective development and operation of all of our public and private enterprises.

— Unbelievably, many of those we reelect to public office, year after year freely and publicly proclaim the belief that those programs are still working!

All of this for what purpose? Lets agree that the provisions of the Civil Rights Act of 1964 were helpful. They addressed a need. Beyond that, there was no evidence of a pressing need or even the desirability for all of that additional related legislation that is killing the country; dividing us into a significant number of self-centered, selfish, special interest groups; creating and sustaining phony feelings of victimization, and creating and fulfilling unrealistic and undeserved expectations for special benefits for members of the special groups; all of which leaves establishment people, (especially young white guys, who are stuck with what is left—if anything—after the others get their special benefits) resentful and in many cases out for retaliation. These fellows have done nothing to deserve such shoddy, unfair, unconstitutional treatment. Society's petty, non-responsive answer is that today's actions are to compensate for past exploitation of some of those people? And society is surprised and itself reacts in holier-than-thou, revengeful ways when "white guys" commit what society refers to as "hate" crimes.

Many of the additional actions were largely directed toward satisfying LBJ's ambitions for recognition in the annals of this nation's history.

In one great fell-swoop they set in motion an attack upon the people's sense of pride and of their dedication to self sufficiency. Individually and as a package these changes communicated to all citizens a new relationship between their government and themselves. The government could and would "do it all!" "Big Daddy" would be there to take care of all of us!

Let me repeat: "The assassination of President John F. Kennedy", impacted the future of this country far beyond the realization of most of us. Changes made by President Lynden B. Johnson totally changed the course of our national history from what it would have been had Kennedy lived to serve out his term.

So again—in President Johnson's time; and today, we find the national theme to be:

## "ASK NOT WHAT YOU CAN DO FOR YOUR COUNTRY, ASK WHAT YOUR COUNTRY CAN DO FOR YOU!"

There can be little doubt that changes made during the Johnson administration serve as the "roots" of the massive, misdirected, costly-beyond-comprehension entitlement program problems that we face today. What a shame! The cancerous lesions that are squeezing the life from our system are widespread; and it is possible that, as is the case of many other types of cancers, there is no effective treatment. One thing seems certain; the situation will not cure itself.

Our society will work if, and only if, we *all respect each other;* we are all honest in our relationships with each other; we recognize and respect the rights of society and others when we reach to claim our own rights; when knowledge, experience, and ability to perform are accepted as necessary, controlling factors in staffing the work place, when people are *selected* for work positions for the correct reasons—ability to do the job best; when we share common goals, and when we all work together to achieve them; when it is recognized that people and organizations must produce effectively and efficiently to continue to exist in the new world order and when we accept the fact that we can't, each of us, always have our own way.

I am reminded of the first time that I went hunting for ducks and geese. My younger brother and I were in our early teens. We had religiously saved our money for a long time, to buy a 3-shot, bolt-action, 20-gauge shot gun. Prior to this first hunting trip he and I had torn apart one of the shells that we were using, to expose the large number (probably over one hundred) of small "shot" pellets in each shell. On this first trip we spent about an hour sneaking up on a sizeable flock of birds that were feeding in a field. I remember thinking; as we stood up, spooked them, and began firing, that with all of those "shot" and the way they spread out after leaving the gun barrel; all I had to do was just point the gun in the direction of the flock, and I couldn't help but hit some of them! Imagine my surprise and consternation when the shots had all been fired and the smoke began to clear away—and I had absolutely nothing to show for my effort! I had missed everything. Now, I am not a slow learner, it didn't take me long to learn the lesson that has served me well in all subsequent experiences in my lifetime. If you want to achieve something really worthwhile in life, you have to identify and aim at a bull's eye that will propel you along the route toward your ultimate goal. When I finally became aware of this truism, when I quit shooting at the flock and started picking out individual birds of the flock as my target, then

I began to be much more successful in bringing food home for our family's consumption. One further point, on occasion we would come upon a group of ducks commingling with geese. On such an occasion, the first requirement was for the shooter to select one of the geese as his target, if the goal was to have a goose dinner. A hunter of ducks and geese will never be successful, as long as he/she shoots at the flock. Success requires that the aim and the effort be directed much more carefully and purposefully at a precise target. Beyond this, the hunter had to know how to operate his weapon and must be able to properly aim the gun, leading the bird just the right amount so that the shot did not go behind the target.

It has been my experience that the lesson learned here has application in almost everything that we do in life, if we are to be successful. It most certainly has application in the arena of public service. New legislation is not always the right answer for solving problems. But, in those instances where it may be the best course of action, they must first identify, precisely the problem they are trying to solve,—the target—and then carefully develop the wording of the legislation to do exactly what is needed.

The Civil Rights Act of 1964 was properly focused, to correct inequalities in the treatment of colored people; to assure them equal access in many activities and to many opportunities that the Constitution guarantees all of us. Additional Civil Rights Laws, *Equal* Employment Opportunity, Environmental Protection, Endangered Species, etc. laws that have been added to the mine fields impeding the public and private enterprise ability to accomplish anything were possibly well-intentioned laws. But! they are not working. That is understandable. They were created by persons of narrow vision; who thought only of what they *might* achieve in the fields to which they were directed. They were shooting at the flock. The goal was not clearly in focus. The evils that were to be corrected were not well defined. Those particulars were left to the people, the lawyers and the courts to define. They shot at the flock, and missed! the problem was greatly intensified when they, and their successors failed to recognize that they had missed the mark! Hunters with such an intellect may occasionally get lucky, but they will never be successful at what they do. Neither will government servants!

If ours was a "melting pot" society, everyone in this country would feel honored to be an "American". And, all who enter the country would cherish the hope that they too would be able to enter into the brotherhood of "Americans". That was true for most of our history. It is not true today. Those "wise?" people who we have chosen to be our leaders, and who have been given the responsibility for the stewardship of this country during the last 20 to 30 years, have managed to destroy those important relationships that our citizens used to enjoy with each other. Relationships that were a cornerstone to the effective operation of our system. They have managed to destroy most of the positive, good relationships that once existed between people of differing nationalities, colors, sexes, ages and stations in life. The have created and empowered a significant number of special interest groups within our society. They have driven wedges into the mantle of society creating needless separation, stress, and friction between its various segments. *They have ineptly and irrationally discovered and implemented ways of bringing out the worst in most of us.*

A large majority of the colored people in this country, perceive that it is not in their best interests, individually or as a group, to join in the brotherhood of the "Americans". The next higher grade of citizenship, available only to members of their race, that of Afro-American, guarantees special privileges, perquisites, and "rights!" that are too important for them to sacrifice just to become regular Americans, one of us. As members of this special class of citizenship, they receive all of the advantages of being, simply an American, plus a multitude of special privileges available only to them. They don't have to compete with others for jobs. Their applications for entry into institutions of higher education, receive special consideration which means that they are selected over others with better qualifications! Their names in these kinds of activities are kept on separate lists. In the selection process, it is not unusual for the list of regular "American" candidates to be totally ignored in favor of names from one of the special lists of candidates; for example, "Afro-Americans".

As has previously been discussed, we should not hold the Afro-American community responsible for all of this. If they are able to outsmart the system and legally obtain special benefits for themselves, that's the way the "ball bounces". Taking for oneself, all that is legally available, has always been an accepted tenet of the American Way. All of this "special treatment", and "special privileges" for minorities and special interest groups have been created by that distinguished group of largely white, male, adult, elected and bureaucratic, leaders of our country. The situation will not improve until we get leadership at all levels of government that is intelligent and managerially competent enough to protect "the people's" interests and those of the country against the cunning, emotional demands of these groups. Until that happens, we can only expect that the situation will get even worse.

It is important to note that there is a movement of significant size in the afro-American community that is recognizing that continuation of this special-treatment environment for their people will have long-term adverse consequences for their race in this country. They make a compelling case for eliminating much of the special treatment received by most of their people. Some insights can be gleaned into the thinking of some of these groups by reading Stephen L. Carter's book, "Reflections of an Affirmative Action Baby"; published in 1991 by Basic Books. For reasons that will become clear later, these ideas are vehemently opposed by that leadership group of the black community that presses for continuing the status quo; people who continue to demand more and more special goodies. The leaders of the status-quo group stand to lose much in prestige, power, and financial gain if the alternate mode of operation is accepted.

The Afro-American community has been singled out here as an example. They are not the only group that benefits from such special treatment; there are many others. The greatest penetration of inequitable actions that are most abusive to the rest of us and that most threatens our way of life, is that of the Femme-Americans, the feminist movement. A small, mostly white, segment of the female population of the country represents the most aggressive, demanding and vitriolic special interest category presently jeopardizing this country. It is interesting to note the passive acceptance of all of their antics and irrational demands by those of us who represent the establishment; people who supposedly have the welfare of the nation at heart. In general, we have not even separated them out, identified them as a special group and given them a name. Publicly, they have continued to be known simply as a part of the "American" group. However, they enjoy special privileges (rights!) that greatly overshadow those of any other group in our society. Benefits that they receive just because they are female. We need to be able to identify this group as we proceed with our discussion. We'll refer to them as Femme-Americans.

Again we need to point out that this group *does not* include all of the women in the country. A large segment of our women are not involved in the vindictive, aggressive attack that the Femme-Americans are waging to increase their power, their influence and their benefits at the expense of the rest of us. Having said that, it is important to note that the lack of participation by the establishment women's group does not insulate them from the adverse affects of the Femme actions, and the spineless capitulation of our politicians, managers, and power brokers to their endless demands for more and more special treatment.

A large percentage of the female population of this country would prefer to live the pattern of life that has been traditionally their's in this country;

family and interpersonal relationships that women in our society have enjoyed over the years. It seems that they may not understand, that that alternative is rapidly disappearing as an option. As the Femmes continue to vanquish the art of reason and win more and more concessions in their unrelenting war against our society; their control over what is allowed and what is not proper grows proportionately. The two concepts are simply incompatible.

For example, a woman who is happily married, who has children, and who wishes to stay home and serve in the traditional roles of wife, mother, and keeper of the home fires, shares the loss when her husband; being a white, anglo-saxon, protestant male (WASPM) can no longer compete in our warped economic system. Should he lose his job; the fact that he may be the only "breadwinner" for a traditional, functioning family unit will be of no benefit to him in his search for new employment. The absolute priority given to females and others in the selection process regardless of any other extenuating circumstances dooms him to be last on the totem pole for employment. Never mind that the special-category person selected over him, is often (usually) the spouse of someone that earns an annual income in the six or seven figures! Is it any wonder that the rich get richer, the middle class is shrinking and the poor are getting poorer? And we all know what happens! The welfare rolls, and demand for food stamps continue to increase at a shocking rate. More importantly, these conditions will cause yet further decline in our family unit statistics. American women who believe in and cherish the traditional role of women in our society must realize that option is being lost as an alternative. Present circumstances dictate that they become aggressively involved if that alternative is to be preserved for those who desire it! They enjoy a unique position in the power struggle that must be waged to correct the problem. White men will not be able or willing to do the job for them. For reasons that defy most logic; the males that we elect to positions of leadership cower in the presence of any and all charges made by the feminist, counter-culture, special-interest group.

The Native-American (Indian) is another group that has deeply penetrated the veil of what is considered fair and deserved in a traditional or Constitutional sense in our society. As a result of their classification as a special group, they receive very substantial monetary and "rights" benefits over those available to persons in the "regular American" group. They too, continue to press aggressively and forcefully for more and more special benefits. And the "great white fathers", with tears on cheek from the ***emotionally tugging*** justification, bow in servitude to their continuing charges and intimidation.

Each of the "special" groups have developed very clever, devious ways of gleaning special treatment for themselves". Their appeals all have in common, the pretense that the members of the special groups have suffered as victims of our system and the white American male. They understand clearly the weaknesses and ineptitude of those who make our government decisions. They are especially clever and effective in capitalizing on and at exploiting the affects of the "EMOTIONAL PLAGUE" on the decision makers; and their deep-seated feelings of sympathy and guilt that is so prevalent in this "ERA OF EMOTIONAL IDIOCY".

In our society today, as it has been reconstructed through the genius of these leaders, all employee selections, public and private, are required—first and foremost—to meet affirmative-action quotas. When "*special*" lists of candidates for all of these "protected" groups are available to selecting officials, and they usually are, the relative level of qualifications of the candidates on the various lists—the ability of a candidate to perform on the job—is meaningless. As a matter of fact, it is not even necessary that the candidate selected be qualified for the position—if she/he is of a protected ethnicity, sex, etc.

There are a number of writers who pose themselves as management experts and consultants, who publish columns on that subject in the hard media. If you read them, as I do occasionally, I'm sure you have encountered there, statements to the affect that Resume's are no longer important or useful in the job-search activity. To a person who has successfully managed large organizations over a period of many years, that statement goes a long way toward explaining the reason for the increasing occurrence of organization failures in this country. It also provides interesting insights as to the value of advice from such pseudo intellectual consultants and the likely competence (?) of managers who hire them and accept and use their advice.

The employer's need for literate, competent, economically feasible employees to get the job done in a timely manner, at a competitive cost is totally and absolutely violated by this "formula for action".

One would like to think that honest, capable management people, especially in the private sector, would say, "to hell with all of this baloney, if I am to survive in my area of local, national and international competition I will have to employ the best qualified, most capable, highly dedicated people I can find"; and that they would then go ahead and do just that! But alas! that is not an option. Anyone who would do that would surely find themselves in court facing the full force of the Federal government with its unlimited supply of lawyers, time and money. Efficiency, effectiveness, and survival of our public and private enterprises will be, and are, sacrificed, as necessary to indulge and acquiesce to *all* of the idiotic laws that the social politicians have forced on the system.

I simply cannot understand why the survival of businesses, and commerce; especially labor intensive, blue-collar activities such as manufacturing; is of no importance to these *leaders*. By what logical process do they impose innumerable, impossible and costly restrictions to our ability to produce and compete in the evolving, new-world order; and then they turn around and enter into "free-trade" agreements with those who have taken and are taking our jobs. People and countries who are still able to hire the best person available to them for the job; who are not subject to quotas; who are not encumbered by outdated labor laws; who are not confronted by endangered species laws, and who are not subject to environmental protection requirements, and costs.

What is the intelligible logic that says to them, "pollution of planet earth's water, air, and soil to satisfy the insatiable demands for more and more material benefits for citizens of the U. S., is acceptable if that pollution occurs in Mexico, Taiwan, Korea, etc.; but not acceptable if it happens in the United States???

By what logic is it considered possible for our system to compete with employers in foreign settings who are allowed to pay their employees substantially less for a days work than most employers in this country are *required* to pay their employees for one *hours* work. Where those competing foreign employers do not provide health care, child care, family leave, sick leave, vacation with pay, retirement programs, social security, etc., ad infinitum.

What is the basis of their rationalization that our system and its elements should be able to compete successfully with these other forces when our domestic competitors in the "new world" market are encumbered with massive taxation penalties levied freely and beyond any sense of practical control by Federal, state, county, and city governments; school districts; health districts; transportation districts; water districts; sewer districts; etc., all of which are grossly mismanaged by elected and bureaucratic persons who are selected for mysterious reasons. Reasons other than their ability to do the job. And who, as a result, are usually inept at what they are supposed to do! Taxation that is predictable; its costs will increase incessantly more rapidly than any of the cost indices in the nation.

Does the impact of such simple, logical comparisons go beyond the level of literacy of those in "high places" in management structures of this country, today? What other reasonable answer might there be? I'm listening!

Lacking understanding and action at those levels, the entrepreneur who is responsible for the success of any particular business operation in this country, does what he must do, to try to save his organization; he moves it to Mexico or some third world country. And this country forfeits all of the jobs, the taxes, and the financial benefits it represents! And, the additional economic benefits that had been generated by a multitude of satellite, support activities are also lost.

Only a politician can understand all of this! Only a politician can help create such a crazy, impossible system and then, turn around, and wonder why so many Savings and Loans are failing; why so many banks are in trouble; why so many businesses are unable to make it; why our institutions are not competitive with those of other nations; why the fabric of our society is being shattered, families breaking up, mothers (and fathers) relegating companionship, care, and development of their children to a priority level below that given relationships on their jobs; why our education systems are in shambles, the bulk of our population apparently semi-literate, or worse, and the situation deteriorating more and more, day after day; year after year; so many young people, with so much to live for, are committing suicide; etc., etc. Only they, the politicians, fail to understand that they and their ineptitude or their unwillingness to do their job rationally, are responsible for all of these appalling, serious failures.

Our leaders never seem to realize that our problems are largely the result of actions they and their predecessors have taken in the past. That solutions must start with the correction of past mistakes; modifying or eliminating existing laws and programs that are not achieving the expected benefits, that are counterproductive, and that require massive expenditures that this country simply cannot afford.

Instead, they bury their heads in the sand, and proceed to enact more and more misdirected missiles that compound the problems and make the situation worse.

Throughout this discussion we have referred to and advocated the scientific method of problem solving as a model for moving to correct our many, challenging, serious difficulties. The system calls for proceeding with the activity in certain well-defined steps. As applied to the government arena, these steps consist of:

— being continually alert and reacting in a timely fashion to symptoms of pending problems.

— defining precisely the characteristics of any problem. Effective solutions require that corrective action be sharply focused and directed at the well-defined problem.

— identifying possible alternative actions that might best serve our needs; considering best-guess effectiveness and *cost*.

— selecting the one alternative that appears to have the best chance for success.

— implement the selected plan, being careful to include "milestones" or measuring points that can be used to monitor its success or failure.

— follow through; with continuing, conscientious oversight, to monitor and record how well the "fix" is working.

— if it is working, and it seems appropriate, make adjustments as necessary to improve its performance.

— if it is not working, and it proves to be the wrong choice of corrective methods, abandon it.

— select another alternative and repeat the above steps.

Management methods utilized in this country have changed drastically during the last two or three decades. Changed from systems that worked to ones that guarantee chaos. Thanks, largely to the enamored, open-armed, unquestioning acceptance and integration into the management chain of hordes of theoretically schooled geniuses that are spewing out of institutions that award Masters Degrees in Business Administration (MBA's) and Masters Degrees in Public Administration.

Having surrendered management of so much of our public, commercial and industrial business activities to these people, their egotistical approach, and their ill-conceived methods over recent past decades, we can identify one absolute difference between the two techniques; the scientific method works—their's is a proven, miserable failure!

It is appropriate that we examine some of the 1960's actions, and identify relationships between them and our present, on-going problems.

# CHAPTER 16

It is not unusual for conscientious, thorough study and analysis of problems we face in this country to lead to a sense of surprise—astonishment that our abuse and neglect of stewardship responsibilities have not already led to collapse of our system.

A brief look at a few of these issues can help corroborate that statement. The discussion will present the view point of the author. If it is to accomplish its intended purpose we must discuss specific details of controversial issues. If, in the process your "OX" is one of those gored, we can understand that your spontaneous reaction will be adverse and emotional. Some logic will be presented to help support the statements made. If, after reading and considering that, you still disagree; we can understand that also. These are very difficult questions. It is unreasonable to expect that we will be able to develop a consensus agreement on all of them. Don't let that experience on one issue "turn you off" to the point that you are unwilling to consider the further discussions; where the action may be less personal to you, it affects others. If you are concerned at all about the welfare of the country you will certainly agree with some of the points made.

Some politicians, even social-democratic party members of the incumbency who have played major roles in creating these menacing problems, agree that correcting the mess will not be easy. As they put it; "fair, effective remedial action will require that we all share the pain resulting from such actions". Unfortunately, their thinking and involvement in correcting the situation begins and stops at that point! There is no follow-up action. *TALK IS NOT ENOUGH.*

Balancing the Federal budget in which we have been spending $400,000,000,000 per year more than we are taking in, will not be an easy task. There simply is no painless way to do that job.

Our understanding of the forces at work in the continuing onslaught on our system, will be facilitated if we introduce and define a new concept. There are individuals involved in advancing each of these "special interest" activities; who are aggressively leading the attack. Their actions, behavior and interests must be illuminated. They project presumed expertise in all fields of activity related to their area of "special interest". They vehemently support the cause of their specific groups. They are experts at exploiting emotional idiocy and the sense of guilt that is so prevalent among the people of good will in this country. They insist that "the establishment" act to meet all of their demands; to hell with the majority position on the issue or what may be best for the country. For reasons that are not obvious, the mass media follows them around like a little puppy dog reporting on and supporting all of their demonstrations, boycotts, and other activities. The resulting free promotion they receive for their cause, greatly magnifies the seeming importance of their small-group actions, often to the detriment of the country's best interests.

These persons project a selfless, deep sense of dedication to their particular special interest. Don't be too quick to embrace that perspective as being accurate. Look at their situation closely and it becomes obvious that their motivation can be attributed to potential for personal gain; benefits that flow to them when they succeed.

Our continuing references to such persons will be simplified if we assign a name to them. In one sense they are "movers and shakers"; they know all the tricks in the book for succeeding at what they do. And they are willing to use them. Issues of morality and ethics are not allowed to interfere."THE GOAL JUSTIFIES THE MEANS".

In another sense, they serve as "mouthpieces" for their cause. Nothing is off limits to them, as they verbally continue their unrelenting pursuit of their cause and assault on all opposition. The ideology of reason is completely foreign to them. They listen to no one. There is only one side to any issue; theirs!

In yet another sense they act as agents for the members of their special interest group. In that role, they are aggressive crusaders, actively involved in the leadership of the group. The concept of agent also gains some credibility from the fact that they, go for everything they can get and they expect to personally share in any gain resulting from their efforts.

Considering all of the above attributes, the title, "Operator" seems an appropriate title for them; with one exception. These people shoot for the stars; the affects of their work can and often does have major impacts on our society. The more appropriate title, then is "Big Time Operator" ("**BTO**" if they operate at the national scale; "**bto**" if they operate at a lesser level). We'll use that.

The fact that we introduce and first use this title in a situation involving African-Americans should not be misunderstood. We are not picking on anyone. As will become obvious, the process and the problem applies to situations far beyond race-related issues.

Our contention that the governments of this country are *grossly mismanaged*, could be demonstrated by discussion of any of tens or hundreds of examples. "Grossly mismanaged", as used here refers to a level below "no management". That is, government actions have made things worse than they would have been if nothing had been done. Such a situation is not uncommon in our society today. It is what happens when "**busy-bodies**", fools, insist on fixing things that aren't broken.

We will restrict our discussion here to just two examples, others deserve identification and definition in future efforts.

We will discuss:

1. The Voting Rights Act of 1965, and
2. "EQUAL" Employment Opportunity Legislation

## * * *The Voting Rights Act of 1965* * *

A look at circumstances surrounding passage of the Voting Rights Act of 1965 will give us an opportunity to make some judgments as to the honesty, the true motivation and the effectiveness of our Federal government at that time; and since. Debate leading up to the passage of this Act was *not* based upon consideration of what was best for the country. In what has become the typical approach to legislation; raw power of the few, and coercion and intimidation of the remaining members of the House of Representatives and the Senate; carried the day. This was not government, "of the *people*", "by the *people*", or "for the *people*"; where the word "*people*" carries its intended definition—the majority of the citizens. I have seen nothing in the record that would indicate that passage of the act was in response to any grass-roots movement by a majority of the citizens in the country; this law probably would not have survived a vote of the people.

In retrospect, this era can be seen as an early foray into the "big daddy" syndrome that continues to grossly plague our system to this day. The concept that the government knows what is best! That the people don't understand! And in a vacuum of public opinion and demand for corrective action; elected officials and their bureaucrats feel free to do it their way. This law and some others, generally similar to it, enacted at that time and since; have questionable bases of support in any literal translation of the Constitution. Instead emotions, personal biases, and political considerations "of the few in power" carried the day.

Biographies and history of the time indicate clearly that pressure applied by President Johnson and a few of his "power-broker" buddies, to the lesser mortals in the Legislative Branch proved to be the determining factor in the passage of this law! Citizens of this country have a right to expect that members of the House of Representatives and the Senate will vote his/her heart; as effected by discussions with constituents. When all of this was totally subordinated to the demands of the ex-Senator from Texas, something was drastically wrong.

If our democracy functioned correctly, as originally intended, a system of "checks and balances" between the three major branches of the government would become operative in circumstances such as this. In this case we would expect the Judicial Branch to step in to assure that legislation produced by the other two branches would be compatible with Constitutional dictates. Unfortunately, that part of the system had been prostituted also.

We and the country would benefit greatly if the selection of judges for the judicial system, were made on an intellectual basis, without regard to political considerations. That had been the case in earlier times; but, alas, that concept has not been in operation for several decades. And so, decisions that had previously been objective and dedicated to an intended literal translation of the Constitution, have been displaced by judgments that reflect the emotions, personal convictions and biases of presiding jurist(s). Adverse impacts of errors in judgment and destruction of the system are compounded by the fact that every decision recorded, sets precedent, and affects the resolution of future cases. The total legal system is like a chain; in which the total can never be stronger than the weakest link. And the cause of real justice is lost!

Most Supreme Courts, prior to the Warren Court, (1953-1969), had viewed their job as one of interpreting the wording and intent of our Constitution to applications in the new day's setting and situation. That was not enough for the Warren Court and those that have followed. They have overtly *legislated* their own biases and beliefs into the laws of the land.

Our Constitution provides lifetime tenure for persons appointed to serve as judges on our Supreme Court. One obvious reason for that provision was to free the Court from political encroachment and intimidation by members of the Executive and Legislative Branches. To assure independence for the Court and its members from demands from those two groups.

Our Constitution limits our President to two, four-year, terms. Term limits for members of the state and federal legislatures have been voted into law in several states and are being considered in others. If we are to continue to allow the operation of the Supreme Court and its supporting judicial system as merely, one more legislative group, free of its originally intended mission of interpreting the Constitution; justification for continuation of the life-time tenure must be questioned. Changing modes of operation of the Supreme Court and the rest of the judicial system impacts the effectiveness of our entire system of government in radical, negative ways. For this and other reasons, term limits for members of the Judicial Branch deserve our thoughtful attention.

Here again, if the checks and balances in our system were working as they should, we would expect the Legislative Branch to aggressively oppose "legislative action" by the Judicial Branch. However, in this case the views and programs being "legislated" by the courts were essentially consistent with the socialistic aspirations of the democratic majorities controlling the Congress. So they said nothing; they did not intervene.

Prostitution of these government systems by those in command continues to contribute in a major way to our rush to impending failure.

Prior to the passage of the Voting Rights Act, people could be required to demonstrate literacy as a condition to voting. The new law changed that. It gave literate and illiterate people equal standing at the polls.

Race-discrimination was not present in the balloting situation that existed prior to passage of this new law; the law was color blind. It denied the ballot to all illiterate persons, regardless of race, sex, age, creed, etc.

But! some Afro-Americans were included in the group that was being denied the vote. BTO's active in that arena saw this as an irresistible opportunity to get involved! They envisioned the possibility of making substantial gains in achieving increased minority control and power over the "rule of the majority".

So why was the law passed? There was no sweeping, grass-roots, public outcry for action in this area. Nor was there a great demand for action by the rainbow group of individuals who were being denied the right to vote.

Consideration of possible adverse impacts that could result from passage of the Act seems to have been ignored. Questions that begged to be asked and answered include: Does literacy of the voter play any role in assuring the success of a democratic system such as ours? Does guarantee of the voting right to all citizens, regardless of their ability to effectively perform the role of voting member, enhance or detract from its chances for success? Is it necessary or desirable that balloting be based on some understanding of how our system is supposed to work? Whether or not it is working? whether or not the incumbents that I elect and who are representing me, are providing a positive contribution? Or are they ineffective and part of the problem?

Are these important considerations? If they are, where will those who cannot read or write (the illiterates that were given the right to vote by this law) seek the knowledge and understanding needed to cast an informed ballot?

From the BTO'S, of course! They will be happy to tell them *how*, or *who* to vote for!

On the other hand, if the above factors are not important, we conclude that a literate electorate is not necessary to sustain our form of government! Acceptance of that hypothesis, leads us to some additional questions. Can we agree that chances of success of our system would be enhanced if all of our electorate was literate? And what of the other extreme? all of the electorate was illiterate? Would that work? I suspect it would not. So! What percentage of illiteracy can we allow and still succeed? How do we measure it? How do we control it?

We are using the concept of literacy and illiteracy as having unequivocal black and white meanings. That is not actually the case. We can see some shades of gray in the following definitions taken from Webster's Encyclopedic Unabridged Dictionary of the English Language; 1989 Edition:

Literate—

1. able to read and write.
2. having an education, educated
3. having or showing knowledge of literature, writing, etc.; literary, well-read
4. characterized by skill, lucidity, polish, or the like
5. a person who can read and write
6. a learned person

Literacy—

1. the quality or state of being literate, esp. the ability to read and write.
2. possession of an education

Literacy test—

— an examination to determine whether a person meets the literacy requirements for voting, serving in the armed forces, etc.; a test of one's ability to read and write.

As a matter of fact, the use of literacy tests to determine eligibility to vote, was not unconstitutional. It was not discriminatory. Such a requirement had good justification then; it has good justification now. *If* conditions related to voting in the 1960's presented discrimination overtones, it was an enforcement problem. Honest, effective enforcement of laws then on the books would have eliminated any discrimination that may have been occurring.

At that time, black people were encountering discrimination in some other activities. Given that fact we can understand that emotions and the level of caring of some members of the electorate was elevated on some issues related to their treatment. This may help explain the passive acceptance accorded the new law at that time. In that social and political environment, there evolved a small, persistent, effective group of African-Americans who stepped up to lead the attack on the establishment's system. Their goal, then and now, being to create windows of opportunity with which to maximize the benefits; to increase the muscle and control of the Afro-American community (about 12 percent of the U. S. population), over the remaining 88 percent.

The social and political considerations that led to the passage of the Voting Rights Act of 1965 can be summarized as follows:

Passage of the Act gave the right to vote to tens or hundreds of thousands of citizens who had previously been denied it. Some of them were Afro-Americans. That fact provided a great deal of motivation for the BTO's of that faction. They understood implications of the situation that obviously eluded most of us in the "establishment majority", of the population. The action created a large *block* of voters whose ability to prepare themselves for casting an **informed** ballot, was very limited. We should not be surprised then, when these persons look to others for suggestions and/or advice as to how they should mark their ballots. And, of course, the BTO's are right there to "*help*" them. That is the point of their whole operation. Great political power comes with such relationships! **ONE MAN (WOMAN); ONE VOTE?** Don't be naive. This doesn't apply to them! It just applies to you and me. We cannot materially affect the outcome of an election with our one vote! But BTO's and bto's can and regularly do so, with their "blocks" of votes.

Thus was created an early prototype of the **voting block** phenomenon; a dilemma that, to this day, effectively abrogates the "one person—one vote" concept within our system. An individual, you or I, cannot cast 50, 150, 500, etc. ballots! But by controlling "voting blocks", BTO's and bto's essentially do so!

High concentrations of the people who gained the vote with this new Act, reside in heavily populated metropolitan areas of the country. BTO's have capitalized on this fact and aggressively organized voter registration drives to increase the number of active voters in these areas. And the number of voters under their control continues to rapidly increase. The bargaining power of the BTOs expands proportionally with the increased numbers of voters under their individual control.

A few individuals, the BTO's, have thus gained control over large numbers of votes. The power that emanates from such relationships is not lost on the politicians. These blocks have contributed importantly to the social-democrats extended, unending control of the Legislative Branch. It has completely changed the nature and effectiveness of government in most states. For example, the results of elections in states such as Oregon and Washington are totally dominated by the voting in the metropolitan areas of Portland, Seattle and Tacoma. And the vote of people who own, live on, and manage 99 percent of the land within the states; and who create most of the wealth and jobs—farming, forestry, mining, manufacturing, etc.—becomes meaningless; outstripped by massive numbers of ballots from the inner cities with their unique problems. And we can begin to gain insight as to why government action is misdirected, ineffective and non-responsive to the problems we face.

Incumbent politicians especially reap the benefits of the "block" phenomenon. Those persons whose main (only?) goal is to get reelected, to stay in power, find it to be very helpful. They get a "free ride", as long as their surrender to the demands of splinter-group blocks, does not result in adverse questions and/or actions from members of the establishment majority, whose rights, welfare and survival they have adversely impacted.

So be it! Then, that misguided actions of our inept elected officials have greatly accelerated the expansion and impact of the block phenomenon. More blocks and massive increases in the number of votes under the control of BTO's and bto's. Blocks representing women, the welfare state, homo-sexual, pro-life, pro-abortion, African-Americans,

Japanese-Americans, native-Americans, disabled-Americans, the elderly etc., etc.

The social-democrats have always been willing to indulge and cater to such groups; at the expense of the nation and the rest of us. This helps explain their perpetual success in controlling the Legislative Branch at the Federal level and in the legislative and executive branches of most state governments.

Please note, once again, that there is nothing illegal about what we are discussing here. It is simply a case of a few ambitious people, the BTO's, outsmarting and intimidating the leadership of the country; of an intellectual vacuum and lack of dedication in our councils of government. And the citizens, who have so much to lose, who are drowning in an era of idiocy and self guilt "buy into" the deal, or passively accept it! And our national dream fades slowly away!

Why is our system failing? The George Bernard Shaw quotation in the box at the beginning of this chapter provides part of the answer.

"A Government Which Robs Peter to pay Paul—Can Always Depend On the Support of Paul"!

If Peter, the constituent being robbed, passively accepts what is happening to him/her and does not aggressively rise to protect his interests and rights, the response of politicians is absolutely predictable. Reelection is not just an important concern with most of them; it is the only one that matters! If you are a constituent who is adversely impacted by your elected agents "caving in" to such pressure, who passively tolerates their "sell out" of your rights, and who continues to vote for and otherwise support them; you give him a free ride! If you expect him to honestly do his job, you simply must participate in generating the necessary pressure supporting your point of view; to counteract that of the special-interest groups.

Politicians understand the price they will have to pay if they do not acquiesce to the demands of the splinter groups. These groups are organized; they are merciless. Their members stick together. They will organize demonstrations and boycotts against non-compliant public officials; subject them to mean, nasty personal and political attacks. They will do anything to force compliance with their demands.

The fate of the country is in your hands. If you, and millions of others like you, don't care enough, if you are not intelligent enough, if you cannot identify and effectively decide between the emotional and the intellectual response alternatives available to you; if you continue to abdicate or surrender your responsibilities of citizenship to others—elected representatives, bureaucrats and the other citizens *who are involved*—these grievous situations we cannot succeed with corrective action. The country and the rest of us who do care, cannot do it alone.

All of which answers some of the questions we asked earlier. This country and our system of government cannot survive if it is harnessed to an illiterate, uncaring, passive, lazy, establishment electorate!

It would be a mistake, however, to leave the subject of literacy and its correlation to the effectiveness of our system of government; without recognizing the probable existence of other important relationships between the two. We have previously spoken of the "**fools that we elect to public office**". We have also admitted to some personal responsibility when we help these people with their campaigns or vote for them when they run for public office. From this perspective, the concept that "**fools beget fools**" gains some credence.

It seems appropriate to end the discussion of this item with three questions that merit public attention and debate:

1. Can a democratic government of the people, by the people endure in an environment of near total illiteracy?
2. "What level of literacy must we have within the general population, for our system to succeed?"
3. Does the present level of literacy of our general population meet that criteria?

Lets now turn our attention to the second subject we have selected for analysis and commentary:

### * * "EQUAL" Employment Opportunity * *

This concept, which has its roots in the decades of the 1960's and 1970's has come to be known and accepted as "EQUAL" Employment Opportunity. Mention the title of this program to anyone in the country, and they will have some familiarity with it. For reasons that totally elude informed observers, it seems to enjoy a general, unquestioning acceptance by vast numbers of members of the "establishment".

Viewed from another perspective, most attorneys, jurists, and judges who work with the legal intricacies of this subject on a continuing basis would express doubts that members of the general public understand it; at all. If quizzed further most of this same group would probably claim that individually, they do understand it. Even if we are willing to admit that they are more knowledgeable about the subject than you and I; I believe that we can demonstrate with a minimum of interrogation the probability that no one **really** understands it! The evolution of the program to-date cannot be rationally explained. Its future is totally unpredictable; dependent upon continuing irrational actions of the legislatures; the nature of the cases brought to court and the biases and personal whims of the judges and the members of any juries involved. Its evolution, to date, defies sane logic or intellectual reason. On the other hand, indications of successful emotional persuasion are abundant.

We can find some helpful, elementary information on this subject in the book, "Primer of Equal Employment Opportunity", Fourth Edition by Michael D. Levin-Epstein. Enforcement and litigation of EEO matters today, involve use of one or more of an extensive list of federal, state, and local laws and executive orders. Some of them are quite new; others may date back more than 100 years. Opportunities for both the complainant and the defense to select from a multitude of diverse legal positions and case histories are abundant. The following list enumerates a few of the statutes, rules, etc., that may come into play in these kinds of actions:

*The Civil Rights Act of 1964*, which we have already discussed briefly, is considered to be a foundation for later additions to the law:

— *Title VI*—of that Act prohibits discrimination based on race, color, or national origin in federally assisted programs.
— *Title VII*, as amended—forbids employment or membership discrimination by employers, employment agencies, and unions on the basis of race, color, religion, sex, or national origin. Title VII was amended in 1978 to prohibit discrimination against pregnant women.

Cases involving this general subject may also be influenced by a large number of other statutes. Some of them are:

— *Title 1 of the Civil Rights Act of 1968*
— *The Civil Rights Attorney's Fees Awards Act of 1976*
— *Title IX of the Education Amendments of 1972*
— *The Age Discrimination in Employment Act of 1967*—prohibits discrimination against employees or applicants for employment between 40 and 70 years of age.
— *The Age Discrimination Act of 1975*

— *The Equal Pay Act of 1963*—makes it unlawful to pay wages to members of one *sex* at a rate lower than that paid members of the other *sex* for equal work on jobs that require equal skill, effort, and responsibility under similar working conditions in the same establishment?

— *The Vocational Rehabilitation Act of 1973*—Section 504—prohibits discrimination against handicapped persons in any program or activity receiving federal financial assistance.

*Section 503* goes the last mile in this preference legislation; it requires federal contractors to take *affirmative* action to employ and promote qualified handicapped persons. (In practice, it is not unusual for this to translate into demands to hire any handicapped applicant over more qualified other applicants.)

— *The Vietnam Era Veterans' Readjustment Assistance Act of 1974*—contractors with federal jobs over $10,000 must take *affirmative* action to employ and advance disabled veterans and qualified veterans of the Vietnam era. (over who? women? black people, or just white guys?)

— *The State and Local Fiscal Assistance Act* of 1972—State and local governments receiving federal revenue-sharing cannot discriminate in employment on the basis of race, color, national origin, sex, religion, age, or handicapped status.

— *The Immigration Reform and Control Act of 1986*—Makes it illegal for employers to discriminate against legal aliens merely because they are aliens or look foreign. (Of course, the other side of this situation is that employers can be {and are} prosecuted and fined heavily if they hire illegal aliens! Counterfeit credentials are inexpensive and readily available to the illegal aliens. The "establishment" employer's liability is not diminished by the fact that the employee conceals his illegal status with bogus credentials! On the one hand, the law forces small and large business entrepreneurs to hire these people; it then bears down with heavy fines and penalties if they are deceived by bogus credentials! sane logic of "the fools we elect to public office?"—our own governments serving as deterrents to honest citizen's attempts to peacefully live their lives and effectively to do their jobs? Why do we tolerate such moronic, ridiculous conditions? Is this the proper role for government? To always interfere?)

As if the above maze of impossible, ill-defined, costly and time consuming legal impediments were not enough! Two additional statutes passed over 100 years ago play a part in the administration of this type of activity today. They are:

— *Section 1981 of the Civil Rights Act of 1886*—gives all persons the same contractual rights as "white citizens".
— *Section 1983 of the Civil Rights Act of 1871*—affects persons acting, "under color of state law" to deprive others of federal rights, including employment opportunity!? (This is a prime example of what is wrong with our justice system today. How many citizens understand what that means? I don't! Probably 99.99 percent of our citizens don't! The wording begs to be interpreted in many different ways by many different courts; resulting in legislation by the courts. **HOW CAN THE PEOPLE BE EXPECTED TO SUPPORT AND OBEY INCOMPREHENSIBLE LAWS THAT THEY CAN'T UNDERSTAND?**

And finally there are executive orders that have been issued by executive departments that affect EEO issues today.

— *Executive Order 11246—(As amended by Executive Orders 11375 and 12086) NOW PAY ATTENTION TO THIS!* Try to understand this Executive Order? They are written of course to apply to mortals such as you and I! As such, it is reasonable to expect that we should be able to understand what they say.
The following is quoted from the previously cited book, Primer of Equal Employment Opportunity,[19]

"Forbids employment discrimination based on race, color, religion, sex, or national origin by first- and second-tier government contractors whose contracts are in amounts exceeding $10,000. In addition, contractors become subject to additional requirements to develop affirmative action plans and to take positive steps to eliminate employment bias when they have government contracts of $50,000 or more a year and employ 50 or more workers."

---

[19]    Primer of equal employment opportunity; by Michael Levin-Epstein; Copyright 1987-The Bureau of National Affairs, Inc. P6

Of course! you understand all of that; now don't you? Be careful! be honest with me and with yourself!

— *Executive Order 11141*—this order bans age discrimination by government contractors.
— *Executive Order 12250*—assigns the responsibility and authority for *leadership* and *coordination* of Title VI of the Civil Rights Act of 1964; Title IX of the Education Amendments of 1972; and Section 504 of the Vocational Rehabilitation Act to achieve consistent and effective implementation.

EEO as we know it in the 1990's stems from the passage of the above legislation and the issuance of Executive Orders. It's evolution is also based on years of interpretation by hundreds of thousands of bureaucrats, arbitrators, judges and juries; large numbers of whom are members of one of the protected classes; a factor that obviously involves conflict of interest; and which jeopardizes objectivity, truth and fairness in the results.

In addition to the above labyrinth of federal EEO edicts; states and some other pockets of authority have contributed their own maze of additional incursions into the rights of the ordinary citizen. We are told that Title VII, for example, "extends about as far as it is possible for Congress to reach under its authority to *regulate interstate commerce.*" (Underlining added for emphasis.)[20] Can EEO activity really be justified by its relationship to "regulation of interstate commerce"? Come now! That is stretching things beyond reason. A cursory review of the information presented in the Levin-Epstein, Primer of Equal Employment Opportunity; demonstrates that actions taken in this arena of activity display a callous disrespect for protection of the civil rights of the masses!

We are told that the EEO movement has its Constitutional support from:

— *The First Amendment* which guarantees freedom of religion
— *The Fifth Amendment* which says that citizens will not be deprived of rights to life, liberty, or property without due process of law
— *The Thirteenth Amendment* which assures citizens freedom from slavery

---

[20]　Ibid P13

— *The Fourteenth Amendment* bars denial of federally conferred privileges by actions of the states.[21]

With the passage of time, the tentacles of this program have continued to infiltrate and impact increasing numbers of people and activities. And rights guaranteed to all of us, by our Constitution are being sacrificed for the benefit of small non-establishment, special-interest groups.

Acquiescent, citizen acceptance of the wide variety of inane actions being taken in the name of EEO should be of deep concern. We must be continuously vigilant of jeopardy to or loss of our own constitutional rights. And, we must do what is necessary to protect them if that becomes necessary! Justification of everything that has been and continues to be done in the name of EEO on the basis of such narrow, vague interpretations of excerpts from our constitution, certainly **stretches** the imagination of vigilant, thoughtful citizens!

Please keep the above four Constitutional citations in mind as we proceed. While admitting that we don't understand all of the gobble-de-gook in the above statutes, executive orders, etc.; we are all able to read the Constitution and judge for ourselves the extent to which we perceive that our individual personal rights are being misappropriated by government.

And although the real meaning and intent of all of the rules, laws, etc. "relevant?" to the EEO issue we have quoted is lost to everyone; that should not temper or in any way influence our own judgments or sense of what is right and fair. If, per chance, our conclusions in that regard are different from those being "*laid on*" us by the our legal system; that does not mean that we are wrong. A fundamental requirement for success of our system of government is that the people, you and I; be able to **read**, **understand**, and **interpret correctly** the basic documents that underlie and control its operation.

It is not wrong for us to question and call for an accounting of this country's legal system. Be aware that it is "*our*" **legal system**; they work for us just as do the Executive and Legislative branches of **our** government. Standing in awe of that group, and failure to demand accountability from the courts, including the Supreme Court, will contribute significantly to our downfall.

It is important to recognize the dichotomy built into that system. Success, monetary income; the very existence of individuals and the families of practicing attorneys is dependent upon two or more attorneys finding things that they honestly or "make believe" disagree on. The country could have

---

[21]    Ibid P7

survived the education of the first lawyer in this country. The trouble began when numbers 2, 3, etc. joined the fray. Real trouble for the country, and all of us came two or three decades ago when the number of practicing lawyers began to exceed the public's needs to settle real, incidental disputes that occur in the transactions of individuals, business and commerce. Continuation of our educational systems to **"spew"** out tens or hundreds of thousands of new lawyers each year is tantamount to training and releasing into our society each year the same number of "Masters of Terrorism". There being no authentic need for them in the legal system, they are left with a choice:

* They can go out and create problems that require their services, where there was none. They have devised very clever, appealing, and effective advertising programs for this purpose. And! in the process of creating work for themselves, they create opportunities for any number of additional attorneys to represent all sides of the synthetic problems so established. The public is saddled with the imposing additional amount of dissention created; and as is almost always the case in any event with the ultimate responsibility for paying the huge bills that are run up for this foolishness. There are seldom any redeeming benefits to society, as a whole!

* They can go to work for organizations and dedicate their efforts to protecting their employer from the delays and expense brought into the system by real problems and/or by the predators discussed above.

* Large numbers of them join the faculties of law schools, where they continue to exacerbate the problem of oversupply. From an outsider's perspective, it appears that this option is especially attractive to those who have personal biases or prejudices that they want to infiltrate into the country's legal system. How better to do it, than to take advantage of the captive audiences of eager, absorptive brains of young people. The country would be better off if it created a program that would close these schools for a decade or so, and give the faculty members tenure in a retirement system that:

  — pays them a livable wage, and
  — requires that they not be active in any employment associated with the system.

To some that may sound crazy. Maybe it is! But we do worse. Have you heard of the program that requires the government, you and I, to pay farmers for not growing crops on their land?

\* And finally, the most damaging of all alternatives; they can go into government service. Here, they will expand the maize of excess, paralyzing government intervention that obstructs proper operation of our system. And, that provides a generous charitable arena of operation for massive numbers of additional "legal beagles".

We have previously conceded that treatment of colored people in our society in the early 1960's needed some thoughtful, remedial legislative action. It is, therefore, interesting to note that Title VI of the Civil Rights Act of 1964 prohibited discrimination based only on race, color, or national origin. Discrimination based on sex, religion or age was not included!

As a matter of fact, sex discrimination was included in the language of Title VII as a casual after-thought; added just one day before its passage. There was little discussion of the subject to clarify its legislative intent. We can guess, probably accurately so, that most of those voting for the bill in the House and Senate had not carefully considered the need for the action; or the consequences of its inclusion. Many who voted for the bill, probably didn't even know that sex discrimination had been included. Nothing new there! most legislators will tell you that they don't take the time to read most of what they vote for! And! the nation that would subsequently reject adoption of an "Equal Rights Amendment", found itself saddled with an even more repressive consequence.

Presentation of some background will help us develop a common basis upon which to consider this EEO question. To do that we will go back to the 1964 Edition of the World Book Encyclopedia. This quotation is found in Volume 4 of that set under the general heading of CIVIL SERVICE; subheading History:[22]

\*   \*   \*

Start of Quote

"CIVIL SERVICE
—History. The earliest Presidents (of the U.S.) generally gave consideration to an individual's qualifications for a job, although they tended to favor their own political supporters. By 1820, it had become fairly

---

[22] World Book Encyclopedia, Volume 4, pp 470-471.

common to use government jobs as political rewards. An incoming President would dismiss a large number of government workers and replace them with members of his own party, regardless of their qualifications.

This turnover was based on the idea that "to the victor goes the spoils." The system became known as the "Spoils System". By 1841, when William Henry Harrison became President, the spoils system had reached great proportions. Into Washington, D.C. swarmed 30,000 to 40,000 office-seekers to claim the 23,700 jobs that then composed the federal service.

Many persons hired through the spoils system had no training for their work and no interest in it. Many were dishonest. In the early days government work was quite simple. But as the government grew, a serious need for qualified workers developed. *The government passed laws in 1853 and 1855 requiring clerk examinations to make sure that new employees would be qualified to do the work.* In 1871, Congress gave the President the authority to establish tests for people seeking government jobs. But this merit-system trial ended in 1875, because Congress failed to provide funds to carry it out. *The experiment proved the merit of the system to be both workable and helpful.*

Many thoughtful leaders were pressing for a more thorough merit system in the federal, state, and local governments. In 1881, a disappointed office-seeker shot and killed President James A. Garfield. *His death brought public demands for civil-service reforms* and led to the passage of a bill introduced by Senator George H. Pendleton of Ohio. The bill became the Civil Service Act of 1883. About the same time, New York state and Massachusetts began merit programs.

*The new federal law called for examinations open to all citizens. It provided for selection of new workers from among those making the highest grades in these examinations. It made unlawful the firing or demotion of workers for political reasons. It relieved the government workers from any obligation to give political service or payments. It established the United States Civil Service Commission to enforce the law.*

At first the Civil Service Act covered only about 1 out of every 10 federal positions. Later laws and executive orders have placed more jobs under civil service. *They have sought to make civil service a true career service, with opportunity for advancement on merit, with benefits in line with those offered by progressive private employers.* For example, the Retirement Act of 1920 set up a pension system for civil service workers. The Classification Act of 1923 provided all government jobs in the Washington departments be analyzed and classified so that workers would be paid according to the requirements of their jobs. A law passed in 1940 extended the provisions of that act to many positions outside of Washington. *By the late 1950's, the merit system covered about 90 out of every 100 federal workers."*

End of Quote

\* \* \*

In the above quotation, information within parentheses has been added by the author. Underlining has been added for emphasis.

Through the following analysis and discussion we will learn something about the way we deal with each other—today! Deceit, subterfuge, betrayal and dishonesty will show through; crystal clear, in so many of our relationships.

We can draw some interesting comparisons between the quality, and integrity of leadership; the way things were done and what motivated citizens of this country in earlier times and today. Such analysis will contribute to our ability to understand the difficult issues we are addressing here.

For example, the reference tells us that in 1820 government jobs were passed out as political rewards; new employees put into government jobs "regardless of their qualifications", or lack of them. By the late 1930's this system came to be known as the **spoils system**. Many persons hired through the **spoils system** had no training for their work and no interest in it. Many were dishonest.

But as the government grew, and it's work became more complex, the people and their leaders recognized that well-qualified, highly-motivated employees were a requisite to providing effective government. And they did something about it! They designed, enacted and implemented a system that dealt effectively with the problem. That is the type of government and response by elected persons that we can accept and respect.

This is interesting!—at that time the federal government employed about 25,000 people and the federal budget was about $45,000,000. In that era, when the masses of the people and their leaders were educated to levels presumably much less sophisticated than what exists in our country today; they were intelligent enough to realize the importance of effective governance of the nation, and that the work required the best qualified workers available. They were then honest and patriotic enough to support and enact legislation that responded to real needs.

Contrast that to our situation in 1992 when federal spending was $1.3 trillion, about 29,000 times as large as that of the early 1800's; and the federal government employed about 3,200,000, 128 times the earlier number.

Never has this country spent more money to provide more years of schooling to such a large percentage of our population! Our new president, Bill Clinton, has been a benefactor of today's most elite, extremely expensive educational opportunities; Rhodes Scholar, Ivy Leaguer, and Law School graduate. One would hope that from all of that exposure to the pseudo intellectual community of our time, he would have learned something useful to him in his new job. But alas, that is not the case, he has openly proclaimed that **merit** will not be a significant factor in the selection of his administration's management team. His plan essentially reverts to use of the spoils system. As the selections have been announced, it has seemed probable that the decision authority was given to or confiscated by the first Lady, Hillary Clinton. The selection criteria used is not at all obvious. He had announced that they would be chosen to represent the "diversity" of the country. "Diversity" being a "buzz" word used in EEO activities. It denotes a concept in which the number of people of each sex, race, age, etc. hired into any job situation will replicate their proportionality in the population. Meeting quotas is the name of this game! Color, race, sex, etc., take precedence over everything else.

In an earlier time in our country's history, prior to the 1960's and the subsequent socialistic reconstitution of our system; good citizenship was viewed as a serious, personal responsibility by our people **and their leaders**. The best qualified persons were sought out for leadership positions in our government. People, of limited qualifications, did not apply for positions beyond their ability; they had the courage and good sense to "say no" when asked to serve in a capacity for which they knew they were not qualified.

But alas, those conditions no longer exist; and the country is stuck with "amateur hour" in its critical executive management function for the remainder of this inept administration.

A point of personal privilege: "The results of Clinton's selection process as it has unfolded?—"What a zoo!" Mostly women, mostly lawyers, and totally lacking in experience that would even begin to qualify them for the positions. Family friends, associates and classmates of the president and his wife are everywhere. Experience, background, and qualifications have been of little consequence in the process. It would be a joke, if it did not portend such tragic consequences for the future of our nation and its people.

In embracing the use of the **spoils system** in selecting his staff the president rejected the **merit system**. The two concepts are totally incompatible. After so many years of exposure to control of our government by the multitude of socialist-democrats; thinking members of the electorate, have developed a fixation in which they are seldom surprised at anything our governments do. Notwithstanding that fact, his actions come as a surprise. His election to the top leadership position in this nation, at a time of great need, is the highest honor that can be bestowed upon anyone by his fellow citizens! You would think that even he would understand that and react in a sane, responsible way.

Could we agree that being president of the United States, is probably the most demanding and important management position in the world. The future of the 250,000,000 plus citizens of this country as well as the general welfare of the total world population is directly dependent upon the effectiveness of the management of this country's affairs.

By what presumption would any able, sane, educated incumbent in such a position call on any but the very best qualified, available candidates to help him with this staggering challenge? What is happening is bewildering. What did our new president learn during all of those years of schooling?

Is his performance indicative of what the country must expect from the progression of his "hippie" generation, of the 1960's, into leadership roles? Thankfully, there is another side to that generation. The side that has stepped up to serve their country in its time of need; who continue to live within the rules of the establishment, who are numbered among today's concerned citizens, working for the betterment of the country, their families, and all citizens of the nation and the world! The challenge facing our electorate in future years is the same test they failed this time around; that of selectively choosing our leaders from those members of that generational group who respect the need for choice in our lives; the need for honesty and compliance with codes of ethical conduct and morality. Who cherish what this country stands for and will work to preserve its concepts for themselves and future generations.

Passage of the ***Equal*** Employment Opportunity Act (EEO), in effect, reinstated the legality and priority use of the **spoils system**. At a time when the Civil Service Laws also demanded the use of the **merit system**; government agencies faced the impossible task of meeting the requirements of two mutually exclusive laws. EEO laws were written in very general terms; leaving the specifics to be defined through court actions. Implementation of EEO became the favored program. A disaster has resulted! Small, activist groups representing any number of special-interest groups that were singled out for special treatment under the EEO have appeared before liberal, socialist-oriented jurists and juries, regularly. The tentacles of abuse to the civil rights of the masses are massive and destructive.

I know of no other situation in the history of this country that has been so infiltrated with double-talk, gobble-de-gook, distortion, and lies as are encountered here! One only gets to the title before stubbing your toe! *Equal* Employment Opportunity; what does that mean? To a person who has spent his entire professional life working with higher mathematics in engineering and scientific work, the word EQUAL, has a very precise meaning. Try as I may, I can find nothing about this program and the way that it has been implemented that would justify the use of the word "EQUAL", as a descriptor of the program, its intent or the way it works.

What about that title? What does it mean? What is it supposed to mean? Equal opportunity to work? Equal opportunity to compete for work? As implemented, it does neither.

The "Equal Employment Opportunity" programs as they exist in our society today have originated and evolved over the last 25 to 30 years. It is important to recognize the absence of public discussion or debate of this subject during this period of time. In this nation which prides itself in guaranteeing the right of free speech to all; this subject has been "off-base", especially for white guys! Remember what happened to TV sports commentator Jimmy the Greek and Andy Rooney of the 60 Minutes program when they ventured completely innocent comments on the subject? On the other hand minorities, women and other benefactors of the program have spoken freely and critically about everyone and everything related to the subject that was not to their liking. Their vitriolic, damning language representing the "anything goes" mentality. They regularly characterize any and all who suggest differing points of view or who question any aspect of the programs as "racists", "bigots" or other similar character-assassination references. Any reaction by those normal white citizens who are insulted or otherwise offended by such malicious treatment is met with specially designed, harsh penalties designed by our "**justice**" system for application only to those white citizens who are judged to be guilty of "hate crimes"!

There is absolutely no doubt but that a wide array of people who make up the establishment majority find themselves limited to a second-class level of citizenship. All categories of persons designated for special treatment by the program, receive first priority when positions are filled. White guy's applications are rarely considered, especially when applications are available for persons in the special category groups. Relative qualifications of candidates across this dividing line are of no consequence. Organizations regularly establish two lists of candidates; one for those identified as members of the special-treatment categories, the other for the rest of us. Selections from the list of special benefactors are made without regard to their relative qualifications standing with those candidates on the other list. And, this has been going on for almost three decades! When is enough, enough? Is it any wonder that the country is in great jeopardy; gridlock everywhere in the public and private sectors? Staggering under debt so massive that its size is incomprehensible to the average citizen? begging for real leadership that will present an honest, authentic vision for the future that the people can understand and will be challenged to achieve.

A tragic reminder of the true gravity of the problem rises in the fact that the justice department continues to buy into the practice! A reflection of the quality and mind set of the people that have been chosen to serve us in prestigious positions of power in the justice system! A sane person can be excused for believing that those who wrote our Constitution and established the original, basic modus operandi of our system of government must be rolling over in their graves.

Government promotion and hoopla used in support of the program has been long on the appeal to emotions. One *implication* has been that the present distortion of the rights of individuals is justified by inequalities that are claimed but never proven to have existed in the past.

It is true, that a typical work place in the early 1960's, may have had a predominance of white people, with men and women usually working at different types of work. That does not prove that there was anything sinister or illegal involved in the situation. At that time people were chosen for the work place, based on justifiably different criteria; candidate qualifications and demonstrated ability to do the work was then a major factor! And the pay for any position, outside of the organized labor movement, was based on two basic concepts that were and still are important to successful operation of any democratic, free-market economic system:

1. The law of supply and demand of people with the talents required to *perform the work*, and
2. The level of pay depended upon the value of an individual's contribution to the success of the total operation.

There is absolutely nothing in either of those concepts that violates any part of our constitution, or any of the other basic precepts established for our nation by the founding fathers. In fact, the hodge-podge of misdirected, special-treatment for some, at the expense of others violates every letter and the intent of every basic document that forms the foundation of our system of government. However, it appears that the situation may not be corrected, unless and until the establishment masses force their "agents" to an accounting for their actions!

What better way to examine this subject, of EEO, than to begin at the beginning. To do so we have to try to deal with the question; Why was this legislation passed? Was there real need? You have to know that "budding BTOs and btos" saw it as the opportunity of a lifetime! Why did the Congress "succumb" to coercion by such a small part of the population? Why did they act with so little consideration or understanding of the adverse impacts that might ensue from such drastic, untested, and unnecessary changes in the management of *all of our public and private* activities? They certainly knew of the existence of the Civil Service, "***merit***" system that was then in use. And, is it unreasonable for us to expect that people we trust to operate and manage our "public" business could look at that situation and appreciate that the merit system was working well? Isn't it also reasonable for us to expect that those "movers and shakers", would be intelligent enough to realize that the total trashing of "merit" considerations in hiring and advancement decisions in our work force would have serious adverse consequences. Such thoughtless, irresponsible action by those to whom we have delegated so much authority and responsibility is totally inexcusable.

As a matter of fact, discrimination was a part of the personnel management system inside and outside of government at the time. But the discrimination was not based on sex, color, race, age, etc. of the persons vying for new positions or for advancement. The discrimination was instead based on qualifications to do the job; education, experience, ability, etc. there is absolutely nothing illegal about such discrimination. It is totally consistent with the word and the intent of our Constitution; and it is an absolutely necessary component of any successful plan to restore our system to proper functioning.

I have discussed earlier my indoctrination into the federal Civil Service personnel system; the battery of tests I took when I graduated from college and went to work for the federal government in 1949. In the 1960's, when the move toward EEO began, I was still working there. By that time, I had advanced into supervisory and management positions, where I had oversight responsibility for a lot of personnel actions.

Any assumption that the make-up of the work force at that time resulted from discrimination against colored people, women, etc., ignores some important realities of the times. People in the non-union job market and in the work place at that time, viewed the work place and their position in a peculiar way; measured against today's standards. They saw the work place as an arena that existed for the express purpose of getting necessary work done in the most effective, efficient, economic way possible; to make their employer as competitive as possible in domestic and world markets. It was understood that employee's security of employment depended upon the employers success in meeting that challenge.

People understood and accepted the fact that qualifications were important. It was recognized that the merit system was in place and operating well. As a result, the system policed itself. Most people simply did not challenge the system and apply for positions for which they were not qualified. Managers and supervisors charged with making personnel decisions were locked into a system that required them to select one of the three best qualified candidates. When colored people, women, etc., were among the best qualified they were usually selected. Even at that time, management was sensitive to the low representation of minorities, women, etc. in certain parts of the work force. There was a tendency to grant them special consideration; to select them any time their qualifications put them within reach of the selecting officer.

Use of the Civil Service System's hiring on the basis of "merit" was essentially destroyed with the rapid adoption of hiring and advancement criteria based solely on factors of race, color, sex, age, etc. The impact of the change of criteria was not lost to all of those opportunists in the select, minority(?) groups who stood to benefit from the change. Large numbers of them began to bid on every vacancy, regardless of whether or not they had skills in the field of endeavor. They expected that the new laws would give them the leverage they needed to get selected. Sometimes it worked for them. Sometimes it did not. Many managers just weren't willing to fight the distasteful, torturous battle required even then to reject unqualified candidates and select the best qualified person. You have to know that existing and potential new BTOs and btos recognized that situation as an opportunity of great possibilities for themselves. They went to work on the situation, and the rest is history. Our system of legislation and adjudication, burdened with widespread "emotional idiocy" was no match for the onslaught that followed. The chaos we are left with is everything that a reasonable, thinking person might have guessed it would be!

There is one other factor working in the EEO arena that is important and needs to be recognized. It helps explain the tenacity with which the program continues to "*live*". The quote from the encyclopedia (pp 522-524), disclosed the gravity of problems posed by the practices of patronage and nepotism that came to dominate the appointment of employees under the "**spoils**" system in the 19th and early 20th centuries. The elected and bureaucratic crowd in office abused their authority by putting family members, friends and supporters on the public pay-role regardless of their inability to do the work. Leaders of the country at that time were honest enough to recognize the enormity of the problem; and to do something about it. They developed and implemented the civil service, "merit system". Although it was not 100 percent effective in eliminating all nepotism and patronage in public service hiring, it did much to choke off the oppressive control that powerful incumbent politicians and bureaucrats had confiscated over the hiring process. While it was in use, the merit system, protected selecting officers from the threats, intimidation and abuse of aggressive, authoritative, politicians who would otherwise, have used this weakness in the system to pay off political debts. Without their intervention the selecting officer was free to select the best qualified candidate.

Legislative, administrative, and judicial actions associated with the evolution of the several parts (EEO, Civil Rights, etc.) of the ineffective, socialist programs that are slowly strangling our society have essentially eliminated "merit" considerations from the hiring practice.

No organization, large or small, can succeed without resolute control of the qualifications, honesty and dedication of its employees. Any system, public or private, that ignores those requirements and hires only on the basis of phony "social" considerations has no chance of success. So we should not be surprised when we look around us and see the sorry state of affairs in our public and private enterprise activities. Try to find any activity in our Federal, state or local government arenas that are well-run! Very difficult to do. What a mess!

It is important that we not lose sight of a very important fact related to the hiring process in our country. As long as the hiring is based on a good, operational system in which merit is the dominating factor for "choice" of applicant, the quality of the work force can be controlled. But! once the concept of merit is breached in the process, for any reason; it is breached for all reasons. Chaos ensues. That is where we now find ourselves! Once the system was breached for EEO reasons management lost control of the quality of its work force. In the public service, political appointments based on patronage and nepotism flourish. Pockets of employees who are members of certain religious groups prosper when one of their group is selected for supervisory or management positions and he/she proceeds to quietly and covertly select new employees for the group based on that factor. Not surprisingly, all of this takes a toll on the performance and productivity of the work-group.

As we have previously noted the visibility of our problems has progressed to the point, that even members of our leadership structure recognize and publicly admit to the existence of serious problems. So, why aren't we all concentrating and working together to correct the situation?

That is an important, valid question. Reinstating a merit system into the hiring process would surely have to be one of the first steps of any system that would have a chance of success. And! unbelievably! that creates a very difficult problem. Any such effort will confront, early on; persistent and powerful; no-holds-barred opposition from the ruling majorities of today's politically entrenched leaders. They correctly see patronage and nepotism as powerful tools in their personal arsenals of political gimmicks that help them stay in office.

And, they seem not to be affected by the pangs of conscience that stirred their predecessors to take corrective action! In fact, controlling numbers of today's leadership seem to like this devious system, "**just fine**". They earnestly nurture and use it. And! Multitudes of people are hired, especially into public service jobs, for every reason but the correct one. Changing the system to one that will work for the benefit of the country may well have to be done over the serious opposition of those presently in power! A difficult; maybe impossible task!

The EEO program was introduced and "sold" to John and Jane Q. Public on the theory that it would achieve an embodiment of ethnicity, sex, age, etc., within the work place that was comparable to their proportions of the population. That is, to match the "diversity" of those categories of people in the work place to their existence in the population.

As is usually the case with actions taken by inept leadership; the whole concept had not been thought through. Emotions ruled the day! Intelligence and reason, if those capabilities existed "there and then" were disregarded. Program plans had not been developed, goals were not defined, the method of implementation had been given no consideration.

After all of these years (decades) of process development and attempted implementation by the public and private sectors of our society the system *still* remains largely undefined! Creation and implementation of mountains of new related rules and regulations; continuing massive streams of litigation on the subject over three decades; and the evolution of millions of pages of "precedent-setting" documentation only adds confusion to the whole process.

The breadth of the unrest between the sexes, the races, the generations, etc. of the citizenry continues to increase; the depth of distrust and animosity deepens; and the people and the country are unnecessarily deprived of the kinds of pleasant, pastoral, productive relationships that previously existed between persons, public entities and private organizations. Relationships that made it possible, "once upon a time", for our system to work and that contributed to our individual and collective enjoyment of life!

One does not get very far into any serious consideration of the social legislation that has been foisted off on us before its total idiocy becomes starkly apparent. That these kinds of things happen, and are unchallenged in what is supposed to be a civilized, moral, ethical society of educated (?) people defies all logic! Women entered the EEO fray demanding 51 percent of the jobs. Their argument was based on the fact that 51 percent of the population was female. Never mind that a significant percentage of the female population was not (are not) seeking full-time, permanent employment. Truth, ethics and the "American Way" were early losers in this new world of lies, extreme greed and manipulation. As implementation and expansion of the EEO programs evolved, it became obvious that the goals enunciated earlier were phony. The 51 percent quota of women, has long since been surpassed in many of our work places: public education, financial institutions, government offices, etc. In many situations the work force has reached 90 to 95 percent women, and yet the same preferential hiring practices continue to be used! Financial institutions; banks, savings and loans, etc., have obviously changed their whole mode of operation to adapt to the requirements of these insane laws; and the public pays the price in decreased service and substantially increased costs! There was a time when you could walk into the lobby of such an institution and get authoritative, reliable answers to most questions from the employees working there. Walk into those same lobbies today and you will find that most of them are staffed entirely by women. And my experience has been that even simple questions must be referred to others; often several times—to people up the organizational ladder. On occasion you are told that they will have to "get the answer and get back to you". In one instance, involving a common real-estate loan transaction my answer finally arrived two weeks later—from Washington, D. C. through the lending institution!

You will find few colored or minority women, in these offices! no minority men! people, over 50 years of age, especially men, are seldom seen in any of these settings. A major provision of the EEO is supposed to protect against "age discrimination". As a matter of fact, it does not do so! The system does not even pretend to enforce provisions for protecting the older employee. There is open-season on older workers everywhere; but especially in the federal service. If you are of that age and employed, it is probable that you have been approached by management with one of any number of ploys to get rid of you. If you are over 50, you are out of work, and you need to work to survive; you are in real trouble. Your applications have an early rendezvous with the waste basket.

What do you conclude from all of this. How would you integrate the word "equal" into what is happening here? Obviously the program is not devoted to equal anything! It becomes apparent that a major objective of the program is to get rid of the white guys and older people in the work force. All of them, as soon as possible.

The BTOs and btos in the women's movement have been tenacious and very effective in forcing total occupancy and control for women in those job classifications that women had previously occupied. The obvious poor operating performance of systems that have been strangled by this process does nothing to impede the continued expansion of the practice.

The femme BTO's have also persistently demanded that women be put into jobs that had previously been largely the preserve of men; examples being police work, fire fighting, military service, etc. Some of this work requires unique abilities and character traits of the people in the job; they require strength, agility, and self-defense skills; they must always be prepared, instant to instant, to meet the most perilous situations that can be devised by the most violent offenders in our society. Realists serving in such positions are constantly aware that in addition to being responsible for their own protection and survival, they bear responsibilities for the safety of their comrades in the service.

The subterfuge that is operative in the EEO process is highly adaptable to their needs in this effort. The most abhorrent of political practices become involved. Anything goes! Nothing is "out of bounds. Our inept, corrupt, milquetoast leaders are but putty in the hands of these uninhibited, greedy activists.

In this situation, it works to the advantage of the women to profess that there are no differences between men and women. To claim that women can do anything men can do; and that they can do it as well, or better than men. (*Keep this alleged hypothesis in mind. We will return to it on occasion as we proceed.*) Of course, not all women believe that. As a matter of fact, probably no one, man or woman, *really believes* it. It has been proven beyond doubt, that women are better at some types of work, while men are better at others. One would hope that, as a country, we would be smart enough and care enough to take advantage of such facts in our struggle to survive in the world economy. But in our society nothing related to this sacred subject comes under question. If the women activists say this is true, as ridiculous as it may be to most of us, the premise goes unchallenged. And a minuscule number of them intimidate our leaders to accommodate their wishes for additional new power and special treatment! Legislators enact; and the courts obediently support and expand upon those actions; ignoring their sworn duty to protect the rights of **all** citizens.

Entry into the armed services has been a primary target for this movement. Some women have been serving there for many years, with limitations on the kinds of activities they can be involved in. I can't imagine anyone that would feel comfortable with the thought of women serving with the infantry in the trenches, the tunnels or the caves of World War I or II; or the Korean or Vietnam wars; engaged in life and death, hand to hand combat with the enemy using bayonets, knives, etc. They have been and currently are not allowed to serve in this way; of course they protest. You can't say no! to anyone in our society today! especially members of the splinter, activist groups. They have rights!

Here, as elsewhere in the work place, they are very aggressive in demanding that they get what they project as their *fair share* of the advancement opportunities. Fair share, here, being an undefined amount, except to say that it requires that everyone of the protected group, who wants a promotion, gets one—not because it has been earned, but just because they want it. Their pleas are emotionally based on a presumed status of victimization and bias. They are expert at presenting the idea that they are excluded from advancement into the executive suites, by a "glass ceiling". They conveniently overlook a cardinal rule of the work place, that men and women have experienced, understood and accepted for decades as they traveled this road before them. The number of "executive suite" positions are extremely limited. For every worker who reaches that pinnacle of success there are thousands who do not. Of course, we can't blame them for using whatever works for them! And the tactics they use do work. They go to work for an organization; they learn the location of the rest rooms; and they learn how to spell the name of the company; and look out! move over! they are ready to take over the top-command and run the place!

I don't want to be misunderstood on these issues. I can bring myself to live with a situation of women in the military and the other places that *some of them* want to be; under the right (fair) conditions. The "some of them" is the problem. Only some women want this; a very small, minuscule percentage of the total.

One set of rules governs the relationship between **all men** in our country and the military. If women insist on participating in the activity; on a basis of fairness and equality, they should do so under the same, identical rules. *All of the rules* that apply to *all of the men* in the country will apply to *all of the women* in the country—not just to those who want to serve. In the event that it may once again be necessary for us to draft people into the military service of the country; and we decide to accept the femme premise, the only fair way to do that is on a unisex basis, using last name and first and middle initial, for all women and men. That is *equal* treatment. I think the idea is insane but I can accept it as being fair, if that is what **the people** decide to do to protect the country.

Proposal of such an "equal opportunity" plan will allow the country to honestly and candidly debate and decide this issue. The phony charges and claims of the femme BTO's will be flushed out and dealt with on a basis of fact! And the demands of a negligibly small number of women will be recognized for what it really is. "**A minor complaint by an insignificant number of female opportunists who are intent on exploiting the weaknesses of the system for their own benefit; at the expense of the rights of the majority of the people and the best interests of the country.**"

Women intent upon selling this foolish idea to the power brokers, will proclaim that; sexuality, the attraction and interaction between the sexes is not an issue in this situation. These women are different; *super women*! they can simply turn those feelings, desires and aspirations off—if they exist at all in the women involved. And the discussion tends to stop there. No mention of the fact that the men they encounter in their new activity are not; and they do not pretend to be, *super men* in this regard. If that kind of numbing of the senses, dumbing of the soul and denial of the feelings and relationships that make life really worth while is necessary for a young man to serve his country in the military; intelligent, sane, temperamentally balanced young men will simply avoid the military as a career. They will migrate to other career choices that are not so totally comatose in their demands.

Ventures into these kinds of irrational operations should not be entered into without careful consideration of the "mine field" that may lay ahead. As a practical matter, the socialization programs presently being forced on the military services may have tragic, irreversible impacts upon our military capability. Any educated person who chooses to put his life on the line for his country, will surely be concerned about the real ability of those who share the responsibility of the trenches and the battlefields with him. His survival in such perilous situations is closely inter-linked with the ability, loyalty and dedication of the peers who share the responsibility with him. Will they be there when he needs them; or will they be seen retreating over the nearest hill seeking what ever haven of safety may be available? If they do choose to stay; will they be an asset to the total effort? or a liability?

I suspect that most of us who have responded to our country's call to military service in the past *would not be willing* to do so if the above proposed intermingling of the sexes in battle situations was enforced. I can tell you that I would not.

There is yet one other way to accommodate this absurd proposal to provide the access women and others are demanding into the military services; and, at the same time minimize many of the associated problems enumerated above.

In addition to forcing insane social adjustments in the military, the "fools" are presently decimating its budget resources. Military bases are being closed throughout the nation, and world.

—Our plan:

> . . . Select a base or bases that are scheduled for closure to serve as the "home bases" of some new, all-female, Army or Marine units. For example, we might call one of them, the 99 99th (Ninety Nine, ninety ninth) Marine Brigade. It and its members will be affectionately referred to as "**The Chargers**" in recognition of the aggression and determination they exhibited in breaking down intelligent, sane rules for service that have served our country well for its entire history. Women in the military will be transferred into these all-female units. Women officers will be put in charge; and given two or three years to develop their people into sharp, aggressive, tough fighting machines. They will be responsible for identifying and budgeting for all of the equipment, materiel, etc.,

that they will need to accomplish their mission. It will be up to the female officers to determine the extent to which they will call upon male members of the other military units to help them do the training job. Officers of the other units are free to accept or reject such requests.

The mission identified for the "The Chargers" is to alternate assignments with units, staffed entirely by men, who have been trained and are deployed on short notice, to any trouble spot in the world where intervention is considered necessary or desirable by our leadership. Male and female units will take turns in responding to and settling these kinds of problems. True equality of opportunity demands that there be absolutely no deviation from the normal alternation of assignments.

*The chance of a lifetime for the femmes to prove the validity of their arguments.*

We, the people of this country, tend to view our military services as massive, organizations that can withstand, without adverse impacts, the kinds of moronic actions being imposed on them by the socialist-democratic party now in power. That simply is not true.

Bill Clinton, that great military strategist, and professed patriot; a person that has been chronicled in our national media to be a draft dodger during the Vietnam War (he didn't believe in the "cause" we were fighting for over there) has been our president for about one year. During that period of time the effectiveness of his service as Commander-in-Chief of the armed forces has been everything that sensible, reasonable persons might expect; a pure and simple disaster. He tried to bully the military into accepting openly-gay persons with all of the ranting, demonstrations and militancy that society has learned to expect from that group! Thankfully; cooler, wiser heads prevailed when his proposal was considered in the Congress. The concept that ultimately prevailed reacted to testimony of military leaders, and ignored most of Clinton's wild ideas. The stress from this issue continues to fester in all of the military services. We can expect the courts to stay involved with the issue. It is reasonable to assume that there are members of that splinter group who serve as judges or other positions of authority in the Justice Department who will continue to keep the issue alive.

As a further demonstration of his obvious groveling subservience to the women's movement, he champions a continuing demand on the military to allow women to serve in combat roles. Not all combat roles, mind you; just those that they think they want to serve in. He has no plan for making such a situation work. Such mere details don't slow him down in his plunge for notoriety.

Most persons in the Washington, D.C. power structure agree that the budget of our Defense Department can be decreased in response to the significant changes in the Soviet Union and elsewhere in the world. But! by how much? Les Aspen, Clinton's Secretary of Defense, came to the job from the Senate; where he served as an influential member of the Armed Services Committee. He is hardly a novice to the historic strategic planning and funding concepts that are so important in that work. During this past year, the Department of Defense (DOD) and the committees of Congress have been moving toward agreement in their efforts to determine a prudent level of funding for the Department. In their infinite wisdom, the president and his Office of Management and Budget are insisting on additional cuts of about $50 billion beyond the "mission supported" level agreed to by the DOD and Congress. This is not an insignificant problem; this world is not yet the bastion of good will, love, and peace that will assure safety and freedom for all men! It would be foolish to get reckless at this time in funding the DOD.

I have previously referred to the Clinton Cabinet as a zoo. The inexperience, and ineptitude there, is a major contributing factor to this problem. The country has no foreign policy statement, mission, or plan to serve as a basis for making these important decisions! And! people's lives are put "at risk" and some are "lost" for undefined, unjustified, or unnecessary reasons.

In this short period of time, the new president's policies toward the military are creating major new morale problems within the ranks. Its organizational units are adrift not knowing how much funding, manpower and other resources they will be allocated or what will be expected of them. Those serving are unsure and apprehensive about the knowledge, commitment, or allegiance of the commander-in-chief to the causes for which they might be asked to make the supreme sacrifice of life itself. Media reports tell us that the ability of the armed forces to recruit new people is already being adversely impacted by this very unfortunate situation.

We must be alert to and guard against the evolution of conditions that might destroy the country's ability to recruit, train and deploy volunteer Army, Navy, Air Force, and Marine forces; a very realistic possibility given the mind-set and incompetence of this administration in this field.

And what then? What if we find, at some future date, that we can no longer muster and depend upon volunteer staffing for our military services? Does conscription (draft) of the necessary manpower, remain as a viable alternative for us? Will it serve our needs to meet possible "super power obligations" to put down barbarian insurrections, wherever they may occur? To enforce the limitation of nuclear weapon development by countries who do not now have them? to protect the innocent or oppressed whenever, and wherever that may be needed? to feed starving people in nations around the word? or to fend off any attack on our own domain by ambitious, adventurous foreign opportunists?

Should we find it necessary to try to reinstate the draft system to provide staffing for the military services, there are some things we could count on:

1. Some will register as conscientious objectors—and refuse to serve on the basis of religious beliefs.
2. Some will work the system (as Bill Clinton did during the Vietnam War) and evade military service by "pulling the strings of power" that link them to the political and financial elite in the power structure of the country. We can expect that because of the greatly increased presence of patronage and nepotism in our society the number of recruits that will escape through this ruse will be substantially larger than in the past.
3. And some will simply "walk away" as they did in the Vietnam and some other previous conflicts—to Canada, Europe; any place where they would be protected from the laws of this land, until the conflict is over.

There is one other thing that would probably happen with any announcement of the country's intent to re-establish the draft. Activists of many minority and splinter groups and the peacenicks who have come to expect to get "their own way" by embarking on noisy, vulgar, and disruptive demonstrations will surely have feelings on this issue; and they will react!

The most important unknown relates to the question of the response of those members of the general population, who have always carried this burden in the past; who have carried the colors into battle and sacrificed life and limb. How will they respond this time?

I hope you will pardon the language, but I know of no other way to say this and have the affect that it deserves. We are talking here about the honest, hard working, dedicated and patriotic group of citizens that has continually been sh_ _ on by all of the social engineering of our society during the past three or four decades and in our military services during the past couple of decades. The group that has been ignored by the politically powerful, has been taxed ruthlessly by the fools we have elected to office, and whose continued loyalty, dedication and support of the nation has been taken for granted.

Referring once again to the findings of the national poll taken and summarized in the book, "The Day America Told the Truth"[23], we find some evidence of changing beliefs, expectations, and allegiance in this group. One section of the book covers the subject of "What Americans Really Think About America". It presents a dichotomy of beliefs that make it difficult, at best, and impossible, at worst, to predict just how this group of people might react to their call to service in any future instance.

It states that 91 percent of Americans are patriotic; yet three to one, they believe that the country needs more, not less patriotism. Americans still perceive their country to be first, among nations. But, first or not—81 percent of them believe that this country has a major role to play in the world. Yet American's find massive faults with their country; their confidence in its institutions has sunk to an all time low—still their love for the country appears to be unshaken.

The traumatic impact of this country's Vietnam experience, and of those who served there would surely be a factor as potential new draftees considered what their response would be to a "call to duty" facing them. They would remember the loud, dishonorable, and vicious demonstrations and lack of support by large numbers of citizens back home; the same lack of direction, plan and mission that characterizes our present administration; the resulting doubts that developed in the minds of so many serving there: why they were there? what were the real interests of the United States (U.S.)? would the sacrifice benefit anyone? the people of the U. S.? Of Vietnam? They will be revisited by visions of the hard copy and electronic media pictures of the treatment so many of our returning heroes received at the hands of some of the "scum" in our society who, themselves cowered in the shadows, and refused to serve there?

And finally, the recent election of a president who dodged the draft at a time the country was at war; and the acts of officially forgiving all those who illegally evaded the call to service in the Vietnam era will come back

---

[23]   The Day America Told The Truth; James Patterson-Peter Kim; Prentice Hall Press; 1991

to haunt us. It is a certainty that decisions made by potential draftees will be impacted by those actions.

There are no free lunches. The country's ability to serve its people and the nations of the world, to meet super-power responsibilities, may well have been sacrificed by the lapses in sanity that allowed those actions to occur.

There is interesting, additional data in the book that gives us some comparisons between public perception in the Vietnam era and now. In 1973 the Vietnam War was drawing to an end. The American people had experienced years of lies, deceit and ineptitude by their leaders. Oil prices were very high; inflation was driving prices up at double digit rates each year. People had little confidence in the ability of its military.

The Executive Branch of our Federal government was in total disarray; the Watergate scandal was unfolding. President Richard Nixon had felt it necessary to publicly announce to the people of the country that, "I am not a crook." He and Vice President Spiro Agnew were ultimately forced to resign.

How bad can things get? You might guess that those conditions in the early 1970's represent the worst that could happen. And yet! the authors of the book conclude from the analysis of their data that, American's confidence in the Executive Branch of government was lower in the early 1990's than it was at the time Nixon left the White House! Even more surprising, Americans' confidence in their military was also lower in the 1990's than it was then!

These factors will surely affect the ability of the country to successfully reinstate a Selective Service (draft) System. One thing that seems certain; it will no longer be possible to "make" people serve in the military service—or any place else that they do not want to serve. The concept of passive disobedience, so expertly developed by early leaders of the ethnic revolution, and taught to the dissidents of our society; combined with the affects of the Era of Emotional Idiocy, result in making it impossible for the "public interest" to prevail in any such struggle!

There was a time when individuals faced with a draft call to serve in the country's military services contemplated their response in a mood of somber dedication to patriotism, duty to country and to fellow citizens. Given today's situation the decision becomes more a response to social questions. "Do I believe that the causes for the conflict are worthwhile? What's in it for me, if I serve? What would I prefer to do with my life during the next few months or years. What the heck! I've got too many other things planned, let someone else do it! Why should I stick my neck out? I could get hurt or killed!"

And the telling truth of the matter is that future possible draftees will have the viable option of walking away, evading service; with the expectation that they too will be able to come back on bended knee, after it is all over, be forgiven; and then, being able to compete on an equal basis for benefits of the society with all of those who did serve! Including the right to be president!

After it is all over; the graves of the fallen have been closed, the maimed are suffering through treatment and rehabilitation; those who successfully survived the "hell that is war" will find themselves, once again, playing second fiddle to the same old beneficiaries of EEO, Civil Rights, and other deformed, corrupt employment practices in the work place! And once again those gnawing, burning questions will present themselves—Why did I do it. Was it really worthwhile? Would I do it again? And as time goes by, it seems certain that more and more will decide to, "sit this one out!"

The "Civil Service" merit system for managing personnel matters, discussed earlier, provided a small beneficial compensation for those who had served in the military. Those who had served, were given an extra five points on their qualifying score; disabled veterans were given that same five points plus an additional five points for the disability. But, in the greedy, political world of nepotism and patronage; of EEO and Civil Rights; all of that is lost. If being a veteran counts at all in today's personnel decisions; and I am quite sure it does not, it counts only in the competition between "white guys" for whatever opportunities are left after the women, the racial minorities, the homophobes, etc.; all members of the "special benefit" groups have taken their choice of the opportunities that are available!

Quite simply, our Constitution guarantees; **"equal treatment for all; using honest assumptions and comparable conditions"**. There is absolutely nothing in that document that will support all of this questionable, devious activity. Females arrive on this earth, in the same way as do males. In much of the world, that is where their troubles start. They are not treated well in many places. In fact, life is very cheap for many of them. In this country, they have been treated more respectably. For most of our history they have been honored, placed on a pedestal, and respected for the indispensable, positive contribution they have made in holding our families and our society together. They nurtured, trained and counseled our youth to be first class citizens of each new, succeeding generation. There is no higher calling than that for any person on this earth. Life was enjoyable, relationships were constructive, our country and its people had a sense of purpose, and the nation prospered.

Large numbers of the women in our midst, still cling to that set of values. They recognize the importance of the positive impact of lives devoted to such roles. They recognize the natural maternal instincts with which they are imbued. But, they find it necessary to navigate through mine fields, if they try to respond to those instincts. Few find it possible to do so. Grossly misguided government actions play a major part in denying them that opportunity. The "zombie", feminine BTOs and btos, represent maybe 1 in every 100,000 people in our land. And yet, the fools we elect to public office obediently respond to their loud, illiterate, zany demands; ignoring the wishes of the other 99.9999 percent; with no studied, intelligent consideration of what is best for the country.

I am tormented by one additional factor when I consider the feminization of the military services. This is the same feminine movement that in other areas of activity, advocate and champion the concept that "winning" is not important; it's the way you play the game that counts. This position is popular with them because it supports other inane tenets that they champion, elements of the "Era of Emotional Idiocy", that they would have us all accept:

Uncontrolled emotional tug, in this era, can and does totally override an intellectual approach to life. Contributions of the psychiatrists; the psychologists; the preachers; the teachers; the do-gooders; the welfare workers; the media, with its constant barrage of pictures of starving and otherwise underprivileged people of the earth that prey on people's perspective. The emotion and empathy that develops in people's minds overpowers their ability to intelligently, logically and realistically think things through. They are struck by the "Emotional Plague" and they become active contributors to the Era of Emotional Idiocy.

In this instance they conclude that we owe it to our youngsters to see that they are allowed to grow up without ever encountering rejection, disappointment, or sadness. "Life is just a bowl of cherries; frolicking! fun! play; great joy! bliss! felicity! happiness! baloney! drivel! balderdash. The lunacy of such thinking and its devastating adverse impacts on our society continues to elude most of them! Children who are reared under such deceptive assumptions reach their teens and early twenties totally unprepared to face the world of brutal realities. A world of every person for himself, insecurity around every corner, personal rejection by a

suitor, an employer or society as a whole! A world of exposure
to regular, continuing mental insults and physical abuse, injury
and in the worst cases death. These are conditions that they are
totally unprepared to meet! Many of them are overcome by the
relentless brutality and intensity of it all. And large numbers of
them simply give up; they take what they see to be the easy way
out; they turn to alcohol, drugs, promiscuity, etc. and for some
the situation reaches such depth that they commit suicide.

And the survivors view the scene with pity and awe; and wonder "what
went wrong?". Why can't those idiots who are doing this to our youth
understand and accept the fact that they and their insane concepts are the
problem? That it don't have to be this way. We can turn things around and
it won't cost anything!

No young person should be denied the opportunity to experience the full
scope of feelings that life has to offer during his/her formative, growing-up
years; the positive influence of discipline, including corporal punishment.
How else will they learn of the temporary nature of the disappointment that
comes with losing; or for that matter, the elation that comes with winning?
Who will really care with any intensity, one month from now or one year
from now, who won and who lost the 1993 McLoughlin Heights Little
League soccer championship; or yesterday's nationally televised, hard-fought
National Football League game between the Kansas City Chiefs and the
Houston Oilers. A contest that was heavily hyped in all of the advance
publicity as a prestigious struggle between the Chief's quarterback, legend
Joe Montana, and the Oiler's defiant, intense and very effective defensive
coach, Buddy Ryan. The emotions of the moment are high, but the decay
curve of the decreasing intensity of feelings is steep.

Allowed to confront such situations in their own activities children
learn the emotions of disappointment, from which the elation of winning
gains new meaning. They learn to put such activities in proper perspective;
to win and to lose gracefully; and as a result to confront tests and difficult
situations during their life time in appropriate, confident ways. The same
logic applies to personal rejection. Respect for others; the mutuality of
caring relationships; the sensations and passions of love in marriage, for
your spouse, family, and friends; gain increased intensity when measured
against knowing the frustration and hurt of rejection. Sadness and sorrow,
self inflicted and those that result from circumstances beyond our control,
are certainties for all of us. The human spirit, if left to its own devices, has

demonstrated its ability to handle such situations effectively. During the last decade or two, those who perceive themselves to be "social scientists" have forced their way into providing counsel and advice for those in such circumstances. A critical examination will demonstrate the probability that their intervention only makes things worse.

When allowed to grow up in normal surroundings, we gain an accurate perspective of the totality of experiences that life has to offer; the breadth, depth and intensity of emotions provoked by disappointment, fear, terror, sadness and despair; and by expectations, gratification, satisfaction, happiness, joy, and exhilaration. It is important that our children be allowed to learn from all such experiences of life. To deny them that opportunity is not a favor to them! it is instead a terrible mistake!

But, let us return to the concept with which we began, "winning is not important"; and consider how the imposition of all of these feminist and social engineering gimmicks play out for those men considering the military as a career? They face serious questions. What is the motivation of those new comrades who will share the foxholes and the trenches with them in future conflicts? Those who they must depend upon for "air cover"? Who must perform all of the multitude of jobs on war ships with precision if they are to be effective fighting machines? Are these female newcomers as fervently dedicated to a "must win" attitude as the men they will replace, and the men they will serve with? Will they be there when they are needed? Will they be able to do the job that must be done? Will the young men be willing to lay their lives on the line to find out the answers to these questions?

The tenet, "winning is not important", to which the feminists pledge allegiance is totally incompatible with the devotion required of military persons in combat! How are these two conflicting ideals to be reconciled in their minds? Can they be?

In war there are no second and third place ribbons. Winning is not just important! *it is all important; it is all that counts*! you win or you lose—*everything*. The consequences of losing are repugnant and tragic. *I know that! you know that! and so must they!*

The tragedy of acquiescing to such absurd doctrines goes far beyond its application to those who would serve in the military. As a matter of fact, winning is everything in much of life. In competing in the job market, there is usually only one winner! You win or lose; you work or you loaf; you eat or you starve; you have living accommodations or you live on the street; you support yourself and your dependents or you sponge off of others! In fact, winning *is* important in *all* of life's critical contests. That being the case, how will new generations be prepared for that reality? if they are reared using the irrational feminist tenet that winning is not important? In managing and nurturing your personal life, your career, and your family, the will to win; to do the very best job that you can do; is *all important*. What a terrible disservice it is to mislead—to lie—to small, vulnerable children about such an important concept.

It is appropriate that we have discussed, at some length here, the socialization and feminization of the United State's military. The ultimate adverse impacts of these actions are potentially very important to those of us who live in this country; they probably are even more important to hundreds of millions of others, throughout the world who enjoy a semblance of peace and tranquility in their lives because our military is there. How many situations are there, in the world, where inhuman, ruthless, ambitious rulers look covetously at the geography and wealth of neighbors; but are deterred from acting on their impulses by the presence and threat of possible super-power military reprisal?

The situation truly deserves further interrogation and analysis beyond what we have given it here. That will have to wait until another time and place; it goes beyond the scope of this work. In summary, however, it involves the following considerations:

*    *    *

We can assume that Bill Clinton's actions during the Viet Nam war era, are a true reflection of his distaste for and attitude toward the U. S. defense establishment, at that time! A cursory review of his actions and experiences in the intervening time, reveals nothing that would signify that he has changed his position on that issue. The idea that the people of the country, knowing that, would then elect him to an office in which he would be entrusted with the responsibilities of serving as the Commander-in-Chief of those same military forces defies logical reasoning, as I know it. But it happened; and barring unforeseen events he will serve in that capacity for some time to come.

This combination of circumstances does give us a reason to carefully follow his performance in this area of activity; always, questioning whether his actions are directed towards the best interests of the country; or are designed to accomplish some sinister, hidden agenda of his own! As we look at his performance in the office, to date, most astute observers would find it difficult to identify any of his proposals that are singularly, "to serve the best interests of the country.

As is so often the case, a review of the documents that serve as a foundation for our society, demonstrates that such situations were anticipated by the creators of those documents; the system of checks and balances could serve our needs. The Senate has approval authority over his appointments to policy-making positions in the Department of Defense (DOD); and the Senate and the House of Representatives must approve his budget proposals for the military forces.

The mechanism for control is there; if the members of the legislative branch are intelligent, diligent, and patriotic enough to select from alternatives presented, the one that will best respond to the country's needs; and then to demand that that option prevail as the program for the DOD. Having written to some members of Congress who serve on the committees involved here; having received some replies; and having followed some of the legislative response in the media; I find little reason for hope that the dedication exists there to make the system work as it was designed to do!

It also seems appropriate for us to raise questions about the other side of this equation. What are the real motives of the feminist's in this activity. There are aspects of the situation that indicate that true feelings of machismo or virility are not true motivational factors with them; and that also casts doubt on the true applicability here of their stated maxim that, "women can do anything men can do, and they can do them as well as men".

Monetary compensation for women is a persistent theme loudly proclaimed in all promotional activities for the women's movement. Of course, the magnitude of the pay check for those in the military service is not large. On the other hand, players in the National Football League (NFL) receive huge amounts of compensation for their work. Some of them earn as much on one fall, Sunday afternoon as some military personnel earn in two or three years. If, in fact,

1. Equal Employment Opportunity laws require that at least 50 percent of all employment opportunities, go to women, and
2. Women can do anything that men can do, and they can do it as well as men do, and
3. Winning is not important, what is important is the way you play the game; don't you wonder why this small, loud, odious, group of activist women aren't on their soap box demanding women's fair

share of that huge cache of opportunity and financial lucre available in the NFL?

I am not aware of any attempts by women to invade the ranks of active NFL players. I have read of several instances in which girls have insisted that they be allowed to play on boys, high school football teams. In one instance, in which the girl wanted only to serve as the place kicker for the team of a small school; she was allowed to do so. In other instances, school officials, coaches, and team members have resisted the requests. Some cases have gone to court; I am aware of no case in which the court denied the girl's request. In one instance that I am aware of a boy sought to play on a girls volley ball team. His request was denied. I know of no case where such a request by a boy has been approved!

In one instance that struck me as being, "very American", "politically correct", school officials denied a girl's request to play on the boy's, high school football team. The girl took the case to court; the court ordered that she be allowed to play on the team. She was seriously injured; in one of her first games. She then sued the school, and others involved and collected a huge financial settlement; based on liability considerations?

This is part of what is a much bigger picture. For decades, the meaning of the word liability has been translated and interpreted by the justice system in strange ways to benefit the plaintiffs in personal and/or product liability cases. The plaintiffs in such cases have often suffered injuries, frequently due to their own negligence. They typically look for someone, anyone even remotely related to the case, to include as defendants. Entities with "**deep pockets**" are especially attractive as co-defendants in such suits.

This is a classic example of how the Justice Department legislates its biases and socialistic predilection onto the general public. In America, such absurd actions are passively accepted by the throngs?

There is one other question, the answer to which might be important in our search for the true health of our society. It is this:

> Many of the women who have been in the military services for an extended period of time, who have advanced into positions of leadership are old enough to have been a part of the same activist movement against the military and its work in the 1960's that enchanted Bill Clinton at that time. Did many of these military women of today participate actively in that rebellion? Might those goals still be part of their purpose in life? Is it possible that

this socialization process is, in fact, simply a continuation of that movement; with an ultimate goal of reducing the country's military to impotent, ineffective organizations?

Put another way, is service in the military services really their career choice? or is it rather a "TROJAN HORSE" by which they get inside of the organizations, gain access to and become part of the power structure to enhance their ability to accomplish their real goals? Their destruction!

\*     \*     \*

There are two other notable situations where the same argument—"women can do everything men can do, and they can do it as well as or better than men"—is being used by the feminists in the game of one-upmanship with which they are pillorying the rest of us. Where merit of candidates qualifications is ignored in the hiring process; replaced by patronage, nepotism and quotas.

Current events in our neighboring city of Portland, Oregon can serve as a "living example" of modern politics in action! The present mayor of Portland has been in office about one year. She comes to the job after many years as a member of and Speaker of the Oregon House of Representatives. The Oregon Legislature might well be characterized as being second only to California, in its non-responsiveness and incompetence. Subjected to its mismanagement Oregon has energetically, thoughtlessly and needlessly followed the nation on its way to socialism and impending financial ruin. They have spent, spent, spent, and taxed, taxed and taxed the people to the point that a tax revolt ensued. Measure 5, an initiative of the Oregon people which passed a short time ago, limits property taxes in Oregon in much the same way that Proposition 13 has in California for a longer period of time. Like California, the Oregon Legislative process has yielded no useful results of consequence; year after year. The people, are left with the unwieldy alternative of trying to do what needs to be done by using the initiative process. The mayor, who has little, if any, supervisory or management experience in business, commerce or police work, put herself "in charge of" the police force of about 1000 persons.

True to form, the white-guy who had been serving as the police chief left the job; the mayor selected an Afro-American to take his place. Many metropolitan areas have gone to minority police chiefs. White men in those positions seem not to be acceptable to the black citizens of the areas? The mayor and the new chief have bought into the concept of overpowering crime with massive numbers of new officers, operating in what they call a "community policing" mode. A "non-solution" idea, popular, especially in the bigger cities; because it presents yet another way to "unload" the costs of managing pockets of discontent and crime onto the law-abiding segments of the communities. The alternative to problem solving that calls for doing the job with more manpower; is seldom the best and almost always the most expensive option available. That is especially true in the public arena today where the wage scale is escalating out of control and where the side benefits (perks) may cost as much as an additional 50 percent of the wage scale!

Hiring new police officers under the umbrella of politically correct, management criteria proves to be a difficult and time consuming job, not to mention the expense involved. It also presents interesting insights into the priority criteria of the practitioners! Oregon is experiencing very high unemployment levels. Political gridlock resulting from inoperable state and federal environmental and civil rights laws create pseudo environmental problems with the spotted owl, anadromous fish, etc.

We are told in the media that there are something over 100,000 unemployed workers in Oregon. It was reported that the Portland police department received over 3000 applications when they advertised some positions not long ago. And yet, they are making recruiting trips to many southern communities including some to Georgia, and North and South Carolina in the search for candidates that will meet their *critical* "diversity goals". This is EEO and civil rights at their very best! ! and at their very worst! !

Forcing increased hiring of women into the police forces of the country has been, and continues to be, a major objective of the feminist activists; the BTO's and bto's! Claims of discrimination, civil rights violations; anything that works will be maintained as a part of their repertoire of charges and justification for achieving their goals. Never mind that the safety of all police officers on the force; as well as your safety and mine will be jeopardized, and the overall effectiveness of the entire operation will suffer serious adverse impacts!

People in police work, as in the military; are often exposed to spontaneous, extremely dangerous situations. In an instant, any instant, they can find themselves facing some of our most deranged, dangerous criminals in life-threatening, uncontrollable situations. The officer's lives as well as those of their associates and members of the general public are in the balance. Death or survival depends upon the individual police officer's own knowledge and skills; as well as those of his colleagues.

To recruit and hire people for this work on any basis other than one that puts the best qualified and most able people on the job, is inexcusable!

I am reminded of a true episode reported on one of the "COPS" type television programs several nights ago. I believe the event reported occurred in Philadelphia. Two women police officers were sent to a bar to take in a man who had been accused of hitting his wife. Although the man did not fight back violently, he refused to let them put the handcuffs on him. The women officers were helpless; they were completely stymied until some of the men in the bar came over and helped them. If the ordinary citizens have to provide the brawn for the police department; then we should rethink the necessity of having such a department!

Another new Portland City Council person with what seems to be even less awe-inspiring credentials was put in charge of the fire fighters. It appears that a major driving force in any hiring activity there will be directed toward increasing the number of women in the ranks of the fire department!

Seattle is referred to in the local fire department staffing situation as being an example that Portland should emulate; because they have a large number of female fire fighters. Once again fire fighting work can be very hazardous. Lives of the fire fighters and members of the general public are dependent upon the knowledge, ability, strength, and commitment of the persons with whom they work. Hiring persons to meet quotas; people who do not meet the rigorous qualifications set up for the jobs, creates unnecessary, serious, life-threatening possibilities that qualified, intelligent men, especially those with family responsibilities will be reluctant to accept. Many deserving, middle-class, bread-winners who would otherwise choose this as a career will go elsewhere for their livelihood. And, as is usually the case, the tax-paying, general public ends up being the big loser. Paying for something that they do not receive.

In Portland and in hundreds of other cities across the country, year after year people who have no qualifications for managing the public work-force, are elected to political office. They lack the knowledge, experience and management ability to do the job. They wilt and surrender to the intimidation and demands of public employee unions. They encounter and succumb to the demands of infinitesimally small bands of "special interest" activists; including the feminist BTO's and bto's! Unsure of their own ability to make proper decisions, they become unduly influenced by media rhetoric and bias!

We should be aware of the fact that continued use of these convoluted hiring practices may well result, a few years hence, in all-female staffing of these activities in most cities. Is that an intelligent option? Is it a workable option? Is that really what we want? If that is being considered, we need to test the viability of fire crews manned entirely by women; create some all-female precincts and fire houses and observe and measure their operational feasibility.

Consideration of the following possible scenario might help to establish your own thinking on this issue. Suppose that you, your wife and two children (an 8 year-old who weighs 70 pounds and an 11 year-old who weighs 100 pounds) are staying on the third floor of a downtown Seattle hotel. A fire breaks out that prevents you from using the hall to get to the fire escapes. The only possible way to safety is out the window and down the ladder of a fire department ladder-truck. The hotel happens to be situated in a section of town that is protected by the all-female part of the department. You eventually look out to see that the ladder has arrived, and a lady fire fighter has come up, ostensibly to save you and the family. She appears to be about 35 years old and weighs maybe 140 pounds. What do you do? How much help will she be? If you, personally, are experienced in working at heights, from ladders etc., you may be able to save yourself and your family. If you are not, you have a major problem; and there is nothing you can do there and then to solve it! If those politicians, who are making these decisions today, realized that their decisions might one day jeopardize the lives of the members of their family, I suspect that they would come to different conclusions.

And the story that has decimated major city after city in this country over the years seems destined to repeat itself yet again in Portland. The people elect unqualified, inept people to run their city government. Those elected are unable or unwilling to effectively manage the business of the city. They spend, spend, spend for everything and anything. They incessantly pass laws that overburden the people financially and that infringe more and more upon the rights of individuals and organizations. Business, industry and commerce simply picks up its marbles and moves to more favorable surroundings. Unemployment increases, the costs of social programs increase, the income to the city goes down; and soon they face major crises. Without exception, at this point, loud and woeful cries are pointed in the direction of Washington, D.C.; and the expectation is that the Federal government will (can) somehow bail them out! And, although not understood yet by the feds in Washington or by the people of the country or in the cities, that is a myth. Billions of dollars have been and continue to be doled out to urban areas over the years for all sorts of reasons; and there remains no tangible evidence of any lasting benefit. In general, masses of federal funds foster graft, corruption and misuse. The sooner people realize the fallacy of the "bail out" expectation; the sooner they can begin effective local corrective action. Most problems of the urban areas are caused by the people and their elected officials of the areas; only they have the ability to ultimately solve them! It is difficult to imagine how this situation could be made much worse. It clearly demonstrates the ineptitude of most modern politicians; their inability to meet even the rudimentary qualifications of the jobs we put them in. And it showcases the chaos that results from their blind intervention in activities that they simply don't understand!

Where in our constitution do we find it stated that such stupidity has to be? Why do we, whether we are white, black, yellow, red; male or female; young or old; etc. tolerate such craziness?

\* \* \*

Finally, let us turn to yet another aspect of the venomous impacts of the LBJ programs, and the social-democratic laws enacted since that time on the ability of a democracy such as ours to survive. We have previously introduced in this book the idea that, to succeed, a democratic society, operating in a free-enterprise-economy mode requires a certain level of literacy in its people. We have gone so far as to postulate that the literacy in this country may be at or approaching that critical level which will result in failure.

There is irrefutable evidence that the literacy level of the people in this country has fallen significantly in recent decades; and that it is continuing its downward spiral. We discussed earlier some of the shocking results reported of tests done in Oregon. The curves formed by the test scores, over the years, for children in the various grade levels of our public education systems show a sobering decline in the performance of our public education systems. That is not news. It has been widely known and discussed for a long time! If money and talk could solve the problem, it would have been solved long ago. Billions of dollars have been thrown at it; with no visible positive impact.

What may be news to many is the probability that the socialistic, bureaucratic, government intrusions (EEO, Civil Rights, etc.) that we are discussing here have contributed significantly to the failure of our public education systems.

A look back to the early 1960's will show that up to that point in time the methods and goals of our public education systems were well established. The public understood and there was general agreement as to the elements of what constituted a reliable and respectable basic education; the kind that would satisfy the ordinary needs of people as they went through life. And! at that time the schools still reflected the values and views of the parents and the public in the communities.

Local school districts were not then, as dependent upon state and federal dollars as they are today. As a result they were not forced to comply with the multitude of bureaucratic, misdirected, back-breaking directives, mandates, red tape and philosophical intervention and bias that is the price they pay today for taking money from the "fools we elect to public office". The relationship between the general public, the teachers and the school systems was positive and constructive. The country still retained the characteristics of a "melting pot". The people shared a common understanding of what was possible; and what was desired. The common bond that we all shared, the desire to be American's and to share all that conveyed; the responsibilities and advantages of citizenship, and access to a share of the "**American Dream**"; had not yet been shattered by these defective, misdirected programs. Programs that drew lines in the sand between people of different cultures, color, sex, age, etc.; that illogically distorted, as predators, the common, ordinary citizens who had invested their lives in making this country what it was; and that created a new power base for the others, based on the groundless conclusion that they had been victims of the system and of the "predators". Prior to this fracture of the unity of the country, self pity and greed were subservient in people's minds to an aspiration for the common good. Developing our youth into intelligent, skillful, competent citizens who could successfully continue the management and operation of our country was given a high priority status.

Teachers were not unionized. They had not yet begun the crusade to equate themselves with doctors and lawyers; and demanding salaries comparable to the grossly overblown compensation collected there. Teachers were just ordinary folk; just like the rest of us! They were our friends and the neighbors next door. They were people in the community who were proficient in the subject(s) they taught. To be sure, earning a living wage was important to them; but that was not an overriding consideration in their decision to make teaching their career. They understood the problems other people in the community faced and they empathized with them in their struggle to "make ends meet"; to stretch their limited incomes to meet the total needs of their families. For most teachers, their overriding motivation came from an intense desire to work with and develop the youth so they would be able to contribute in a constructive way to the evolution of our society. They accepted their station in life as employees of the system. They had not yet started to try to run the whole operation!

Teaching was a person to person relationship between people who respected and cared for each other. Society's expectation (demand) for success of the effort was well established. It was measured by the quality of the citizens it produced. Individual transcripts were available for each student which were a *true reflection* of his or her potential for a positive contribution to society. Children were taught the subjects of reading, writing, arithmetic, english, history, personal health, home economics, etc. And, in the process they were taught how to think; not what to think. They were not subjected to pressure to listen to and accept masses of revolutionary, reactionary and activist drivel that represented the teacher's personal and the school administration's biases and causes-celebre.

Most teachers through the high school level had only under-graduate degrees. A few high school teachers in the math and science areas had master degrees in those subjects. Their minds were not cluttered with a lot of social-science fluff and superfluous trash related to the psychology of children, and teaching; to pacification; to civil rights; to the subjugation of the study of our own culture to that of many other different cultures around the world; etc. They did not suffer under the illusion that they were blessed with *the* grand vision for the future and that it was up to them to produce clones of their perspectives who would bring their vision to fruition in future generations. They did not feel the need to continually frustrate the educational process by inventing *new* methods of teaching math and some other courses; creating new methods that do not work to replace existing ones that will work, if the application is competently administered.

There was an unspoken sense of trust. If we imparted to our children the knowledge and skills they would need to navigate life's bumpy avenues, we could trust them to use those skills honestly and effectively in furthering the evolving objectives of the country.

School administration organizations were not massive as they are today. It was not unusual for a superintendent's staff to consist of one very able, and personable secretary/assistant. The constant meddling with school organization, changes in curriculum, changes to new texts, general confusion, misdirection, and red tape resulting from these large staffs today; was thankfully absent!

People hired into superintendents positions were citizens of the community and the world; they were not career "students", social scientists, or theorists with advanced degrees in exotic, unrelated fields. Most superintendents in those days had worked at real jobs; for real businesses; for the real wages that those jobs paid. They understood the real world that their students were graduating into; and that knowledge was uppermost in their minds as they went about doing their job, day to day. They were trustworthy; they could be trusted to make decisions that reflected the best interests of the students, the parents, the community, and the nation. They did not take advantage of the timidity and ineptitude of members elected to the school boards by employing endless feints and diversionary tactics, designed specifically to distract the people's attention away from the educational system's blatant failure to do the only job they are hired to do; to transform students into literate, knowledgeable, patriotic and dedicated citizens who are equipped and motivated to meet their needs and those of the country throughout their lifetimes.

Look at your own, local school situation. How much time, effort and discussion in the community is centered on solid, honest issues that will improve the quality of education for the children. As contrasted to time, effort, discussion and money spent on building new school related buildings; moving the sixth grade from elementary to middle school; moving the ninth grade from high school to middle school, or vice-versa; changing curricula; devising useless, inoperative *new* methods to teach math or some other subjects, usually sacrificing the quality of the product to improve its acceptability to a larger number of students; changing to a four-period day using 80-minute classes; or to a six period day with 55-minute classes; shifting to a trimester school-year, with three segments of 60 days each; or to a two semester school year with 90 days each; etc.; etc.; ad-infinitum.

These concepts are but a part of an unending list of clever ploys designed and used by the educational pros to divert the public's attention away from the critical necessity to improve the quality of the education dispensed.

Be alert! guard against falling for the special, endearing, gobbledygook explanations used in the presentations of such *new* concepts; designed to impress (con) the non-intellectual lay person as to the purpose and merit of the changes.

Prior to the integration and socialization of the public education systems, performance of schools was tested, as it should be now; using testing systems that made possible the objective, reliable comparison of results; from year to year, and from location to location. School boards, superintendents, and teachers were held accountable for the effectiveness of their efforts. If they weren't getting the job done, they were replaced!

This brings us to the genesis of major government intervention and socialization as a destructive force on our public education systems. Analysis of the data from the testing programs in use at that time, showed that children in many of the inner-city school systems were not realizing the same quality of education achieved by children who attended other schools.

We have previously discussed the scientific method of problem solving that carried this country to some of its finest achievements. Use of that system on the inner-city school problem would have dictated the meticulous diagnosis and analysis of the situation there to identify:

1. All of the symptoms of deficiencies in the systems;
2. The possible contributory roots of the problem; and
3. A list of possible alternative plans for improving the performance.

But, as is so often the case, this situation was complicated, by a lot of unnecessary rules and limitations some of which are unwritten, yet sanctified, and strictly enforced in our society.

Most of the children in these inner-city schools were Afro-American or other minorities; as were many of the teachers. This seriously restricted the resources that could be brought to bear on the problem. Thinking, objective, white people who were (are) knowledgeable of such subjects, and who could obviously contribute a great deal to the analysis and corrective action, are simply barred from making any effective contribution! Of course, once the decision was made, as to the plan that would be adopted, sacrifice by the whites and confiscation of their financial resources to pay the bills would be mandated; in the name of legislative actions and Constitutional interpretations!

Any reasonable approach to solving this problem would have required open, critical consideration of the:

1. intellect, interest, and aptitude of the children involved,
2. education and ability of the faculty and administration persons serving the systems, and
3. compatibility between the type and quality of instruction provided to the needs of the children.

Of course, in this country where we proclaim "freedom of speech" rights for all; white people simply cannot become involved in any activity where value-judgments involving minorities must be made and acted upon. To do so invites loud, public, scathing, hateful charges of being a racist, bigot, or worse.

The process used to study this problem and develop the proposed solution is not clear. We can assume that it was primarily a decision made by the minority communities involved, led by their BTO's and bto's. The result of their effort implies that even they were not willing to consider the three major factors enumerated above.

**The plan that was developed and that was willingly accepted and implemented by the "fools we elect to public office" and that was given Constitutional support by the courts of the land consisted of the following:**

1. The problem was seen as one of *inequality*, the children in the inner-city schools were victims of the white man's system,

2. The only acceptable solution to the problem was to *"integrate"* the schools—do whatever—was necessary to combine white and minority students in the school systems,

3. It was decided that the way to do this was through a massive, costly and very disruptive "bussing" program. That program was implemented. Massive numbers of inner-city, minority students, of all ages, were loaded onto busses and transported to urban and sub-urban schools that had previously been almost totally white. In turn, white children from these districts were bussed into the inner-city schools. We have read that some of these children were forced to spend as much as two hours per day on these busses! (It is difficult to imagine any mother or father, white, black, or of any other nationality that would feel secure in having their small elementary school children hauled to some far-off destination to spend the bulk of the day with strangers. But the plan dictated that and parents passively accepted its implementation. {And this is a government of the people, by the people and for the people?})

4. It was decided, and our legislators and courts obediently conceded that a concept of, **SEPARATE AND EQUAL** schools was not acceptable. Schools had to be **INTEGRATED** to meet the legal and *Constitutional?* Requirements of the nation!

A thoughtful person who studies the possible logic leading to this decision encounters some difficult questions. The first and foremost being, "What were the real motives for the change?" To improve the quality of the education received by: inner-city children? by children in the urban schools? Or of all of the children? Interrogation of that question, surely and unerringly leads to a conclusion that improving the quality of education for any of those children was not a major consideration in arriving at the decision.

It was known then, as it is now, that putting a number of children into a common setting and learning experience, would not produce identically enlightened clones. That, instead, each individual came to the school activity with unique backgrounds and experiences; each would learn at his/her own speed; and each would reach an individual level and diversity of education, based upon his/her personal ability, the interest and effort he/she exerted in the effort to learn, and the unique compatibility between each student and the teachers he/she encountered along the way.

Any structured, well staffed, thoughtful consideration of the problem would certainly have identified a number of alternative solutions, most of which would have been superior to the one adopted. It had to be obvious to the parents of the children involved, to school staff people and to everyone else that the hundreds of hours children would spend riding busses each year, could have been spent much more productively in a class-room, learning setting. Not all children rode busses; but some accommodation was felt necessary for those who did. The new plan had not been in effect long when the school day, the time spent in class, was shortened in most schools. Where it had been seven or eight hours per day, the time was shortened by one or two hours to accommodate those affected by the bussing ruling.

Had information that was known about the problem been more honestly and effectively integrated into the solution, much more responsive results would have been possible. Differences in students' desires to learn, their ability to learn, and the differing methods and abilities of teachers could have been integrated into a preferable plan that would have been much less costly in dollars, in the utilization of personnel, and fuel resources. Facts available, strongly suggest that if, in fact, improving the quality of education, for the children of the country was the primary goal of this effort; that could have been achieved most expeditiously and at least cost of resources by leaving all of the children in the schools near where they lived and providing them with the additional resources necessary to do the job.

However, even a cursory view of the situation, indicates clearly that improving the quality of education was not a major objective of the effort. My sense is that the integration, bussing plan was the brainstorm of the minority BTO's and bto's; the black leadership of that time. To them and to the Legislative and Justice Departments that forced the plan on the American people of all colors; it was just one more step in achieving their socialistic goals for the country.

Without dwelling on the issue, it is appropriate to point out the sense of what happened here. In the eyes of our Legislatures and Justice Departments, providing citizens with an *equal opportunity to learn* does not satisfy the requirements of our Constitution. Instead, it is their position that "equal results" must be realized! Everyone must achieve identical levels and scopes of education in our public school systems! An idiotic idea! An obviously impossible task!

How does it happen that we find ourselves in this dilemma? A studied examination of the operation of our government over the past two or three decades demonstrates clearly that such a condition is not unusual; it is the rule. At least, on a subconscious level the people of the country realize that something is seriously amiss. There was almost unanimous agreement by the members of the electorate during the 1992 campaign and election that "change" was vital to the survival of this country. A large percentage of the people who voted in the November 1992 election, voted *for change*. But the unanimity ended there. All three candidates campaigned on a platform that presented *him* as the "choice candidate" that could and would make the changes needed. But, the scope, nature, and causes of the problem were not discussed by the candidates. Neither did they provide any detailed information about how they would propose to solve the problem.

Recognition of some of the fundamental characteristics of this widely diverse social agenda; President Johnson's Great Society, the profusion of Civil Rights and Equal Employment Opportunity and social program rulings, ad-infinitum helps us to begin to understand the roots of problems we encounter in our everyday relationships. Add to that, feelings harbored by members of the establishment, of distrust, disbelief, and animosity toward the continuing inept, misdirected social-democratic incumbency that has forced the resultant grievous inequalities and injustice on the masses of the American people. And finally the situation is complicated by the fact that by their wording and provisions, all of the programs establish bogus bases for the recipients of "all the benefits" to claim to be victims of the "system". Greed overcomes all reason and the prospect of "getting more" fosters continued unrest and claims for more and more! It is understandable that the elements of dissention and discontent is creating subliminal strife and confusion for all of us. The wonder is that more aggressive reactions have not followed.

Our discussion has enumerated a number of new principles that have *evolved* from local, state and Federal; legislative and judicial actions by incumbents in elective office, justice officials and the massive bureaucracies of our times. Principles that have been passively accepted by the American people; regardless of well-founded questions of their Constitutionality. Questions that gain legitimacy, by the spontaneous, loud, hateful, vindictive reactions from members of the groups who reap the benefits. A sure sign that they harbor doubts about the possible outcome of any legitimate, objective discussion and debate of the issues.

It is important that we all understand what has happened here, the real issues, the motivation for the actions, and the damage they are causing! These programs, essentially denounce basic elements of the foundation of our form of government and of our country! They establish the premise that government, "of the people, by the people, and for the people," will not work. That, at least in our case, the American people, in a melting pot sense (all Americans); cannot be trusted to live together, to relate to each other, to take care of each other, to work together to identify, understand, and solve the problems we encounter, etc. We are incompetent to establish our own priorities for the schooling we receive and that we provide for our youth; for the careers we choose; for the way we spend *our* money; for the kinds of people we and our children associate with; for the ethical and moral development of our children, our communities and our country.

The evolution, enactment, implementation, and enforcement of all of this social legislation and court action, essentially consecrates the conviction of those in power that they must impose their own personal level of intelligence and understanding; their own personal priorities, of warped morality, and of ethics on the rest of us, if things are to be done *right*? In the United States of America! How does that strike you? God help us all, if we don't, find a way to correct such a blatant, grievous flaw!

And don't forget that there are certain limits to the application of their conviction. All of this intervention and all of these controls apply to you and me; members of the general public; it does not apply to them! Those who impose all of this on the rest of us; do not feel compelled to live by the same laws they have established for us!

I urge you to carefully study the Constitution and all of the other base documents of our society, looking for anything there that supports or justifies these actions. If you are satisfied with what you find, and feel that things are going along OK; relax. If you do not find that; "Don't just sit there! Get going! There are things for you to do! Things that only you can do effectively!"

## # # THE END # #

# INDEX